BYRON: AUGUSTAN AND ROMANTIC

Also by Andrew Rutherford

BYRON: A CRITICAL STUDY
KIPLING'S MIND AND ART (ED.)
BYRON: THE CRITICAL HERITAGE (ED.)
TWENTIETH-CENTURY INTERPRETATIONS OF 'A PASSAGE
  TO INDIA' (Ed.)
RUDYARD KIPLING, 'A SAHIBS' WAR' AND OTHER STORIES;
  'FRIENDLY BROOK' AND OTHER STORIES (Ed.)
*THE LITERATURE OF WAR: STUDIES IN HEROIC VIRTUE
RUDYARD KIPLING, *PLAIN TALES FROM THE HILLS* (Ed.)
EARLY VERSE BY RUDYARD KIPLING 1879–1889 (Ed.)

*Also published by Macmillan

Byron: Augustan and Romantic

Edited by

Andrew Rutherford

Warden of Goldsmiths' College
University of London

in association with
The British Council

First published 1990

Published by
THE MACMILLAN PRESS LTD
Houndmills, Basingstoke, Hampshire RG21 2XS
and London
Companies and representatives
throughout the world

Printed in Hong Kong

British Library Cataloguing in Publication Data
Byron: Augustan and romantic.
1.   Poetry in English. Byron, George Gordon Byron,
Baron, 1788–1824 – Critical studies
I.   Rutherford, Andrew, 1929– II.   British Council
821'.7
ISBN 0–333–51723–7 (hardcover)

Contents

Notes on the Editor and the Contributors

Andrew Rutherford is Warden of Goldsmiths' College, University of London. He was formerly Regius Professor of English in the University of Aberdeen. His publications include *Byron: A Critical Study* (1961), *Kipling's Mind and Art*, ed. (1964), *Byron: The Critical Heritage*, ed. (1970), *The Literature of War: Studies in Heroic Virtue* (1978, rev. 1989), and *Early Verse by Rudyard Kipling 1879–1889*, ed. (1986). He is a Vice-President of the Byron Society and Chairman of the Literature Advisory Committee of the British Council.

Anne Barton is Professor of English at Cambridge University and a Fellow of Trinity College. She is the author of *Shakespeare and the Idea of the Play* (1962), *Ben Jonson, Dramatist* (1984) and *The Names of Comedy* (1990), as well as of a number of essays on sixteenth- and seventeenth-century literature and on Byron and other Romantic poets.

Bernard Beatty is a lecturer in English and Chairman of the Board of English at Liverpool University. He has published numerous articles, especially on Romantic literature, continuity in poetry, Dryden and Bunyan. He is author of *Byron's Don Juan* (1985), and *Byron's Don Juan and Other Poems* (1987), and co-editor of *Literature of the Romantic Period 1780–1830* (1976) and *Byron and the Limits of Fiction* (1988). He is the academic editor of the *Byron Journal*.

Marilyn Butler is King Edward VII Professor of English Literature at Cambridge University and a Fellow of King's College, Cambridge. Her books include *Jane Austen and the War of Ideas* (1975) and *Romantics, Rebels and Reactionaries* (1981). She is currently working on a study of Romantic Orientalism.

Michael G. Cooke, Housum Professor of English Literature at Yale University, is author of *The Blind Man Traces the Circle: On the Patterns and Philosophy of Byron's Poetry* (1969), *The Romantic Will* (1976), and *Acts of Inclusion: Toward an Elementary Theory of Romanticism* (1979). He writes and lectures regularly on Byron. He is currently Director of The Common Wealth of Letters, an international organisation centred at Yale and devoted to illumination of English literary culture.

Hermann W. H. Fischer held the Chair of English at Mannheim University from 1965 to 1987, and founded the German Section of the International Byron Society in 1974. He has published extensively on seventeenth-, nineteenth- and twentieth-century literature, and his works include *Romantic Verse Narrative in England* (1964, in German; English translation forthcoming), and a German translation of Wordsworth's *Prelude* (1974). He is an Honorary Trustee of Dove Cottage.

Michael Gassenmeier is Senior Lecturer in English at the University of Mannheim and President of the *Gesellschaft fur englische Romantik*. His publications include *The Man of Feeling as a Literary Type* (1972), *Imagism* (1976), a booklet on tendencies of modern English poetry, *Poeta Interruptus* (1976), a booklet on *Tristram Shandy*. He has also co-edited *Beyond the Suburbs of the Mind: Exploring English Romanticism* (1987), and *Poetry as Politics: Texts and Contexts of London Poems from the Restoration to the Walpole Era* (1989).

Malcolm Kelsall is Professor of English in the University of Wales at Cardiff. He has taught in the universities of Exeter, Hiroshima, Oxford, Reading and Paris. His main publications have been in the fields of neo-classical literature and the theatre, and his recent books include *Christopher Marlowe* (1981) and *Byron's Politics* (1987). He is currently writing a study of the country house in English literature.

Leslie A. Marchand, who was born in 1900, taught at Rutgers University in New Jersey for many years, and was visiting professor at UCLA, NYU, Columbia, Illinois and Harvard, and Fulbright Professor at the University of Athens. For the past forty years he has devoted himself to the study of Byron and is chiefly noted for his three-volume *Byron: A Biography* (1957) and for his twelve-volume edition of *Byron's Letters and Journals* (1973–82) which won him the James Russell Lowell Prize and the Ivan Sandrof Award of the National Book Critics' Circle. He is the doyen of Byron scholars.

Jerome McGann is Commonwealth Professor of English, University of Virginia. His publications include *Fiery Dust: Byron's Poetical Development* (1968), *Swinburne: An Experiment in Criticism* (1972), and *Don Juan in Context* (1976). His most recent book is *Towards a Literature of Knowledge* (1989), delivered as the Clark Lectures in 1988. He is editor of the Clarendon Press edition of Byron's *Complete Poetical Works*, the last two volumes of which will be published in 1990.

Claude Rawson is currently Professor of English at Yale University, and an Honorary Professor at the University of Warwick. His publications include *Henry Fielding and the Augustan Ideal Under Stress* (1972), *Gulliver and the Gentle Reader* (1973), and *Order from Confusion Sprung: Studies in Eighteenth-Century Literature from Swift to Cowper* (1985), as well as many other books and articles chiefly on eighteenth- and twentieth-century literature. He is a Past President of the British Society for Eighteenth-Century Studies.

Donald H. Reiman, editor of *Shelley and his Circle* at the Pforzheimer Collection, The New York Public Library, has published editions and critical studies of the English Romantics, most recently *Romantic Texts and Contexts* (1987) and *Intervals of Inspiration: The Skeptical Tradition and the Psychology of Romanticism* (1989). He is General Editor of *The Bodleian Shelley Manuscripts* and *The Manuscripts of the Younger Romantics* and was Lyell Reader in Bibliography at Oxford during the academic year 1988–9.

William St Clair was until recently joint chairman of the Byron Society, of which he is now a Vice-President. As a senior official in HM Treasury, he has been responsible for introducing and developing new methods of evaluating British government programmes. His books include *Lord Elgin and the Marbles* (1967, rev. 1983), *That Greece Might Still Be Free* (1972; awarded Heinemann prize), *Trelawny* (1977), and *The Godwins and the Shelleys: The Biography of a Family* (1989).

Acknowledgements

My thanks are due to the following: the British Council and the Byron Society, for making possible the Cambridge seminar on Byron; Ian Scott-Kilvert and Harriet Harvey Wood, for their help in planning the lecture programme; the contributors, for permission to include their essays in this volume; Liverpool University Press, for permission to include a revised version of Marilyn Butler's essay "The Orientalism of Byron's *Giaour*," first published in *Byron and the Limits of Fiction*, eds. Bernard Beatty and Vincent Newey, Liverpool University Press, 1988; the *Yale Review*, for permission to reprint Michael G. Cooke's essay, "Byron, Pope, and the Grand Tour", first published in the *Yale Review*, 1988; and Lawrence Pollinger Ltd and the Earl of Lytton for permission for Anne Barton to quote from the Lovelace Papers.

Unless otherwise indicated, quotations from Byron's poetry are from *Lord Byron: The Complete Poetical Works*, ed. J. J. McGann (Clarendon Press, 1980–); and quotations from his letters and journals from *Byron's Letters and Journals*, ed. L. A. Marchand (John Murray (Publishers) Ltd, 1973–82). My thanks are due to both publishers for their permission to use this material.

I greatly regret the fact that restrictions of space make it impossible for me to include all the lectures given at the seminar.

A.R.

Introduction

1988 was the bicentenary of Byron's birth, and to mark the occasion an International Seminar was held at Trinity College, Cambridge, under the joint auspices of the British Council and the Byron Society. The essays collected in this volume were delivered as lectures at that seminar, the aims of which were to reassess Byron's poetic achievement in the light of modern scholarship and criticism, and to reconsider his relation to the literary movements by which he was influenced and to which he himself contributed.

A major figure in the history of European Romanticism, Byron continually asserted his commitment to Augustan values; yet even the most Procrustean of literary historians could hardly fit him into an Augustan mould, while to theorists of Romanticism he is a tiresome misfit. His elusiveness to such categorisation may well reinforce existing doubts about the value of the categories themselves, but more immediately, and inescapably, it compels us to explore the nature of the poetry which he actually wrote. Such exploration is the object of this volume.

The contributors come to his work without preconceptions as to where achievement may be found. *Don Juan* retains its self-evident supremacy, but there is a readiness to discover new interest and indeed new riches in works as diverse as 'A Sketch' and *Manfred*, the Turkish Tales and *The Deformed Transformed*. The most recent biographical and textual scholarship is taken for granted, as are earlier works of critical interpretation: the purpose of the contributors is to carry the enquiry further, to evolve new methodologies appropriate to the material, and not to restate conventional, established judgements, but to offer reinterpretations and revaluations – sometimes radical – of the Byronic *oeuvre*.

Andrew Rutherford

xiii

1

The Impact of Byron's Writings: An Evaluative Approach

WILLIAM ST CLAIR

In this paper I suggest an evaluative approach for assessing the impact of Byron as a writer. It is adapted from the methodology being developed in the Treasury for the evaluation of government programmes, on which I recently wrote a brief guide.[1] This approach is not intended to replace more traditional methods but to add to them and to improve the rigour. In particular I look for opportunities to bring measures of quantification to the analysis.

A simple evaluation framework for the impact of Byron would look like Figure 1.1. Literary studies have traditionally concentrated on the first box. There is also a good deal of writing about the last box, Byron's influence, where the scholar offers his or her own selection and interpretation of the evidence but where the reader cannot easily judge whether the examples adduced are truly representative or are unusual in some way. What we are increasingly finding in government, where the same problems arise, is

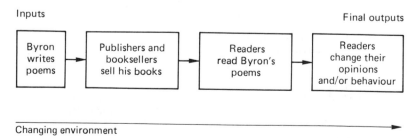

Figure 1.1   The impact of Byron

1

that there are big potential gains to be made from analysing and quantifying the intermediate steps. For one thing, if we are wrong about these links, the chain as a whole is insecure and it is easy to slip into unwarranted assumptions. For example, if we have a mistaken idea about who actually uses health services or the extent to which different groups have access to health services, our conclusions about the effectiveness of health policies will be wrong. Studying the intermediate steps may bring out surrogate indicators which are almost as good as direct measures. Most important, we have a formal framework within which scattered empirical evidence can be placed and judged.

In applying this approach to Byron, we begin at the second box by considering Byron's books not as texts but as the physical vehicles of communication which conveyed texts to readers in the circumstances of the time. In Byron's day poetry came in two main sizes, quarto and octavo. The quarto format has large type and broad margins. At a time when much reading was done by candlelight, it was more comfortable on the eyes, although not on the arms or wrists. The octavo, though smaller in size, is also well-produced by modern standards. Both quartos and octavos were usually bound in leather, as was the custom, but they did not come like that from the bookshop. All Byron's poems were originally sold in boards or paper wrappers. If they were not rebound they quickly fell to pieces and it was low tone to have unbound books on your shelves – like putting milk bottles on the table. Table 1.1 gives figures for copies produced of *Childe Harold's Pilgrimage*, Cantos 1 and 2, and of the tales. They are drawn from Murray's archives or estimated from incomplete records.[2]

The first conclusion to note is that there is no correlation between number of editions and number of copies produced. An average figure for *The Giaour* gives less than 1000; for the *Corsair*

Table 1.1   Production 1812–18

	Editions	Numbers
CHP 4°	1	500
CHP 8°	9	20 000 (estimated)
Giaour	14	13 500 (estimated)
Bride	6	12 500
Corsair	7	25 000

3500. We cannot therefore use numbers of editions, as writers on the impact of Byron so often do, as a measure of popularity. Some early editions were kept short to avoid tying up capital. Some later editions were made from existing sheets or were run off from metal left standing from earlier editions. Others were, I suspect, deliberately numbered to keep up the public belief that Byron's poems were being sold as quickly as they could be run off the presses. For example I know the first edition of *Lara* and the fourth, but have found no trace of a second or a third.

The first question for the evaluation is – who bought these books? In Byron's day there was no sharp distinction between publisher and bookseller. Murray sold direct to the public but also to other booksellers in London and elsewhere. In Scotland his books were distributed by Blackwood of Edinburgh whose name appears on the title page along with that of Cumming of Dublin, who did the same in Ireland. Table 1.2 gives the prices with estimates for binding.[3]

The next question is – what did these prices mean in Byron's day? At this distance of time it is not enough to deflate for the effects of general inflation. To understand these prices we need to devise a contemporaneous standard of the value of money which reflects the social and economic structures and expectations of the time, as well as income distribution and prices of other goods which made up the cost of living. In constructing such a standard we have, I suggest, a consistently reliable foundation in the parsimony of the British Treasury. In 1815, the long war with France at

Table 1.2 Estimated prices (shillings)

		Wrappers	Bound
Childe Harold 1 and 2	4°	30	50
	8°	12	25
Giaour, Bride, Corsair	8°	5.5	–
A volume of Tales	8°	22	32

Table 1.3 Pensions and half-pay, 1816

Widow of an admiral	£120 per year
Captain, Royal Navy	14/6 – 10/6 per day
Commander, Royal Navy	10s – 8/6 per day
Surgeon with 6 years' service	6s per day

last came to a decisive end. It had been going on almost continuously for twenty-two years and many men knew no other occupation. In 1816 the Government set new rates of pensions and half-pay to reflect the peacetime conditions, and they remained in force for many years, generally accepted as fair. Table 1.3 gives a few examples from the Navy.[4]

These rates represented a reasonable but not extravagant lifetime income for members of the upper or upper-middle classes, many of whom were still only in their twenties or thirties. Drawing on these figures and adding a margin for other income, I should like to suggest a benchmark of 100 shillings a week. That would be a typical income of a senior retired commander in the Royal Navy. That is my standard of gentility.

The figure of 100 shillings has special advantages. For if we look again at the prices of Byron's books in Table 1.2 we need no longer think of them as shillings, but as percentages. Thus a bound copy of *Childe Harold*, Cantos 1 and 2 in quarto cost 50 per cent of the weekly income of a gentleman. One of the Eastern tales, in paper wrappers from the shop, cost only 5.5 per cent. What about those lower down the income scale? We know that the highest-paid skilled workers in the country, the printers, were paid 36 shillings a week from 1811. Carpenters were paid about 25 shillings.[5] *Childe Harold*, even in octavo, was clearly out of range for them, as a third or a half of a week's income. We can interpolate for groups in between, younger sons, clergymen, officers, ladies on annuities, clerks and so on. According to evidence given to a Select Committee in 1818, the price of books was higher then than it had ever been.[6]

How many rich families were there? Table 1.4 gives the numbers of taxpayers rounded to the nearest thousand. They are unfortunately drawn from 1801, the only year for which we have figures.[7] The figure of £200 a year is rather lower than my gentility standard

Table 1.4   Income-tax payers, 1801

Annual income	London	Great Britain
£65–£200	52 000	252 000
£200 and over	22 000	69 000
	74 000	321 000

of 100 shillings a week, but we can assume a broad equivalence and there had been some increase in prices and incomes in the meantime. As you can see, in a population of about 10 million for Great Britain, the middle and upper classes were still a small proportion.

Unfortunately the Treasury did not preserve a breakdown of the pattern of income distribution above £200 a year. But we have other indicators. Road books of the day list 10 000 noblemen and gentlemen's seats, many not at all grand. And we have Byron's own figure for the wealthiest section of all, the families who had homes both in London and in the country.

> In the Great World, – which being interpreted
> Meaneth the West or worst end of a city,
> And about twice two thousand people bred
> By no means to be very wise or witty.[8]

The same figure is repeated later in the poem:

> I've done with my tirade. The world was gone;
> The twice two thousand, for whom earth was made,
> Were vanished to be what they call alone, –
> That is, with thirty servants for parade.[9]

There is another point about the economic environment which is highly relevant. The weather – climate, we may almost say – of the 1810s was the most severe in England since the 1690s.[10] A cloud of volcanic dust settled in the upper atmosphere, giving rise to the wonderful orange sunsets portrayed by Turner. But it kept out the sun and there was a mini-ice-age. All over Northern Europe the glaciers advanced, the sea froze. In 1814 there was an ice-fair on the Thames. In Byron's day it was not only books which were at their highest price ever. In the summer of 1812, the year of *Childe Harold*, the price of bread, the main staple of the cost of living, rose to one shilling and eight pence, and it was almost as high in 1813 and again in 1816, which was one of the coldest years on record.[11] These prices, which were the highest in real terms in the history of British bread, benefited landowners, as can be seen from the steep rise in rents and in the number of enclosure bills.[12] Since books are always marginal purchases, i.e. discretionary expenditure to be considered only after more pressing needs have been met, this means that the marginal cost to the rich was falling, while to the

Table 1.5   Sales relative to taxpayers (percentage)

	Above £65 p.a.	Above £200 p.a.	'Twice 2,000'
CHP 4°	0.2	0.7	12.5
CHP 8°	6	29	
Giaour	4	20	
Bride	4	18	
Corsair	8	36	

poor it was rising way beyond reach. The main conclusion is clear. When these books by Byron were first published, they were luxury items even for those on my gentility standard. Most people below that line must have found them prohibitively expensive.

The figures I have quoted for Byron's books refer to production, not sales, a difference readily appreciated by authors. In fact for these early poems where editions were short, we know that all were sold by Murray, either direct to the public or to other booksellers. Table 1.5 divides the figures of books produced (Table 1.1) into the figures for the numbers of middle and upper income families (Table 1.4). It also relates the quarto edition to the group at which it was directed. These ratios give an indicator of market penetration and therefore, to some extent, of impact.

We can see how Byron awoke to find himself famous on an edition of 500 copies. When the Duchess of Devonshire wrote that *Childe Harold* was 'on every table',[13] she meant on about 12½ per cent of the tables of the few thousand families who could afford 30 shillings or 50 shillings from their weekly budget. More seriously, if we regard the main purchasers of the octavos as people at or above my gentility standard, then Murray was selling to astonishingly high proportions of the potential market, no less than 36 per cent for *The Corsair*. If we regard the potential market as every family in Great Britain with an annual income of £65 or more – that is, everyone who could only just afford to buy a book if he skimped on bread – a very unlikely assumption – the figure for *The Corsair* is still an astonishing 8 per cent.

These estimates are, of course, dependent on the accuracy of the tax statistics and we can be quite sure that they are unreliable. Not everyone who was liable to tax paid it, and of those who did, not everyone would have declared his full income. But the exact figures do not much matter for the two main conclusions are not much affected. Even if you halve the figures, they still reaffirm the same two conclusions. These books were sold to the richest section of society and a high proportion of that section bought them.

Figures of total sales do not take account of the fact that the books were sold at different rates. For light on this question we can use Murray's advertisements. Thus a printed note dated February 1814 advertises *The Corsair* as forthcoming, plus the 7th edition of *Childe Harold*, the 9th of *The Giaour*, and the 6th of *The Bride*. By April he is advertising the 8th of *Childe Harold*, the 11th of *The Giaour*, the 7th of *The Bride*, and *The Corsair* is already in its 6th edition. And there are others.

As I mentioned, however, we must beware of taking editions as surrogates for totals. I can suggest a further, more objective, measure which elides the element of commercial exaggeration. In 1815 Murray started to sell editions of Byron's *Collected Works*, first in two volumes and then in three. They are not reprints, but copies made up from the individual poems with a new title page inserted. A set dated 1815 may be made up of the 8th edition of *Childe Harold*, the 6th of *The Giaour*, and so on. The 1817 set still contains the 8th of *Childe Harold* but the 12th of *The Giaour* and so on. By comparing the make-up of sets of this kind we have, I suggest, information about the rate at which stocks of the individual poems were being run down.[14] We have indicators of speed of sales and of comparative popularity.

Putting all this evidence together we are now able to complete this part of the analysis. The best-selling of Byron's poems was undoubtedly *The Corsair*, which sold very rapidly in 1814 and 1815. It was closely followed by *The Giaour*, with *The Bride* some way behind, both selling briskly over the same period. We have no exact record for total production of *Childe Harold*, Cantos 1 and 2, but I estimate 15 000 to 20 000 before 1818, putting the volume in the same range as *The Corsair*. Although it was more than twice as expensive, this poem sold very briskly from 1812 right through till 1816 when Canto 3 was published, after which interest falls away. Some of the cheaper poems also sold well and quickly, notably the *Ode to Napoleon Bonaparte* and the *Lament of Tasso*. The slower movers include the *Siege of Corinth*, the *Hebrew Melodies*, *The Prisoner of Chillon*, and *Manfred*.

This quantified analysis broadly confirms conclusions which we might have come to on the basis of the other evidence alone. However, the approach is most interesting and most useful when it challenges conclusions based only on scattered anecdotal references. Take *The Prisoner of Chillon*. Murray told Byron in December 1816 that he had sold 7000 copies at a booksellers' dinner, which is puzzling, since his records show that only 6000 copies were produced.[15] Even so there seem still to have been plenty of copies of the first edition unsold in 1818, the last year Murray sold made-up remainder editions.

My first thought was that there must be something wrong with the figures for production. In fact I suggest we have here an illuminating example of how a quantitative approach can offer a salutary corrective to misplaced assumptions. Firstly, it provides further confirmation that we cannot take Murray's claims at face value. Secondly, we must take care to avoid presumptions based on hindsight. Nowadays we love *The Prisoner of Chillon* as one of the clearest expressions of Byron's commitment to liberty. We may forget that liberal views were by no means shared by the classes of society who bought his books in these early years. These were the same landowners who were benefiting from high bread prices, who were terrified of the unrest which high prices were causing, and who as Members of both Houses of Parliament and as magistrates were passing and enforcing law after law extending the scope of the death penalty, lengthening prison sentences, and imposing transportation to Australia for minor crimes. The sympathies of Byron's readers at this time lay more with the prison authorities of Chillon than with the rebellious Bonnivord. The reviewer for the *Quarterly Review* implied that the poem demonstrated how humane the English death penalty was, compared with the long prison sentences favoured on the Continent.[16]

The quantitative analysis also led me to ask why the *Lament of Tasso* was more popular than *The Prisoner of Chillon*, for they have, superficially at least, much in common. Again what appears to be a puzzle is in fact a confirmation of what we should expect of the groups who bought the books. The *Lament of Tasso* is not primarily about prison, certainy not about oppression – indeed Tasso accepts that his imprisonment is just. It is a poem about hopeless love. It is also an overtly Christian work, a point of great importance to many readers of the upper income groups during the anti-jacobin years. I wondered for a while whether the comparatively poor figures for *Hebrew Melodies* indicate a degree of anti-semitism among the same groups, but that may be anachronistic – some of the individual poems were undoubtedly popular as songs.

So far I have relied on figures for production and sales. But there

Table 1.6   Estimates of readership (to 1819)

	Sales	× 5	× 10
CHP 1 and 2	20 000	100 000	200 000
Giaour	13 500	66 500	133 000
Corsair	25 000	125 000	250 000
Hebrew Melodies	6 000	30 000	60 000
Prisoner of Chillon	6 000	30 000	60 000
Manfred	6 000	30 000	60 000

were, of course, other means of access to Byron's books – notably borrowing from family or friends and hiring from circulating libraries – and not all books bought were necessarily read. The net readership figures must, however, be several times greater than the sales figures, although probably still within the same groups. Those few non-gentlemen like Thomas Cooper and Francis Place who mention borrowing from gentlemen, boast of it as an exception. Nor were circulating libraries which required an entrance fee of about £20 and a daily borrowing rate, accessible to those on lower incomes.

I know of no objective way of estimating the multipliers to convert sales figures to readership figures. But note that any multiplier greatly widens the comparative impact. Table 1.6 gives illustrative figures for readership if we assume that on average each copy of a book was read by five people, and corresponding figures if we assume 10. The letters and diaries of people of the time contain more references to reading *The Corsair* and *Childe Harold* 1 and 2 than to other poems, although unfortunately I have not found a big enough sample to attempt a quantified citation analysis.

I should now like to offer another indicator. If you love a poem, there is no substitute for having your own copy, even if you have to do the copying yourself. One thing which even the less well-off members of the upper and middle classes had in abundance was time. This was especially true of ladies by which I mean the wives, sisters, and daughters of noblemen and gentlemen above my gentility index. They were a group who did not necessarily buy Byron's works themselves but had ready access to books bought by men, and I believe we can regard them as an identifiable constituency. Just as the sailing ship continued for a hundred years after the invention of the steamship, so the manuscript co-existed with the printed book long after it was technically obsolete. Manuscript copies of *English Bards* are plentiful.[17] What was more common was to write extracts from favourite poems into one's own album or commonplace book. I have a number in my collection and have examined many more. Most were written up at different times and treasured over several years. Sometimes they had locks and keys to keep out peepers. In an age when the reading of ladies was controlled and they had almost no privacy, the albums can tell us something about women's concerns when they were alone with their thoughts and their emotions.

Interpreting the evidence of the albums is bound to be more impressionistic than quantified. But a few conclusions can, I believe, be ventured. First, they give yet more confirmation of Byron's overwhelming impact – I do not think I have seen a single album of the 1810s or 1820s which does not contain some Byron, and most contain a great deal. They provide confirmation of the rapid spread of *Childe Harold's* popularity from the date of its first publication. But most of them also contain poems by Samuel Rogers and Thomas Moore, Walter Scott and Thomas Campbell, to say nothing of Bernard Barton and James Montgomery and later L.E.L. and Mrs Hemans. There is almost no Wordsworth or Coleridge, and no Shelley or Keats.[18]

Most significantly, the albums ram home the uncomfortable truth that the poem which was by far the favourite in Byron's day, at any rate among ladies, was not any of those I have so far mentioned, but *Fare Thee Well!*. That, you will remember was the poem which Byron addressed to Lady Byron at the time of the separation in 1816, and did not intend for publication. There were no less than 57 separate printings of this poem in book or pamphlet form in 1816 and 1817, not counting appearances in the newspapers and musical settings. It is by far the commonest poem transcribed in the albums.

We can speculate about the causes of the extraordinary interest in this less-than-remarkable work – and indeed why there was such fascination with the circumstances of Byron's separation from his wife. Part of the explanation, I suggest, is that among the readership prior to 1816, Byron's poetry was not much associated with liberal causes. He was as yet not a poet of ideas at all. He was thought of by many readers, men and ladies, primarily as the poet of romance, especially of long-suffering constant tragic love. That was the appeal of *The Corsair*, of *The Bride*, of *Childe Harold*, Cantos

1 and 2, and even, I suppose, of *The Giaour*. It also explains the popularity of *The Lament of Tasso* compared with *The Prisoner of Chillon*.

The stanza from *Childe Harold* which was most commonly copied into ladies' albums, as far as I can judge from a limited sample, is 23 of Canto 2, not a passage likely to appear in any modern anthology or book of quotations.

> 'Tis a night, when Meditation bids us feel
> We once have lov'd, though love is at an end:
> The heart, lone mourner of its baffled zeal,
> Though friendless now, will dream it had a friend,
> Who with the weight of years would wish to bend,
> When Youth itself survives young Love and Joy?
> Alas! When mingling souls forget to blend,
> Death hath but little left him to destroy!
> Ah! happy years! once more who would not be a boy?

When Samuel Rogers reports stories of ladies in Buckinghamshire weeping over *Childe Harold* it is, I suggest, this aspect which touched them.[19] Again this kind of evidence only confirms what we should have expected to find from what we know of the readers. During the years before 1816 officers were still going off to the wars as they had done since 1793. We can identify a distinctive constituency of Byron's readers among the many ladies deprived of love by separation and, of course, among war widows.

In general, if we jump straight from text to impact, we will underestimate the importance of the shorter poems. Take, for example, the poems published at the end of *Childe Harold's Pilgrimage*, Cantos 1 and 2. In modern editions we read *Childe Harold* straight through and these poems are printed elsewhere, but to Byron's readers between 1812 and 1819, they were a considerable portion of the book. In the second edition, for example, *Childe Harold's Pilgrimage* takes up 112 pages, the other poems 71. More poems were added in later editions. You can also see the increasing importance of the short poems in the design of the books. The first editions, the quarto and the octavo, are entitled simply *Childe Harold's Pilgrimage, a Romaunt*. But the third edition, which must have been put on sale within days or at most weeks of the success, is retitled *Childe Harold's Pilgrimage, a Romaunt, and Other Poems*. And the phrase 'Other Poems' is in larger letters than

Childe Harold. It is not a true edition at all. Murray, sensing the interest in the Other Poems has simply inserted a new title page in the second edition. For the fifth edition the words Other Poems were made even larger.

You will remember too the incident of the shorter poems printed at the back of *The Corsair*, which included the lines *To a Lady Weeping* which were mildly critical of the royal family. The pages containing these poems were withdrawn from the first edition by Murray after first printing in response to an outcry in the pro-Government press but were reinserted soon afterwards at Byron's request. Murray's 'ruse', as he called it, was not to withdraw them altogether but to print them instead at the back of *Childe Harold* Cantos 1 and 2 which was then in its seventh edition. As he told Byron, he expected to sell off the whole edition on the strength of this one poem.[20] His customers, he knew, would be willing to pay 12 shillings for a copy of a book many of them must already have possessed in order to be able to read the 52 words of this poem.

One of the other poems most often copied into albums was *To a Cornelian Heart*. Highly popular too were the lines which Mary Godwin copied to Percy Bysshe Shelley before running away with him in 1814.[21]

> Ours too the glance none saw beside;
>   The smile none else might understand;
> The whisper'd thought of hearts allied,
>   The pressure of the thrilling hand.

They are from one of the Thyrza poems at the back of *Childe Harold*. It was these poems which Lady Falkland believed were personally addressed to her, and she was repeating a view that many other ladies felt.[22] The albums also contain a good deal of short poems in the same style which are not in fact by Byron but were believed to be highly Byronic at the time.

Let me now turn to the books published after 1816, leaving aside *Don Juan* for the moment. We all know that the break with Lady Byron altered Byron's reputation. The ferocity of that episode, the British public's most famous periodic fit of morality, has always been puzzling. I think it is partly explained if we accept that one of Byron's previous reputations was that of a poet of love and constancy. By 1816 it was also more clear to upper-income-group readers that Byron was not a safe poet like Scott or Rogers. In the

Table 1.7   Production

CHP 3	12 000
CHP 4	10 000
Manfred	6 000
Marino Faliero	3 500
Sardanapalus and *Cain*	6 000
Werner	5 000

language of a later political leader, he was 'not one of us'. Moore's *Lalla Rookh*, first published in 1817, was waiting to fill the gap Byron had vacated.

The falling-away of interest in Byron can be seen in the production figures. Few of the books which Murray published after 1816 went beyond their first edition. This was true of *Childe Harold*, Canto 3, *Childe Harold*, Canto 4, *Manfred, Mazeppa, Marino Faliero, Sardanapalus*, and *Werner*. Table 1.7 gives the figures. These are well down on the figures for *Childe Harold*, Cantos 1 and 2 and the tales. According to a letter of 2 April 1818 from Murray to Blackwood, he had by that time sold 10 000 copies of *Childe Harold*, Canto 4.[23] That is the whole edition. As with his claim about *The Prisoner of Chillon*, this claim cannot therefore be accepted. And there is plentiful evidence that some of these books moved very slowly indeed. You find copies of the 1821 first edition of *Marino Faliero* with advertisement leaves of 1828, and others in remainder bindings of the 1830s. I have a copy of *Childe Harold*, Cantos 1 and 2, 9th edition, 1815, in a remainder binding of about 1835, unsold from the boom of 20 years earlier.

Now let me turn to *Don Juan* where a different picture emerges. As we know, Murray was unenthusiastic about publishing the poem at all, but his plan was evidently to follow the example of *Childe Harold* and print first in quarto, then reprint in octavo, with the later Cantos available only in octavo. Table 1.8 shows the prices and the quantities. As you can see, the prices are similar to those for *Childe Harold* but the quantities are lower, reflecting the general slump in Byron's reputation since the separation.

Murray assumed that the potential purchasers would be the same groups as had bought Byron's earlier works. As a Tory himself he knew their main characteristics. They were rich and mostly members of the landed classes. They were in favour of strong government, the royal family, high grain prices, and estab-

Table 1.8   *Don Juan:* price and quantities

	Price (shillings)	Numbers
Murray 1 and 2, 4° 1819	31.5	1 350
1 and 2, 8° 1819	9.5	not available
3, 4 and 5, 8° 1821	9.5	1 500
Onwhyn 1 and 2, 1819	4	not available
Sherwin 1 and 2, 1820	4	not available
Murray 1 and 2, small 8° 1820	5	not available
3, 4 and 5, small 8° 1821	5	not available
Hunt 6, 7 and 8, 1823 8°	9.5	1 500
small papers	7	3 000
18°	1	17 000

lished religion. They were against democracy, rights for women, reform of Parliament, reform of anything. I need not repeat the details of their reaction. As a barometer of opinion, we can usually rely on Robert Southey, who described *Don Juan* as 'a high crime . . . against society'; 'mockery . . . mingled with horrors, filth with impiety, profligacy with sedition and slander . . .'.[24] Andrew Rutherford in his *Critical Heritage* volume notes the critical description of the poem as 'moral vomit' and 'ordure'.[25]

Some booksellers refused to handle the book, including Blackwood in Edinburgh who had shared in the earlier successes. The quarto edition did not sell out and some copies were sent for waste paper. There is an interesting remark by Lockhart about the book being read in 'furtive quarto' which implies that even those who did buy it were ashamed of reading it or of letting it fall into the hands of ladies.[26]

But *Don Juan* produced a new phenomenon. 1819 was the year of the notorious Six Acts when the Government cracked down hard on political dissent. One of their objectives was to suppress newspapers and in this aim they were immediately and totally effective. However, one of the unintended side-effects was that the radical newspaper publishers looked for other ways of employing their printing presses. Even before the octavo version of *Don Juan* was put on sale, a man called Onwhyn reprinted a pirate edition. It is described on the title page as 'An exact copy from the quarto edition' and priced at 4 shillings. It was published without even paper covers. Murray obtained an injunction, but the laws of copyright are not always effective against the laws of economics, and another piracy was published in 1820 by a man called Sherwin, again at 4 shillings.

Byron had never been altogether sympathetic to Murray's policy of high prices. When the American visitor, George Ticknor, presented him in 1815 with an American piracy of his poems, Byron 'expressed his satisfaction at seeing it in a small form because in that way, he said, nobody would be prevented from purchasing it. It was in boards, and he said he would not have it bound . . .'.[27] Byron believed that Murray could match the pirates if he chose. As he wrote to Kinnaird on 12 September 1822:

> As to what regards Murray – that great man ought to be narrowly watched – don't you be talked over by the fellow. – He will prate of piracy – but recollect that he might neutralize this in a great measure by publishing *very cheap* small editions of the *same type with former piracies* – at the same time – reserve his *smooth octavos* – for former [purchasers] – of the same more expensive Calibre.[28]

It is reported that when *Don Juan* was published there was a rush in Albemarle Street with messengers filling the street and parcels being given out through the window.[29] But again quantification modifies and corrects an impression given by anecdotal evidence. The numbers printed were small and there was little demand for reprints. At least one of the 'new editions' of Cantos 1 and 2 was made up of old sheets with a new title page. The volume containing Cantos 3, 4 and 5 jumped straight from a first to a so-called fifth edition. The slide which had started in 1816 was continuing. In 1820 Murrary started to produce cheaper editions at 5 shillings, but they do not seem to have made much difference.

By the end of 1822 when Byron had six more cantos waiting to be published and others on the way, he finally broke with Murray. An arrangement was made with John Hunt for an entirely new type of publishing. The next four volumes of *Don Juan* were published at close intervals simultaneously in three different sizes. Firstly, a traditional octavo just like Murray's with which it could easily be bound. Secondly, a smaller and cheaper version, and thirdly an extremely small and cheap version available for a shilling. Of that so-called common version no less than 17 000 copies were printed of each volume. It was by far the biggest single edition of any Byron book. If you look at Table 1.8 you can see the dramatic tumble in prices in four years from thirty-one shillings and sixpence to one shilling, and the equally dramatic increase in production numbers. And these prices do not include binding costs, for the shilling edition was hardly ever bound. *Don Juan* was affordable by many groups who had played almost no part in the

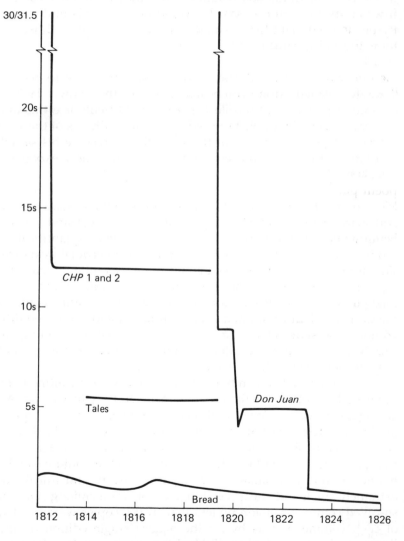

Figure 1.2   Byron and bread

earlier boom, all the middle classes, but also shopkeepers, trades-men, artisans and other higher-paid manual workers, many of whom were politically active and much more sympathetic to Byron's ideas than his previous readership. The change from earlier years and the reason for it can be seen vividly in Figure 1.2, which shows the price of Byron relative to the price of bread.

The book sold rapidly. Even at 1 shilling, however, it was not able to compete with the pirates of which there were about twenty, in the first ten years alone, all producing small-size editions. In some the print is so tiny that it can scarcely be read with the naked eye. These books were probably read on Sundays, the only day of the week when workers had access to enough light. In 1823 a court lifted the injunctions against one of the pirates on the grounds that *Don Juan* was such an immoral book that it could not be protected by the law. The effect was splendidly perverse.

Until I tried to compile an estimate, Table 1.9, I did not realise quite how overwhelming the numbers are. In the 10 years after publication I have found 51 separate editions of all or part of the poem published in London. Of official editions, that is those by Murray and Hunt, the records of production are fairly complete and they total about 94 000. Of pirate editions I believe the Benbow, Sudbury, and Dugdale editions which competed with Hunt's shilling 'common' edition were probably printed in large numbers, but I have no direct evidence. However, on an average of

Table 1.9   *Don Juan, 1819–28*

Editions of individual volumes

Official	19
Pirate	32
	—
	51

Number of copies

Official	94 000	94 000
Pirate	32 000 (estimated)	64 000 (estimated)
(average edition 1 000)		(average edition 2 000)
	126 000	158 000
Readers (× 5)	630 000	790 000
Readers (× 10)	1 260 000	1 580 000

one thousand copies per pirate edition, we reach a total of 126 000 copies of all or part of the book. That is 5 times the number for the *Corsair*, and nearly twice the total for *Childe Harold* Cantos 1 and 2 and the early tales put together. If we apply what I think is a more realistic figure of 2000 for the average size of edition, the estimate rises to above 150 000. You can easily work out the total for 3000 or more if you think they are preferable.

Again we need a multiplier to convert copies to readers. The poor probably share more than the rich. On the other hand, many of the readers presumably read all six parts of the poem and there must be considerable overlapping. But if we take five readers per copy, that gives well over half a million. If we take 10 readers per copy the figures become so great as to be scarcely believable.

Whatever assumption we use in building the estimate, the main conclusion is established. Within a decade *Don Juan* had penetrated far deeper into the reading of the nation than any other modern book, with the possible exception of Tom Paine's *Rights of Man*, and new pirate editions were still being put on the market in the 1830s. The poem was read, in part at least, by many thousands who did not read any of Byron's other works, and it was probably read by thousands who read no other book of any kind except the Bible.

The readership of *Don Juan* was not only far larger, it was different. The number of copies produced for the higher income groups – the octavos – are a fraction of those for earlier years. Of course it could be that the upper- and middle-class families bought the cheap editions instead. But I do not think so. After 1822 *Don Juan* was sold in a different class of bookshops, not the elegant premises at 50 Albemarle Street but centres of the radical culture which were regularly raided and their owners fined and imprisoned. Shops run by John Hunt, Dugdale, Sherwin, Carlile, Benbow and others, some of which specialised in subversive literature, anti-religious propaganda, advice on birth control, and pornography. The publisher Benbow was the first to print Lord Byron's name as the author. He hung a picture of Byron outside his shop and called it the Lord Byron's Head as if it was a tavern. It was these shops which Southey described as 'preparatory schools for the brothel and the gallows'.[30]

This new class of readers was not much interested in the former Byron, the Byron of *Childe Harold* and the *Tales*. For one thing these poems still remained out of reach financially, but we can learn something more from the pattern of piracies, of which there were only a few. For example, among those produced by Dugdale in 1824, was the *Prisoner of Chillon* which was so slow to move at the higher price. Prices for other Byron works are quoted on the back. Fourteen Cantos of *Don Juan* were by then available for 4 shillings and sixpence for the lot. The *Corsair* was 2 shillings and so on. There is no mention of *Childe Harold*. This is a dog which did not bark.[31]

We have always known that there were two Byrons, the Byron of *Childe Harold* and the *Tales*, and the Byron of *Don Juan*. What this analysis suggests is that there were also two readerships, although with some overlap. The first consisted largely of noblemen and gentlemen and their ladies. They were fairly rich, illiberal and conventional, and attracted to Byron, among other things by his treatment of love. Their interest was at its peak in 1814 and 1815, but after the scandals of 1816, and the realisation that Byron did not share their views, it fell away, and Byron's readership among this social group dropped perhaps by as much as a half or two-thirds. Meanwhile in the 1820s a growing new readership developed among a different class of society, who can be loosely categorised as the educated lower middle and upper working classes. They read *Don Juan* with enthusiasm but were largely indifferent to *Childe Harold* and the *Tales*.

There is another constituency of Byron's readers who deserve a mention and who may have spanned the gap. After the end of the war many British people settled on the Continent, where the cost of living in sterling terms was a fraction of British levels. There are plenty of them in the Byron story – Scrope Davies, Medwin, Trelawny, Captain Roberts, the Gisbornes, the Masons, the Shelleys. Some had strong personal reasons for leaving England, but the majority of people in these British communities across the channel were simply trying to survive on fixed incomes below my gentility standard of 100 shillings a week. On the whole their lives were dull, for they had nothing to do and no role in society. But one thing they did have in plenty, to help while away their days – in France, Belgium, Germany and elsewhere you could buy locally-published editions of Byron very cheaply. Galignani and Baudry in Paris advertised their huge volumes of Byron's collected works 'at a third to an eighth of London prices' and you could buy individual poems for a few francs. It is clear from the sheer numbers, not only that these books were immensely popular among the expatriate rentier class, but that many copies found their way to this country.

Although the evidence is necessarily scattered, I suspect that they were obtained by people who had always been interested in politics, literature, and ideas, but who had previously been kept on the periphery by the high prices.

If we had more time I could try to take the analysis forward to the 1830s and 1840s although the further we move from the early editions and the bigger the number of collected editions in circulation, the harder it is to quantify. By the 1830s, however, we know that many of the volumes of *Childe Harold* and the *Tales*, which had been sold so expensively in the years before 1816, had reached the second-hand market. Unsold new stocks were remaindered. By that time there were almost no reprints being produced for sale to the upper or middle classes, presumably because there was no market. Instead Murray started to produce reprints of individual poems for sale at a few pence each. The price of all of Byron, not just *Don Juan*, was by the 1840s well below the price of bread, and well within the reach of clerks, artisans, and even carpenters, and we know that demand was brisk and that turnover was high.[32] In this respect, as in the earlier period, the history of Byron's books is very different from that of, say, Wordsworth or Coleridge, let alone Shelley or Keats.

Byron was still far from being accepted into the canon of English literature. *Don Juan* could only be assimilated by the dominant culture if its more objectionable sentiments were suppressed. Thus we see efforts to blunt the impact by producing anthologies and bowdlerised versions, 'Beauties of Byron', one of which was endorsed as safe by a clergyman. *Don Juan* is not, however, a poem from which it is easy to extract specific 'beauties' – the irreverence is in the tone of voice as much as in the specific sentiments. I wonder whether the concentration on the 'Isles of Greece', does not derive from this time and this attitude? The song is a fragment of the previous Byron, quite out of character with the rest of the poem. It is almost the only passage you can find which could safely be given to ladies. The complete poem meanwhile continued to be reprinted in full throughout the early Victorian period by the slightly disreputable firm of Milner, successor to the earlier pirates.

Let me now offer a word about the illustrations. From near the beginning, Byron was a visual as well as a literary phenomenon. The Phillips portrait which Murray started to sell for binding in Byron's poems in July 1814 was re-engraved dozens of times until it became one of the most recognisable images of the age. Even when the pictures of Byron were poor as likenesses, they usually share two characteristics – an extravagant open-necked shirt and curly, slightly receding hair.

The idea of illustrating the poems occurred first to an artist called Thurston who rushed out a series of line-drawings to *The Corsair* in the spring of 1814. At the end of 1814, when interest was near its height, Murray started to sell a set of 12 plates by Stodhart which could be bound into books. These are much better in every way and were still being advertised in 1816.[33] They were expensive, three guineas for quarto, thirty shillings for octavo, and eighteen shillings for small paper edition, but it is easier to look at pictures than to read poems and the multiplier is probably much higher than five or 10 which I suggested for the texts. In 1819 Murray produced another set, this time by Westall. They held the field until the early 1830s when Finden and others produced sets of landscapes and portraits illustrative of the poet's life as well as illustrations of the other Byron beauties, the heroines of the poems. All these pictures from Stodhart onwards reaffirm the notion that Byron and Childe Harold were one and the same person. Almost every Byronic hero has curly hair and an open-necked shirt. These pictures also give powerful reinforcement to the image of the submissive Byronic heroine. Some were cut out by ladies for their albums. Later we see them reproduced in the printed gift books, *The Keepsake*, *The Gem*, *Forget Me Not*, *Friend-ship's Offering* and so on which are such a feature of the 1830s. But there they are Byronic images without Byron, for in the hundreds of gift books there is scarcely an extract from any of Byron's poems. If, as I suspect, these appallingly insipid books were intended to replace the personal manuscript albums which ladies kept in earlier years, they not only completed the censoring of unsuitable aspects of Byron but deprived ladies of one of their last corners of private space.

Again when we turn to *Don Juan*, there is a difference. Neither Murray nor Hunt produced any illustrations to *Don Juan* during Byron's lifetime. But in art as in literature the pirates supplied the deficiency. There are not many pictures, but those which were produced reaffirm vividly the essentially subversive nature of the poem. If Byron was Childe Harold he was also Don Juan. The poet whom ladies had worshipped as the hero of long-suffering roman-tic love has been transformed into a sex object. The submissive heroines are now women who know their own desires and are ready to take the initiative. This tradition persists into the cheap Victorian reprints and was presumably among the reasons why ladies were kept away from them.

Let us now sum up so far. We have identified two major different impacts and a number of minor ones. Numbers of copies sold, books read, and pictures looked at are all indicators of impact, and probably of influence as well. We could leave the analysis there or elaborate it with other historical evidence. But for the evaluation to be complete we should try to take it to the final stage. We need to return to the original model in Figure 1.1 and consider the last link between reading and influence. This is, of course, very difficult. But here too, I suggest, our conclusions are likely to be more reliable if we have an explicit methodology for what exactly we are trying to judge. In particular we need to consider the nature of the link. Not everything Byronic in the nineteenth century can be attributed to the influence of Byron, any more than all good health can be attributed to doctors. We do not have what evaluators call a base case, a statement of what would have happened otherwise in the absence of Byron, and I doubt if one can usefully be constructed. But what we can do, I suggest, is devise one or more cultural equivalents of my economic gentility index, some standards for assessing the conventions within which readers interacted with the texts they were reading, some benchmarks of discourse which take account of the differing circumstances and expectations of different groups of readers. We will then have something to measure change against. Ultimately of course every reader has a unique experience of the text, but this does not mean that there are not identifiable patterns.[34]

It is for this purpose I suggest that we can best exploit the evidence of the reviews rather than using them, as scholars have tended to do, as direct indicators of the impact on readers. In evaluative terms, reviews are outputs from Byron but inputs for Byron's readers. They are intermediaries looking both ways – offering their own comments on the texts but trying at the same time to take account of the expectations of their expected readership. Thus, to establish the conventions of the discourse between Byron and the upper-class early readers of *Childe Harold* and *The Tales* we should look to the *Quarterly* and, to a lesser extent, the *Edinburgh*. By looking at a range of comments, not just those on Byron, we can build up a picture of the implied cultural standards, for example the notion that literature is primarily entertainment – and a social entertainment at that – the search for specific 'beauties', the delight in the exotic, and so on. We can see that Byron is being judged as a possible successor to Scott, whose poems had been published a few years earlier in similarly huge editions of quarto and octavo, with illustrations to match. For the discourse of *Don Juan* and the readers of the pirated editions, on the other hand, we should look to the reviews in the radical press and the prefaces which some of the pirates usefully provided. We can build a standard which sees literature as a critique of society, as a potential agent of change and an ally in the struggle against the empire of cant. Byron in this discourse is seen primarily as a poet of freedom including sexual freedom, and *Don Juan* a poem, as Benbow wrote, composed 'in the spirit of an epicure and a libertine'.

Our normal literary categories may have to be revised or added to under this procedure, for they are, I suspect, too often descriptive only of the inputs of literature. We have Augustan writers but does it make sense to talk of Augustan readers? Thus, in the case of Byron, we might call the earlier discourse the romantic respectful and the later the realistic subversive.

When we have done this we are probably near the limits of the evaluative approach. However we are more informed than we should otherwise have been both about the nature of the questions which arise in the last box and about how we might set about judging the answers. We cannot do what we would do with the evaluation of a government publicity programme at this stage, that is ask the identified groups directly whether they believe they have been influenced or have changed their behaviour (and then discount their answers). But what we can do is look at what they say in letters, diaries, autobiographies, and so on.

Following the *Don Juan* realistic–subversive strand we are therefore led to consider the possible influence of Byron on the Reform movement and the Chartists, and we duly find that many of the leaders read the book and even wore open-necked shirts *à la Byron*.[35] For the romantic–respectful, we can establish a link with the Philhellenes who went to fight for Greek independence. As for the more general impact, I looked through the records of the early reading of a few dozen Victorians, writers, politicians, and others who grew up during the years of Byron's early fame or shortly afterwards. Contrary to what I had assumed, among the writers at least, almost everyone seems to have read and admired Byron's poetry, even if they disapproved of the man. But it is the early Byron they like, not *Don Juan*, and it was the women writers,

Charlotte Brontë, Elizabeth Barrett Browning, and George Eliot who disliked that poem most. The two main impacts which diverged in 1819 are still noticeably separate a generation and more later, and so are the modes of discourse.

Here I will end. My figures and conclusions about Byron can no doubt be revised and improved upon, and in some areas I have done little more than suggest further lines of investigation. More generally, however, I hope that I have done enough to show the value – and the practicality – of developing a formal, explicit, empirically-based and empirically-testable methodology for evaluating cultural impact and cultural change.

Notes

1. *Policy Evaluation, A Guide for Managers* (London: HMSO, 1988).
2. The production figures, extracted from the Murray archives, are quoted in Thomas James Wise, *A Bibliography to . . . Byron*, 1933. In the Preface, Wise includes a handsome tribute to the young man who helped him find the figures, Mr John G. Murray, the future John Murray the Sixth.
3. Prices from Wise, Murray's advertisements, and surviving copies. Binding costs estimated from contemporary records quoted by Charles Ramsden, *London Bookbinders 1780–1890*, 1952, and Michael Sadlier, *The Evolution of Publishers' Binding Styles*, 1930.
4. Extracted from *Navy List* 1816.
5. R. D. Altick, *The English Common Reader*, 1957, p. 262. Other figures in Thomas Tooke, *The History of Prices*, 1838, and elsewhere.
6. Altick (op. cit., p. 260), quoting a Select Committee of 1818.
7. J. Marshall, *A Digest of All the Accounts*, 1833, p. 44.
8. *Don Juan*, xi, 45.
9. *Don Juan*, xiii, 49.
10. See H. H. Lamb, *Climate, History and the Modern World*, 1982, p. 239.
11. Figures in Tooke and in *Annual Register* for the various years. Prices are for a quartern loaf of about 4 pounds weight.
12. Tooke, i, p. 313.
13. Quoted in Andrew Rutherford ed., *Byron, The Critical Heritage*, 1970, p. 35, from a letter quoted in Vere Foster, *The Two Duchesses*, 1898, where no date is given. The remark may therefore have been made later when copies of the octavo edition were available.
14. The sample I have examined or seen described gives the following pattern.

	CHP	Giaour	Bride	Corsair	Lara	Ode	Lament
1815 (2 vols)	8	6	10	7	5	11	3
1815 (3 vols)	9	13	10	8	4	11	3
1817	10	14	11	9	4	11	–
1818	–	14	11	9	4	12	6

The other poems in the collections are mostly first editions. The curiosity of *Lara* in 1815 suggests that books were not always sold in exactly the order in which they were produced.

15. Samuel Smiles, *Memoir and Correspondence of . . . John Murray*, 1891, i, p. 369, quoted a letter of Murray of 13 December 1816.

16. *Quarterly Review*, October 1816.

17. The frequent copying of *English Bards* is noted by Thomas Jefferson Hogg, *The Life of Percy Bysshe Shelley*, i, p. 300.

18. The album of Augusta Browne, sister of Mrs Hemans, contains an extract from *The Revolt of Islam*, but that is an exception which confirms the rule, for we know that Shelley had a direct link.

19. Quoted *Critical Heritage*, p. 35, from *Recollections of the Table Talk of Samuel Rogers*, 1856, p. 233.

20. Wise, i, p. 94; Smiles, i, pp. 224ff.

21. Copied into a copy of *Queen Mab*, Huntington Library.

22. Leslie A. Marchand: '"Come to me, my adored boy, George"': Byron's Ordeal with Lady Falkland, *Byron Journal*, 1988.

23. Blackwood archives, National Library of Scotland.

24. Southey to the Editor of the *Courier*, 8 December 1824, reprinted in Prothero's edition of Byron's *Letters and Journals*, 1898–1901, vi, p. 398.

25. *Critical Heritage*, pp. 2–3.

26. *John Bull's Letter to Lord Byron*, 1821, quoted in *Critical Heritage*, p. 184.

27. *Life, Letters and Journals of George Ticknor*, 1876, i, p. 62. For a description of the actual volume, see Coleridge's edition of Byron's *Poetical Works*, 1904–5, vii, p. 90.

28. *Letters and Journals*, 9, p. 207.

29. Smiles, i, p. 413.

30. See note 24.

31. Dugdale did produce a pirate of *Childe Harold* in 1825 but only after *Don Juan*, *The Vision of Judgment*, *Hebrew Melodies*, and six other poems.

32. See Altick, p. 253 and other specific references to Byron's books in the accounts of the second-hand booksellers in Henry Mayhew's *London Labour and the London Poor*, 1861, on which Altick draws.

33. They are reproduced in the McGann edition of Byron's *Complete Poetical Works*.

34. Here I believe I am making a similar point to one made by McGann who writes about the quarto edition of *Don Juan* having 'a different meaning' from the first pirated edition. *Textual Criticism and Literary Interpretation*, 1985, quoted in *Byron Journal*, 1988, p. 95.

35. See Michael Foot: *The Politics of Paradise, A Vindication of Byron*, 1988. For the Byronic shirts, see Thomas Frost: *Forty Years Recollections*, 1880, pp. 49, 57.

2

'My Brain is Feminine': Byron and the Poetry of Deception

JEROME J. McGANN

I

I begin with a mouldy anecdote, a late supplement to that once-flourishing industry – now part of the imagination's rust belt – called 'Curiosities of Literature'.

In 1894 a short article appeared in *Notes and Queries* under the heading 'Byroniana'. Its subject was a poem entitled 'The Mountain Violet' which the author of the article, Henry Wake, attributed to Byron.[1] The case for authenticity was argued on two counts, one archival and one stylistic. The archival argument observed that the poem was printed in an anthology of verse collected by one Charles Snart under the title *A Selection of Poems*, published in Newark in two volumes in 1807–8. Wake said that he was in possession of a set of Snart's edition with 'Mrs. Byron' written in pencil in her hand on the front flyleaf, and with the following notation on the end flyleaf of Volume II: "66 from Nottingham Journal'. The latter was a reference to 'The Mountain Violet', which was printed on page 66 of Vol. II. The poem, it turns out, was in fact first printed in *The Nottingham Journal* on 9 April 1803. Neither printing attributes authorship, but according to Wake the pencil notation at the end of Snart's book is in Byron's hand.[2]

Wake went on to argue that the poem's style showed remarkable congruities with the style of Byron's early verse. Such matters are difficult to decide, of course, especially when one is dealing with juvenilia. At that stage of a career, an author's style will be derivative, and one expects to observe features which will be

26

common to any number of other contemporary writers. Nonetheless, the stylistic similarities are striking; and this fact, coupled with the archival evidence, led Wake to his attribution. Wake's judgement was seconded by the distinguished Byronist Richard Edgecumbe, who wrote a brief supporting article which appeared shortly afterwards in *Notes and Queries*. (I pass without comment the importance of Nottingham and Newark since, as all Byronists know, these are places strongly connected with Byron's early verse – the writing of it, the printing, the publishing.)[3]

I initially became interested in this minor literary incident when I began editing Byron's poetry – that was in 1970. 'The Mountain Violet' had never been included in a collected edition of Byron's works, and I had to decide what to do in my edition. For sixteen years that poem remained in my files under the heading 'Dubia' – in other words, in an editorial limbo, neither in nor out of the authoritative corpus. In 1986, however, I discovered the truth about 'The Mountain Violet'. Byron did not write it. The poem is the work of Charlotte Dacre, and it was published in her two-volume poetry collection of 1805, *Hours of Solitude*.

I made my discovery while I was reading Dacre's books, reading them for the first time, I am ashamed to say. It was a discovery I was very happy to have made. But the reading led to another, related discovery about Byron's poetry, and that second discovery is what I want to talk about today.

The title *Hours of Solitude*, for one who knows Byron, can suggest only one thing: *Hours of Idleness*, Byron's first published book of verse issued two years after Dacre's book. This verbal echo is in fact only one part of the massive act of allusion to Dacre which constitutes the title page of Byron's book: the format of the latter imitates Dacre's title page in the most remarkable way. As might be expected, the title page signals a series of textual echoes and allusions which are scattered through the 'Original' parts of the book Byron subtitled 'Poems Original and Translated'. Indeed, Byron's misguided plea, in his book's Preface, for the reader's 'indulgence' because the poems are 'the productions . . . of the lighter hours of a young man, who has lately completed his nineteenth year' was a move he took over directly from Dacre. In her prefatory note 'To the Reader' and then throughout the text, she called attention to 'the age at which [her poems] were written' (that is, all before she was twenty-three, and many when she was sixteen or younger).

What most impressed Byron in *Hours of Solitude* were the poems
of sentiment. The poems he addressed to various female persons
in his first three books (the volumes culminating in *Hours of
Idleness*), as well as lyrics like 'The First Kiss of Love', call back to a
number of similar poems in Dacre's work – for example, 'The Kiss',
'The Sovereignty of Love', 'To Him Who Says He Loves', and so
forth. In the last section of *Hours of Idleness*, which comprises a kind
of critical reflection on all of his poetry to that point, Byron includes
a new poem, 'To Romance', where he reluctantly (and sentimen-
tally) acknowledges a failure of the muse of sentiment.

This instance of a neglected influence on Byron's juvenile poetry
might appear just another item in the shop of literature's curiosities. But the event has an aftermath of real consequence in the
history of Byron's work. The event has perhaps an even greater
consequence for an understanding of the history and significance
of so-called sentimental poetry, especially as it was written by
women – but that is a large subject which shall not, unfortunately,
be able to take up here. Today I shall concentrate on the smaller
and more local matter, on Byron.

We start to glimpse the complications involved by recalling
Byron's attack upon Della Cruscan poetry in *English Bards and
Scotch Reviewers*. The celebrity of that group of writers had waned
since Gifford attacked them in his nineties satires *The Baviad* (1791)
and *The Maeviad* (1795).[4] Nonetheless, their influence on contemporary writing remained considerable, and can be traced even in
writers who are still given prominent positions in our somewhat
skewed literary histories: in, for example, Moore and Shelley, as
well as Keats and Byron. Dacre published under the Della Cruscan-
style pseudonym 'Rosa Matilda',[5] and in *English Bards* Byron
attacks her under that name, and through her the late flowers of
the Della Cruscan gardens:

> Far be't from me unkindly to upbraid
> The lovely ROSA's prose in masquerade,
> Whose strains, the faithful echoes of her mind,
> Leave wondering comprehension far behind.
> Though Crusca's bards no more our journals fill,
> Some stragglers skirmish round the columns still,
> Last of the howling host which once was Bell's,
> Matilda snivels yet, and Hafiz yells . . . .

(ll. 755–62)[6]

In an attached prose note Byron characterises Dacre as a 'follower of the Della Cruscan School', the author of 'two very respectable absurdities in rhyme' as well as 'sundry novels in the style of the first edition of the Monk' (*CPW* I, 413). These remarks are laced with witty innuendo. 'The first edition of the Monk' (1796) created such a scandal that Lewis was driven to delete and revise the sexual passages which were so offensive to many readers. Byron links Dacre's novel *The Confessions of a Nun of St. Omer* (1805), which was dedicated to Lewis, with the latter's notorious novel, and when he characterises Dacre's poetry as 'very respectable' he wants his irony to be taken. 'Sentimental' poetry like that by Dacre, Mrs Hannah Cowley ('Anna Matilda'), and Mary ('Perdita') Robinson (or by Moore and Byron and Shelley) did not go in for the sexual fleshliness that one finds in certain Gothic novels and plays; nonetheless, the sexuality of such writing was explicit even if the diction and imagery were kept, as Byron delicately puts it, 'very respectable'.

In this context let us recall the crucial bibliographical facts: that *Hours of Idleness* was published in June 1807, and that *English Bards* was initially composed between October 1807 and November 1808. It took Byron less than a year to break off his literary liaison with Rosa Matilda, and to publicise their separation. In fact, the breakup took somewhat longer than that, as one can see by glancing at Byron's first two books of verse, both privately printed. *Fugitive Pieces* (1806), Byron's first book, is distinctly marked by that sort of 'very respectable' poetry which *English Bards* ridiculed in the 'sentimental' verse of various writers, and particularly in the work of Dacre and his later close friend Tom Moore.[7] Byron's second book, *Poems Original and Translated* (1807), he himself characterised as 'miraculously chaste'[8] because it represented a deliberate effort to tone down the 'sentimentalities' which had so heated up, in their presumably different ways, the readers of *Fugitive Pieces*. By the time he gets to writing *English Bards* Byron has abandoned the sexually-charged poetry – the 'sentimental' poetry – which had initially seduced him. Byron becomes 'very respectable'.

In doing so, however, we have to recognise how Byron has changed the character of his own changes. His turn (between 1808 and 1816) from what he would later call 'amorous writing' (*DJ* V, st. 2) to a concentration on satire, travelogue, and heroic poetry was a turn from 'feminine' to 'masculine' modes, a turn from Anacreon to Horace and Homer. When *English Bards* announced this shift in Byron's work by an appeal to Gifford, the poem was

specifically invoking a memory of Gifford's own satiric attack on
the Della Cruscans in his two popular satires of the nineties. In
Byron's case, however, the turn involved a key self-referential
feature which was entirely absent in Gifford's work. Gifford had
never felt anything but abhorrence for Della Cruscan and sentimental poetry, while Byron cut his poetical teeth on it. In this
respect, *English Bards* represents a typically Romantic act of dis-
placement. Charlotte Dacre, among other amorous sentimental-
ists, is ridiculed in Byron's satire, but in truth he simply attacks her
for a kind of writing which he himself had been driven from
because the writing had offended certain provincial readers.[9] The
attack on Dacre in the satire is distinctly an act of bad poetic faith.

But Byron was not happy with himself for having bowed to the
prudery of Southwell society in suppressing *Fugitive Pieces*, and
Hours of Idleness was an effort to keep some faith with Charlotte
Dacre even as he acceded to certain of the wishes of Southwell's
'knot of ungenerous critics'.[10] In *English Bards*, however, Byron
made a complete – but as we shall see, not a final nor a clean –
break with Rosa Matilda, and he did so because *Hours of Idleness*
was still judged too mawkish and sentimental – this time not by a
provincial audience, but by the mighty and male *Edinburgh Review*.
Of course, Byron struck back at his accusers with his first famous
satire, but in doing so he adopted the style and the language of his
attackers. Byron became what he beheld, and in the process Rosa
Matilda fell, in Byron's eyes, from grace. The process is one in
which Byron tries to redeem himself and his work by making a
scapegoat of writers and writing which had given literal birth to his
own imagination.

And so 'The Mountain Violet' drops away from the Byron canon.
It is in fact a spurious text, quite inauthentic; nonetheless, it stands
as a sign of a deeper kind of authenticity which Byron would
struggle his entire life to regain.

II

'Sentimental' poetry – the term will be taken here in its technical
and historical sense – was associated with women writers in
particular, though a great many male poets wrote sentimental
verse. As a pejorative term it came to stand in general for writing
which made a mawkish parade of spurious feelings. In the late

eighteenth and early nineteenth centuries, however, such work
was as frequently deplored for immodesty and even indecency;
and the attacks were all the more virulent because so many
women, both as writers and as readers, found important resources
in this kind of work. To many, and especially to those (men and
women both) who felt called upon to guard public morals, the
whole thing seemed improper or worse; nor were the attacks
without foundation.[11]

Crucial to sentimental poetry is the centrality of love to human
experience and – more significantly – the idea that true love had to
involve a total intensity of the total person – mind, heart, and (here
was the sticking point) body. Love could be betrayed at any of
those centres, and a betrayal of the body (through either lust or a
prudish fastidiousness) was as disastrous as a betrayal of the mind
or heart. Indeed, a betrayal at any point was the equivalent of a sin,
for the 'sentimental' soul was equally diffused through the entire
sensorium. The stylistic index of sentimental poetry, therefore, is a
peculiar kind of self-conscious fleshliness. Dacre's poem 'The Kiss'
provides a good example of the style – for instance, the first stanza.

> The greatest bliss
> Is in a kiss–
> A kiss of love refin'd,
> When springs the soul
> Without controul,
> And blends the bliss with mind.

Sentimental poetry strives to be both emotionally intense and
completely candid. Its purpose is to 'bring the whole soul of man
[and woman] into activity', an event which, in the context of such
writing, means that it is to bring along the whole person – mind
and body as well. So the paradoxes of this poem swirl about the
demand for an experience that is at once completely impassioned
('without controul'), completely physical, and yet perfectly
'refin'd' as well. The poem solicits a wild erotics of the imagination
where blissful consummations occur in and through, or 'with', the
'mind'.

Byron and all the Romantics wrote a great deal of sentimental
poetry – this is precisely why they were attacked by modernist
ideologues like Hulme, Babbitt, and Eliot. Keats and Shelley are
probably our greatest sentimental poets, but even Wordsworth's

verse is marked by sentimentality. Wordsworth, however, made a life's work out of 'subliming', as it were, the project of sentimentalism – attempting to show that the 'sensations sweet/ Felt in the blood and felt along the heart' were actually the impulses of 'something far more deeply interfused', something he called 'the purer mind' ('purer', that is, because it had to be distinguished from the sort of mind that Dacre was describing).[12]

But as Wordsworth was moved by a spiritual transcendence of sensuality and sexuality, Byron plunged completely into the contradictions which sentimentalism had come to involve for him. While these contradictions no doubt have deep psychological roots, I am incompetent to explore such matters. What is clear, at the social and personal level, is that Byron reconstructed those contradictions in his work.

We begin to see this in the myth of the relations between men and women which he deploys in his poetry between 1808 and 1816. This involves a misogynist inversion of a central myth of the sentimentalist programme. According to the sentimentalist idea, when an individual only pretends to the intensities and sensitivities of sentimental love, he (or she) betrays not merely the persons who are love-engaged, they betray love itself in its fullest expression. Byron accepts the sentimentalist terms of the entire transaction: that love-relations will be cast along the norm of heterosexuality; that the partner (in Byron's case, the figure of the woman) is his epipsyche; and that a total love-experience – physical, mental, and spiritual – is the goal.

The 'reality-principle' in this myth (and the term must be put in quotation because it stands only for a myth of reality) is that Byron's sentimental beloveds (who turn out plural, if not legion) continually betray the contract of love.[13] At times Byron will implicate himself in these betrayals of love – for example in the early *Childe Harold* when, in the lyric 'To Florence', he writes of the 'wayward, loveless heart' of the wandering – in several senses – Childe. But even in his Childe Harold mode Byron typically represents himself as a man devoted to love yet continually driven from it, or deprived of it, by circumstance. Byron wants to imagine himself true to love, but cruelly kept from it by interventions beyond his control: the time will be right but the place will be wrong; both time and place will be right, but the social or political structure of the events will make an impediment; or all circumstances will be provident, except the ages of the parties; and so forth. In any case, love is lost – mysteriously, fatally lost, but not by the will of Childe Byron, who is at all times and in all places love-devoted.

That Byronic constancy maintains itself despite the fact that its ideal–object, the feminine beloved, appears as a figure of repeated deceits and betrayals. Sometimes the beloved is lost circumstantially (for example through an untimely death) but she also moves away by her 'wandering', by attaching herself to someone else. Mary Chaworth, Susan Vaughan, Lady Frances Wedderburn Webster, even Lady Caroline Lamb: according to this legend, all prove to be, if not positively 'false', then at least 'fickle'.[14]

This Byronic myth is set down between 1808 and 1816 in a series of lyrics composed with these and perhaps several other women in mind.[15] The three most important, and even astonishing, poems in this series are '[Again Deceived! Again Betrayed]', written to the servant-girl Susan Vaughan; the lyric addressed to Lady Caroline Lamb that begins 'Go – triumph securely – that treacherous vow'; and lastly 'When We Two Parted', a poem written in memory of Lady Frances Wedderburn Webster. The 1816–17 poems written to and about his wife and his sister, including *Manfred*, involve a culminant and critical turn upon the entire pattern, and establish the ground on which the last six years of Byron's poetry will be written.

Though a general myth of social and psychic dysfunction, the Byronic malaise is most acutely expressed as a failure of love. A central representation of the myth is forthrightly stated in the opening lines of the first of the works just mentioned, the lyric addressed to Susan Vaughan.

> Again deceived! again betrayed!
> In manhood as in youth,
> The dupe of every smiling maid
> That ever 'lied like truth'.–

The poem's idea is that Byron, for all his experience in love, simply never learns – that he is too fond, too sentimental. Not that he fails to recognise his own fickleness; as he points out in the third stanza,

> In turn deceiving or deceived
> The wayward Passion roves,
> Beguiled by her we most believed,
> Or leaving her who loves.

But the typography and syntax here deflects the self-accusation even as it presses its charges against the 'smiling maid'. What 'roves' here is not 'Byron' or even the speaker of the lines, it is 'The wayward Passion', the latter word capitalised in order to depersonalise further Byron's involvement. Besides, Byron's persona in these transactions never smiles, like the deceitful 'maid'; he is too heartbroken for that, too sentimental.

The poem, in other words, is a peculiar exercise in 'lying like truth', a work which once again deceives and betrays sentimental love by its pretences to faithfulness and candour. The occasion of the poem, we know, was Byron's discovery that he was not the only lover of the Newstead servant girl Susan Vaughan. In the illusion that he was, Byron was equally deceiving himself and deceived by her. But the greater deception of the poem, and the source of its strength, lies in its assent to its own self-deceptions. This is the deception which makes the poem turn its sting back on itself, like the famous scorpion in *The Giaour*. The epigraph Byron placed at the head of the poem appears finally not to be a comment on Susan Vaughan or women generally, but a gloss on the poem itself.

> I pull in resolution and begin
> To doubt the equivocation of the fiend
> That lies like truth.
>
> [*Macbeth*]

Finally this poem shows itself to be most concerned with how the mind and its constructions wound and betray one's life. *Manfred* will be the culminant text in this important line of Byronic work. It is not the historical Susan Vaughan who is the deceiver in this poem, it is the *figura* of the woman which the work conjures up and sets in motion. It is, in short, Byron's own mind and imagination – the 'author' of this figure of Susan Vaughan who uses his writing to 'lie like truth' both about her and about the *persona* of himself offered in the poem. By the time this author writes *Manfred* he will be able to see the entire pattern of this kind of writing more clearly. 'I loved her, and destroy'd her!', Manfred says of his epipsyche Astarte (II, ii, 117), thereby expressing what amounts, in this Byronic myth, to a double tautology (for both pronouns and verbs in this sentence are equivalent).

The poem Byron wrote about Lady Caroline Lamb is perhaps an even more breathtaking display of 'lying like truth'.

> Go – triumph securely – the treacherous vow
> *Thou* hast broken *I* keep but too faithfully now,
> But never again shall thou be to my heart
> What thou wert – what I feel for a moment thou *art*.

> To see thee, to love thee! what breast could do more?
> To love thee to lose thee 'twere vain to deplore;
> Ashamed of my weakness however beguiled,
> I shall bear like a Man what I feel like a Child.

At first these lines seem hard to understand – at least as we read them in their topical context, that is, in 1812, and at the height of Byron's torrid affair with Lady Caroline.[16] The poem distinctly recalls the lines to Susan Vaughan, which Byron had written only shortly before and which, in one of the two manuscript versions, he had begun 'Again beguiled! again betrayed!', not 'Again deceived'. Once again we meet the *figura* of the repeated deceiver whose name only changes. The problem is, however, that *in fact* Lady Caroline remained perfectly faithful to Byron in 1812. What does the poem have in mind, then, when it speaks of her 'treacherous vow'?

The answer is: her marriage vow to her husband! The agony of the lover here, of Byron, lies in his awareness that he is love-devoted to a woman whose return of love for him involves a betrayal elsewhere. The poem therefore sets out to imagine the futurity of such a love-relationship, to imagine the certainty of Byron's loss of her and the corresponding certainty of her 'career' of deceit.

> For the first step of error none e'er could recall,
> And the woman once fallen forever must fall;
> Pursue to the last the career she begun,
> And be *false* unto *many* as *faithless* to *one*.

Such words! – from a lover to his beloved, from Byron to a woman whom he knew had broken her marriage vow only for him! Priggish? Ungrateful? The lines defy adequate characterisation because they represent such a fundamental betrayal of love and of truthfulness. Sentimental poets like Charlotte Dacre – and like Byron earlier (and later) in his career – declare that love may be betrayed not only by unfaithfulness, by 'wandering', but equally by moral priggishness and prudery. This truly amazing poem shows how the two kinds of betrayal are, as the sentimentalist programme insisted, reciprocals of each other, a dialectic of what Blake described as the love-torments of spectre and emanation.

'When We Two Parted' in a way completes Byron's portrait of this circle of deceptions – completes it, first, because the poem explicitly links itself to 'Go – triumph securely'; and second, because Byron for the first time deliberately casts the poem as a work of deception.[17] In later years he told his cousin Lady Hardy, in what was only apparitionally a 'private' communication, that the poem was written about his affair with Lady Frances Wedderburn Webster, and that when he published it in 1816 he printed it with a purposely 'false date', 1808. The poem was actually written in 1815, he said, about events in 1814–15.[18] The poem was published in Byron's slim volume of *Poems* (1816), the book which also contained the notorious 'Fare Thee Well!' and which, as a whole, was fashioned as a kind of summing-up of Byron's life since he left school and entered the fast and false world. The 'false date' suggested, among other things, that the events in Byron's life between 1808 (the 'date' of 'When We Two Parted') and 1816 (the year when Byron's wife left him – *left him*, as Byron so theatrically lamented in 'Fare Thee Well!') represent a history of Byron's sufferings at the hands of lying and unfaithful women. And the crown of thorns in that series of sufferings was, *mirabile dictu*, Annabella Milbanke.

Byron states his poetical case against her in his 'Lines on Hearing that Lady Byron was Ill', which he wrote late in 1816, while he was working at *Manfred*. The poem turns her 'illness' into a symbolic event, an outward and physical sign of an inward and spiritual condition. Lady Byron, the poem charges, was in fact the unfaithful one in their relationship, the wife who, whatever his faults, would not remain 'faithful' to him when he was begirt with foes. Indeed, as Byron's 'moral Clytemnestra' (l. 37) she is made to epitomise Byron's wonderful idea of 'moral' adultery:

> And thus once enter'd into crooked ways,
> The early Truth, which was thy proper praise,
> Did not still walk beside thee – but at times

And with a breast unknowing its own crimes,
Deceit, averments incompatible,
Equivocations, and the thoughts which dwell
In Janus-spirits – the significant eye
Which learns to lie with silence – the pretext
Of Prudence, with advantages annex'd –
The acquiescence in all things which tend,
No matter how, to the desired end –
All found a place in thy philosophy.

(ll. 47–58)

The terms are familiar: like Susan Vaughan and so many others, Annabella is a fiend of equivocations, a woman – *the* woman – who knows how to lie like truth, in this case, to 'lie with silence'. As applied to the historical Lady Byron, the charges are not unwarranted; nevertheless, the woman addressed in this poem is just as imaginary as the Susan Vaughan, the Caroline Lamb, and the Frances Wedderburn Webster we saw in the other poems. However applicable to Annabella, therefore, this passage has to be read primarily as the key element in a poetical structure of reflections, has to be read – in short – as a self-portrait, down to the very details of its own unconsciousness ('And with a breast unknowing its own crimes').

Byron's texts about unfaithful women were the schools in which he learned to lie with silence. His writing, he told his wife, was an art of equivocation, and its greatness, in a lyric mode, is that it comes in the end to fall under its own judgements:[19]

For thou art pillow'd on a curse too deep;
Thou hast sown in my sorrow, and must reap
The bitter harvest in a woe as real!

(ll. 22–4)

Like the other lyrics we have examined, Byron appears to address this poem to another person; nevertheless, it finally speaks to, and of, himself alone – that is to say, himself as an individual, *and* himself as a Romantic solitary. The poem is a deception at every level, and most patently at the level of its rhetoric, where its massive self-absorption comes masked as the spoken word. This work was spawned in 'hours of solitude'. The pronouns shift their referents because the curse Byron refers to is a kind of secular Original Sin: moral or imaginative righteousness, the sense that one knows what is true (one's self) and what is false (the Other), and that the truth one 'knows' will set one free. The actual truth, however, as Blake equally saw, is nothing but a 'body of falsehood' fashioned in a state of Urizenic solitude. Consequently, the function of poetry – of this poetry of Byron's – is to reveal that body of falsehood, to expose the lies which the mind through its imagination conjures up.

The unfaithfulness of Byron's many women, therefore, is in the end a Byronic *figura* of the betrayed and betraying imagination, which is a specifically male imagination. *Manfred* is a crucial work in Byron's career, then, because it fully objectifies the self-destructiveness of this imagination. Astarte dies not at a blow from Manfred's hand but by a look into his heart. Her 'heart', Manfred's epipsyche, 'gazed on mine and withered' (II, ii, 119). That catastrophic event involves the deconstruction of the self-deceived and self-destructive Romantic imagination. The death of Astarte is a poetical representation not of the death of a woman, Manfred's sister/beloved, but the death of an idea, an idol, even an ideology. Astarte is Manfred's homunculus, his imagination, and the triumph figured in this play is the triumph of Manfred's 'life' over the long disease of his imagination. Manfred's death, in this sense, is the sign that he has finally found it possible to live (or at least to imagine living), has finally escaped those fatal and Romantic illusions of living and loving which *Manfred* names, significantly, Astarte.

Nothing more dramatically reveals the play's awareness of lying and equivocation, and of its own investment in such things, than the so-called 'Incantation' uttered over the unconscious body of the play's hero. As I have argued in some detail elsewhere, this poem, first published separately by Byron as a curse and denunciation of his wife, is so incorporated into *Manfred* as to become a judgement on his play's hero, and thereby a judgement on himself.[20] The *Manfred* text of the curse 'reads' the earlier, separately published text and exposes the reciprocal truth of its lying representations. 'A Voice' speaks the truth over the unconscious Manfred – that his 'unfathomed gulfs of guile', 'the perfection of [his] art', 'call upon' him through this voice, and 'compel' him not merely to *see* that he is a hell unto himself: they compel him 'to *be* thy proper Hell!'

(I, i, 242–51, my italics). Manfred's Romantic imagination, which represented itself to itself as a resort and an escape from an imperfect world, is actually an Original Sin committed against that world, a way of seeing that, just because it is *merely* a way of seeing and not a way of reciprocating, becomes a way of life which is properly called 'Hell', the final solitude. The 'Voice' that speaks over Manfred is, as it were, the silenced voice of Astarte, Manfred's epipsyche now not to be represented as a visible figure (which is her emanative form as Manfred's superego) but rather as an audible voice (which is her spectrous form as libido). The character Manfred is not permitted in his play to see or understand this action literally, but Byron's play – both as an intrinsic dramatic event and an extrinsic communicative exchange – is a declarative embodiment of that action. Thus, when Manfred at last falls in with Lady Byron and all of Byron's other figures of lying and betrayal, the entire structure of Byronic betrayal, initiated through Charlotte Dacre and *her* betrayal, is exposed and confessed.

In tracing this literary history I have taken for granted that we understand how literary texts – poems, novels, plays – are always deployed in the practical mode of 'communicative exchanges': simply, that they are produced in some material way or another. (In terms of those exchanges, the choice to write and *not* to publish, or to circulate privately, is just as important as the choice to publish.) The bibliography of a literary work is therefore the archive, the memorial machine, which defines and preserves those exchanges.

In the case I have been dealing with here, several of the crucial texts were not published by Byron: the poem to Susan Vaughan was not circulated at all, the poem to Lady Caroline was allowed to circulate among a small group of Regency intimates, and the poem on Lady Byron's illness was also shown only to a few people. None of the texts appeared in print in Byron's lifetime. Furthermore, the crucial lines in 'When We Two Parted' which repeat the misogynist message of 'Go – triumph securely' were also not published by Byron; he took them out of the published poem and only revealed them later, toward the end of his life, in a letter to Lady Hardy.

In his published work between 1808 and 1816, therefore, Byron's myth of the fallen women is distinctly muted; indeed, the fact that an elaborate mechanism of concealments has been set in motion is itself concealed. 'I speak not – I trace not – I breathe not thy name': this notorious line from what is perhaps Byron's most notorious unpublished poem may stand as the epigraph of the Byronic mode. The Byronic hero suffers under some secret sin, and the entire structure of alienations which he both exposes and represents is a function of that sin, which is never identified. The poems we have been reading, however, show quite clearly that the unrevealed sin is the offspring of a habit of imaginative deceptions and misrepresentations. It has no name, this sin; it is the sin which dare not, which cannot, speak its name precisely because it has imagined itself *as* the Unspeakable. And *that*, exactly, is what Byron's work in this period communicates: that the inability or unwillingness to communicate is always an essential feature of the communicative exchange.

III

From 1817 to the end of his life Byron's work is consciously preoccupied with Poetry and Truth. As in the first part of his career, therefore, he is much concerned with the topic of lies and deceptions, with what he liked to call, generically, 'cant'. But the issues are treated with greater self-consciousness, if not greater intensity and poetical force, in the later work. This comes about largely because from 1816 Byron tried to include himself in, even identify himself with, that company he had imaged as the forever fallen: the company of women. When the Byron of 1808–16 writes about those who 'once fallen, for ever must fall', he struggles to distance himself from the judgement they are subjected to. His righteousness is the moral adultery he will imagine as, and call 'Lady Byron', Annabella, Clytemnestra. That is to say, it is himself.

The Byron of 1817–24, however, including his female imaginations, is very different. The difference is registered in the dramatic shift in public judgement. No longer the bad but adorable creature of Regency England, the Byron of the *Don Juan* period is an all-but-hopeless case even in the eyes of those reviewers who had earlier celebrated his work most loudly. And this general abandonment of Byron by the reviews is a true reading of his latest work, for the poetry of 1817–24 has itself abandoned some of the key moral imaginations which drove and tormented the work of 1808–16.

The Donna Julia of *Don Juan*, Canto I, is the governing type of his new feminine imagination. In a sense, of course, nothing has changed, for Julia is both a liar and an adulteress. In her incompar-

able letter to Juan, she even acknowledges that she is one of the
forever fallen, bound fatally to 'pursue to the last the career she
begun', that is, 'To love again, and be again undone' (I, st. 194).
The difference lies not in her circumstantial life, but in her consciousness of those circumstances. Julia knows herself – wants to
know herself – *in herself*, and not be constructing her Self through
stories of self-justification.

> Yet if I name my guilt, 'tis not to boast,
>   None can deem harshlier of me than I deem:
> I trace this scrawl because I cannot rest –
> I've nothing to reproach, nor to request.

> (I, st. 193)

This is a new image of the Byronic epipsyche, a female *figura* who
represents not so much sinfulness as the knowledge of sinfulness,
a figure of sympathy and understanding. Julia is the figure who, in
refusing to cast reproaches, heaps coals of fire – a curse of
forgiveness – on her lover. In the lyric works we glanced at earlier,
the male speaker – the Byronic *persona* – speaks to his faithless
lover in very different terms. The power of such works comes
precisely from their non-consciousness, from their ability to create
what the writing does not understand – finally, to create and then
themselves represent a figure of self-deception and lack of
understanding.

Julia's letter is in the genre of those earlier poems. It represents,
however, the Byronic epipsyche's response to her creator – as it
were, the 'word[s] for mercy' which Manfred had begged in vain to
hear from Astarte (II, iv, 155).

> My brain is feminine, nor can forget –
>   To all, except your image, madly blind;
> As turns the needle trembling to the pole
> It ne'er can reach, so turns to you, my soul.

> (I, st. 195)

Here the structure of the Byronic myth of the feminine is fully
revealed. For there are two writers of these lines: Julia, the 'soul'
and 'image' and epipsyche of Byron and his alter-ego Juan; and

Lord Byron himself, who here conjures a way (something Manfred failed to do) for that 'image' to turn and speak to him in more than simply cryptic tones. The 'Julia' of these lines says that her lover Juan is her 'soul', her epipsyche. In making this revelation, however, she speaks as the epipsyche of her poetical creator Lord Byron, out of that structure of creation we have been looking at in Byron's various sentimental lyrics. This speaking image, Byron's feminine brain, thus makes explicit a concealed truth of the dynamic of sentimental love as it plays itself out in his poetry: that it is a mechanism of truth-telling, a procedure whereby figures of imagination tell the truth about their creators, whether the latter are aware of those truths or not.

In moral terms, this change in the character of the Byronic epipsyche appears as a new set of ideas about what it means to tell the truth and what it means to lie.[21] *Don Juan* projects many kinds of lies and liars, of course, but the poem's quintessential figure of lying is, appropriately and characteristically, female. This feminine brain, which Byron ultimately defines as 'mobility', reigns from Julia's bedchamber to Lady Adeline's drawing-room. Far from standing as a figure of reproach, however, Byron's feminine brain becomes in *Don Juan* a device – both a figure and a mechanism – of redemption.

This change is especially clear in Canto XI when Byron digresses from a thought about the duplicity 'Of politicians and their double front,/ Who live by lies, yet dare not boldly lie':

> Now what I love in women is, they won't
> Or can't do otherwise than lie, but do it
> So well, the very truth seems falsehood to it.
>
> And after all, what is a lie? 'Tis but
> The truth in masquerade; and I defy
> Historians, heroes, lawyers, priests to put
> A fact, without some leaven of a lie.

> (sts 36–7)

The stanzas weigh in the balance the lies of women and the lies of men (from politicians to priests). The difference lies in this: that the lies of the feminine brain are imagined to be clear, conscious, even brazen, whereas the male brain is unaware of either the substance, the structure, or even the fact of its lying. Indeed, it is this lack of consciousness which turns the lies of the male brain into that central Byronic nemesis called 'cant'. The hero of this late discourse on the art of lying is, of course, the Julia of Canto I, whose magnificent lying tirade against her cuckolded husband – delivered to his face, in her bedroom, while her lover hides under the bedclothes – is a vision of judgement against him. It is such a vision because the poem means to expose the figure of Julia to us fully – means to expose her even in her awareness of herself as a liar and an adulteress. In this exposure she stands in sharp contrast to Don Alphonso, whose presence in his wife's bedroom stands as the poem's first great figure of 'cant', that figure of 'double dealing' who conceals his lies and deceptions under a parade of openness and truth.

Both 'lying' and 'cant' are departures from the truth. Nevertheless, Byron comes to argue that the distinction between these two 'forms of life' is neither trivial nor false. Everyone is involved in deception; only the canting person reifies these deceptions, seeks to turn them from images of falsehood into figures of 'truth'. The latter is precisely the extension of the meaning of the word 'cant' which Byron's work carries out. Southey is therefore called not merely a liar in *Don Juan*, he is 'that incarnate lie' (X, st. 13) – lying which has assumed a fixed and material existence. Southey assumes such a form almost necessarily because, in Byron's imagination, Southey's vision of judgement is a vision of absolute truth, of which he is the spokesman. Paradoxically, therefore, the Byron of *Don Juan*, like his feminine imaginations in that work, is a deceiver, whereas men like Southey are taken as the representatives of accepted Truth – 'truth' being understood now, however, according to that excellent modern proverb, 'Truth is lies that have hardened'.[22]

Manfred is once again the key text for constructing this distinction between lying and cant. As Manfred contemplates suicide on a cliff of the Jungfrau he observes:

> There is a power upon me which withholds
> And makes it my fatality to live;
> If it be life to wear within myself
> This barrenness of spirit, and to be
> My own soul's sepulchre, for I have ceased
> To justify my deeds unto myself –
> The last infirmity of evil.

> (I, ii, 23–9)

Manfred does not redeem himself from 'evil' here, he redeems himself from the 'last infirmity' which evil deeds tempt one toward: the justification of those deeds, the effort to (mis)represent them as something other than what they are. In determining to cease his processes of self-justification Manfred speaks most directly to the Byronic texts of 1808–16, explicating them as texts in which these deceptive dramas of self-justification were playing themselves out.

The connection between self-justification and cant is concealed, or revealed, in the Miltonic allusion executed through the phrase 'The last infirmity of evil'. Here the text glances at Milton's 'Lycidas' (ll. 70–71), where 'The last infirmity of noble minds' is identified as the desire for fame, for a 'public approbation'. This desire is a recurrent topic in *Don Juan*, where Byron both seduces and abandons the public's approbation, mocks it and pursues it. The success of the work might well be represented, in fact, by the resoluteness with which it negotiates those ambivalent impulses, just as that resoluteness will be usefully traced in *Don Juan*'s ambivalent reception history. Indeed, the highest praise that might be given Byron's masterwork is that, although recognised as a masterwork, it never became a cultural touchstone. When the need has arisen for oracular consultations, we have usually gone to Wordsworth and *The Prelude* rather than to Byron or *Don Juan*. (This has been good for Byron, but bad for – a travesty of – Wordsworth.)

Marino Faliero offers another example of a canting self-justification which is pertinent to this discussion. It occurs in Act IV, just after Faliero has overcome his class scruples and determined to carry out the *coup* against the Venetian aristocracy. Faliero reflects on the fact that the oligarchs of Venice, after having insulted him, 'trusted to' his aristocratic character, trusted

> To the subduing power which I preserved
> Over my mood, when its first burst was spent.
> But they were not aware that there are things
> Which make revenge a virtue by reflection,
> And not an impulse of mere anger; though
> The laws sleep, justice wakes, and injured souls
> Oft do a public right with private wrong,
> And justify their deeds unto themselves.

> > (IV, ii, 100–107)

Here the Manfredian phrase works to expose the self-deception of
Faliero. The Doge means that his 'private wrong', his revenge
against his fellow aristocrats, will work in the end a 'public right',
will bring social justice to Venice. But the Doge is massively self-
deceived, for the foundation of his part in the plot against the
nobles has nothing to do with social justice or public service and
everything to do with a private grievance and personal revenge.
The ringing, 'noble' phrases ('though/ The laws sleep, justice
wakes', etc.) are *post facto* special pleading, rhetorical obfuscation.
Nevertheless, as in Julia's letter, this text comes to us through two
voices. One voice we hear is the Doge's self-deceived voice, whose
self-justification and apparent firmness of purpose only mask a
deeper moral 'infirmity'. But that voice is itself defined by a deeper
textual voice, which turns the Doge's personal 'revenge' into a
'virtue by reflection' in a sense entirely unintended by the Doge.
This deeper voice, in fact, translates the entire passage into a
positive expression on behalf of personal integrity and social justice, the two values here falsely proclaimed by the Doge, and
thereby actually revealed through the text.

IV

Byron's interesting new theory of the truth of art is obviously a
critique of the Romantic theory of artistic truth, i.e. a critique of the
idea of Romantic sincerity. Byron's theory is a defence of a certain
kind of poetic artifice which he calls 'the truth in masquerade'. This
remarkable phrase involves an important allusion, indeed, a self-
quotation. I cited the originary passage earlier:

>   Far be't from me unkindly to upbraid
>   The lovely ROSA's prose in masquerade . . .

The allusion tells us that Byron's theory of truth as poetic artifice is
itself a masquerade of some larger truth, including some deceptions and absences of truth. The allusion reminds us, for example,
that Byron's theory has concealed origins in that primary type of
the poetry of Romantic sincerity, sentimental verse. When Byron
in *English Bards* calls Charlotte Dacre's verse 'prose in masquerade'
he is ridiculing her work along the same lines that he ridiculed,
throughout his life, the greatest Romantic poet of sincerity,
Wordsworth.

Of course, in *Don Juan* Byron's attack comes from one who repeatedly insists that his poetic artifice aims for a higher kind of sincerity. Furthermore, if the poetry of sincerity is, as Byron says, dull and prosy, *Don Juan* has made an explicit contract with 'pedestrian muses' ('Dedication', st. 8). Indeed, if the phrase 'prose in masquerade' could ever be applied to any English poem, it could be – as all readers have understood – applied to *Don Juan*, the poem in which Byron 'rattle[s] on exactly as [he] talk[s]' (XV, st. 19).

We can sort through some of these complexities by recalling Byron's attacks on some other children of the sentimental muse. When *Don Juan* was first read, the poem struck a number of readers as wickedly obscene. Byron bristled at the charge, and argued that his work would never induce a person to lustful acts because it was a comic poem. 'Lust is a *serious* passion and . . . cannot be excited by the *ludicrous*', Byron says, and he goes on to contrast his comic writing with serious and sentimental poetry such as his friend Tom Moore's work (*CPW*, V, 679n.). Elsewhere he pursues the same line of argument, only more vigorously, in his brilliant if malicious remarks on Keats's similar sentimental eroticism.

Byron's argument is that the verse of erotic sentimentality – Charlotte Dacre's 'prose in masquerade', John Keats's *'p[i]ss a bed poetry'* (*BLJ*, VI, 200) – turns sex from a matter of the body to a matter of the brain. Sex in poetry becomes 'serious' when it is delivered over to the imagination. At that point the pleasure of the text becomes not moral but, literally, erotic. It is in this sense that Byron will insist, and with good reason to support his position, that sentimental poets like Dacre and Moore and Keats are the true immoralists. Through them eroticism appears as a behaviour of *conscience* – as 'sex in the head'. Unlike sentimental verse, which Byron calls 'the *Onanism* of Poetry' (*BLJ*, VI, 217), *Don Juan* takes up its erotic subjects in a deliberately *un*sentimental way – 'it strips off the tinsel of *Sentiment*' (*BLJ*, VI, 202), he says, and thereby causes offence among those who, while they want sex in poetry, want it in more 'refin'd' forms.

Byron's argument, made in a context when the Romantic ideology was establishing itself, will now seem to us, who stand on the other side of the ideology's historical reign, remarkably insightful. And in truth his imagination of the truth is here quite important. Nevertheless, this Byronic imagination is not 'the whole truth, and nothing but the truth'. It carries its own form of special pleading, and that (what must surely be unconscious) allusion to Charlotte Dacre and his earlier act of poetic betrayal returns in *Don Juan* as a critical opening in Byron's own text, unknown to itself.

Following the concealments and self-deception practised in the poetry of 1808–16, Byron's exilic poetry made a virtue of candour and truth-telling. I pass without comment the important contribution which sentimental poetry like Charlotte Dacre's made toward a poetic ideal of candour and the fulness of truth. These matters we have already touched on, and we have seen the depth of Byron's debt to that poetry. Like Blake's Swedenborg, Byron in 1816 had broken some of the nets that had bound him up, and his escape is registered in his later work. Nevertheless, part of the truth of *Don Juan* still operates in the mode of deception and untruth.

We observe this by interrogating Byron's masterwork on the issue of the erotics of the imagination, the issue of sex in the head. This is the territory occupied by people like Dacre and Moore and Keats, a territory Byron says he has abandoned, as he abandoned his canting homeland. Byron's critique of cant, however, was partly negotiated through a recovery of certain sentimental attitudes – a turn away from the muscular and moral values which so dominate his work between *English Bards* and *Childe Harold* Canto IV. Juan's liaisons with Julia and Haidée are both completely sentimental affairs. Furthermore, Byron's new poetic theory of 'truth in masquerade' is grounded in a sympathetic meditation on a certain kind of 'feminine' lying. Earlier that sort of deception had served only to drive a wedge between Byron and his sentimental attachments, but in *Don Juan* he begins to rethink the issues.

The behaviour of Julia (at the beginning of *Don Juan*) and of Lady Adeline, *la donna mobile* (at the end), epitomises how theatricality and masquerade – deliberate strategies of deception – can serve the cause of deep truth. These strategies will do so, Byron's work argues, only if they are deployed with complete self-consciousness – that is, only if the theatre of deception, or the masquerade, labels itself as such, and includes itself in its own illusory displays. (To the degree that these displays are sentimental productions, to that extent they are part of the theatre of love in the full sentimentalist sense.) In this erotic theatre, the central figure, for the man, must be the woman, 'Whence is our entrance and our exit' (IX, st. 55).

A theory of art, however, once it is deployed through a work, becomes a two-edged sword, and the case is no different for *Don*

Juan. Byron's critique of the sentimental eroticism of Moore and Keats, for example, seems hardly less applicable to many parts of Byron's epic, not least, I suppose, to the scenes in the harem. Criticism might conclude, from this kind of contradiction, that Byron was fabulously self-deceived in thus criticising Moore and Keats; and criticism would no doubt be correct in this judgement. But the exposure of Byron's personal self-deception is far less significant than the way his poetry transforms truth and lies through the artifice of its masquerades. Indeed, the brilliance of the harem episode depends exactly on its having shown so clearly – despite Byron's quotidien pronouncements – the positive relation which operates between sex and the imagination.

This relation is (as it were) dramatised for us in the persons – in the dreams and imaginations – of the young harem women. But the narrator's specular involvement in that drama (and our involvement through him) is equally drawn into the orbit of the poem's theatricality. The harem episode is, in one very obvious sense, nothing more than a distinctly 'male' sex fantasy, and hence a voyeuristic spectacle. The narrator is unaware of his voyeurist perspective, however – or rather, he sees nothing in his act of seeing to be critical of. *We* see this innocence of his mind in his blithe assumption that the scene and events could only be imagined as he has imagined them.

This assumption acquires a critical edge in Byron's poem, however, just because it is a contrived assumption, an artifice. Indeed, the essential wit of the episode arises from the narrator's *conscious* assumption of an innocent eye, his pretence – as in the narrative of Dudu's dream – that he is himself unaware of the word-plays and double meanings of his own discourse. Unlike Julia in her letter in Canto I, Dudu does not narrate her own dream; the narrator tells it for her in indirect discourse. That indirection underscores the theatricality of his talk, the masquerade in which he is involved. The critical consequence, however, is that the narrator is himself pulled on to the stage of the poem. In that event the narrator is released from the bondage of his own imagination. We are not only able, for example, to 'see' and criticise his voyeurism, we come as well into contact with that supreme objectivity which poetic discourse, alone of our discursive forms, seems able to achieve. 'Byron' would not have wanted to be told that his masterwork was itself deeply invested in sentimentalism and sex in the head; nonetheless, this is the case, and it is his own masterwork which tells us so.

In the harem episode we see *Don Juan* operating under the illusion of its own self-consciousness. The narrator's amusement is the sign that he is satisfied with his understanding, that he possesses understanding. But his wisdom is an illusion of knowledge which, however, tells a truth about feeling. The harem episode is a theatrical display of a certain kind of 'sex in the head' – an onanism of poetry fully the equal of Keats's. And it is an onanism of poetry precisely because its eroticism, founded in the sentimentalist project, here executes that project in a space of solitude. The harem episode is an image, in short, not of fulfilled but of frustrated desire. Its pretence to be something else – its pretence to display an ultimately fulfilled eroticism – is an essential feature of its deepest truth.

In Charlotte Dacre's poetry, 'hours of solitude' are hours of critical reflection, hours in which one experiences the loss and deprivation of love and in which one recognises the state of the loss. The harem episode in *Don Juan* means to imagine a way of escaping such solitude and loss, but in the event it succeeds in defining those illusions of escape which serve only to deepen one's awareness of what the experience of loss entails. In this respect the episode is something of a retreat from the philosophical achievement of Canto I. But the text does not revert to the style of the period 1808–16. Byron's feminine and sentimental brain, which emerged between 1815 and 1817, made such a lapse impossible. The eroticism of the harem episode is in certain obvious respects ludicrous and self-deceived, but – like 'The Eve of St Agnes', which is quite a comparable piece of work – the episode does not (at any rate) torture sexual feeling with moral instrumentations. It catches, therefore, the true voice of Romantic feeling – even if the feelings involved are not so rich or complex as the feelings at the conclusion of Canto I.

Notes

1. *Notes and Queries*, 8th series, VI (25 August 1894), pp. 144–5; and for Sir Richard Edgecumbe's piece, noted below, see ibid., p. 515.
2. I have never seen these books described by Wake but his identification of the pencil notations is persuasive. Byron often wrote in pencil in books in this way, especially in his early years.
3. Byron's four early books were all printed in Newark, and of course Byron's life between 1803 and 1807 was closely connected to the Nottingham area.

4. A good brief summary of the Della Cruscan phenomenon is given in John Mark Longaker, *The Della Cruscans and William Gifford. The History of a Minor Movement in an Age of Literary Transition* (Philadelphia, 1924).

5. The Della Cruscans typically published under pseudonyms, and 'Rosa Matilda' is a direct allusion to Mrs Cowley's adopted cognomen 'Laura Matilda'. It is important to realise, however, that Dacre was not a Della Cruscan herself, but a slightly later writer who came under their influence. Dacre's work exhibits a much more self-conscious employment of the Della Cruscan style: see for example her poems 'Passion Uninspired by Sentiment', 'To the Shade of Mary Robinson', and 'The Female Philosopher'.

6. Citations from the poetry are to *Lord Byron. The Complete Poetical Works*, ed. Jerome J. McGann (Oxford, 1980–); when it is necessary to refer to this edition, the abbreviation *CPW* will be used.

7. Throughout his life Byron commented on the erotic elements in Moore's verse, and especially in Moore's *Poetical Works of the Late Thomas Little, Esq.* (1801). This book, a minor classic in the sentimental style, went through numerous printings, and had an important influence on Byron's early work. For a fuller discussion see Jerome J. McGann, *Fiery Dust. Byron's Poetic Development* (Chicago, 1968), Chapter 1.

8. *Byron's Letters and Journals*, ed. Leslie A. Marchand (Cambridge, Mass., 1973–82), I, p. 103; hereafter cited as *BLJ*.

9. The fullest discussion of this event in Byron's life is in Willis W. Pratt's *Byron at Southwell* (Austin, Tex., 1948).

10. 'To a Knot of Ungenerous Critics' is the title of one of Byron's poetical replies to his Southwell critics: see *CPW*, I, pp. 19–22 (and the related poem at pp. 17–19).

11. Some of Gifford's best lines in *The Baviad* and *The Maeviad* involve witty sexual wordplays which call attention not only to the sensuality of Della Cruscan poetry, but to its self-conscious (and hence, from Gifford's point of view, irreal) sensuality. When Byron later saw a similar poetic mode in Keats's work, he ridiculed it as 'the Onanism of Poetry' (*BLJ*, VII, p. 217) – a distinctly Giffordian line of attack.

12. In this respect Wordsworth's was a more successful deployment of the Della Cruscan programme, whose sentimentality inclined toward a travesty of platonic engagement. This travesty, and platonism, are especially clear in the famous poetical 'love affair' which Della Crusca and Anna Matilda carried on in the pages of *The World* in the years 1787–9. The two had in fact never even met.

13. Thus Byron's male friendships come to represent a more stable form of love. Even such love is not completely steady, however, as a number of poems written to his male friends show. In the myth of love Byron deploys, only one figure is imagined as perfectly faithful – his sister Augusta.

14. See the work of 1813 called 'A Song' ('Thou art not false, but thou art fickle'), *CPW*, III, pp. 105–6.

15. Byron's misogyny appears in some of his early poetry as well,

although his commitment to sentimentalism at that stage distinctly undercuts his anti-feminist views. See especially the poem 'To Woman', printed toward the end of *Hours of Idleness* (*CPW*, I, pp. 45–6).

16. For an extended discussion of this poem's text and context see Jerome J. McGann, 'The Significance of Biographical Context: Two Poems by Lord Byron', in *The Author in his Work*, ed. Louis A. Martz and Aubrey Williams (New Haven, Conn., 1978), pp. 347–66.

17. For a full discussion of the linkage see ibid. The essential fact is that the stanza of 'When We Two Parted' which Byron dropped from the printed version was originally a stanza in the poem to Lady Caroline Lamb.

18. See *BLJ*, X, pp. 198–9.

19. See Malcolm Elwin, *Lord Byron's Wife* (New York, 1962), pp. 394, 400. The matter is more fully discussed in my (unpublished) essay 'Byron and the Truth in Masquerade' (forthcoming in 1991 in the papers of the bicentennial Byron conference held at Hofstra University, Hempstead, New York, in 1988).

20. See ibid.

21. For a related discussion of these matters see my 'Lord Byron's Twin Opposites of Truth', in *Towards a Literature of Knowledge* (Oxford, 1989), pp. 38–64.

22. This is the first line of Alan Davies' excellent prose-poem 'Lies', reprinted in *Signage* (New York, 1987), p. 11.

3

Byron and the Romantic Heroine

MALCOLM KELSALL

A simple archetype is my point of departure: the feminist representation of the male as phallocentric patriarch. Byron fits. He is both
libertine and lord. The 'masterwork' is recognised as *Don Juan*. The
title reaffirms the archetype.

But an alternative representation has an equivalent symbolic
status: Byron as revolutionary and voice of freedom. The repeated
subject of Byronic verse is the overthrow of the patrician order. He
expresses sympathy for the subjugated, and identifies with them.
Byron's political libertinism has a feminist context in his acquaintance with the Godwin/Shelley circle. The 'masterwork' is a
'mistresswork' for its subject is 'the ocean, woman', and the ocean
is for the poet a potent symbol of the natural force of revolution.

Beneath lies what Kristeva calls 'the semiotic' – in Byron
unvoiced and historically unvoiceable, the ambivalence of his
sexuality.

I begin with silence and passivity, absence and death – the
heroine of *The Giaour*, Leila, who 'sleeps beneath the wave'. One
sees a mysterious burden sink. One hears, at a distance, the wail of
women – a wordless utterance of misery. Another conflict has
arisen for another Helen; aberrant sexuality has disturbed the
world of men. The guilty Giaour retires from the world to free
himself of sexuality, the curse of the woman Eve; his confessions
are to a Christian patriarch, a holy Father.

The passive woman dies easily: Zuleika and Medora from excess
of grief; separated from the male, the female cannot survive. Her
mind is soon unhinged, for she is passionate as well as feeble.
Kaled and Parisina run mad. Sanity depends upon the male lover.
A woman's happiness lies in service to her lord:

                    . . . dearest! come and share
The feast these hands delighted to prepare;
Light toil! to cull and dress thy frugal fare!
See, I have plucked the fruit that promised best,
And where not sure, perplexed, but pleased, I guessed
At such as seemed the fairest: thrice the hill
My steps have wound to try the coolest rill;
Yes! thy Sherbet to-night will sweetly flow . . .
Think not I mean to chide . . . .

                                (*The Corsair*, I, 420f.)

Medora is represented here as the happy slave.[1] She is both the beautiful odalisque of sensualist fancy, and the devoted house-wife. It is a redeeming virtue for Conrad to love this creature, and Byron's admiring female readership bought such texts in their tens of thousands. There is no need to elaborate upon this romantic stereotype of woman as blancmange.

Yet, in Medora's invitation to share the feast 'these hands delighted to prepare' something else creeps through. Three times she has climbed the hill to get cold water for his sherbet: 'Think not I mean to chide . . .'. That complaint, suppressed, leans towards another stereotype: woman as nagging housewife; but its very domestication in a realist mode would undercut Conrad, his moodiness and his frugal affectation. The entry of the woman's voice into the masculine narration of the poem suggests something else too: the oppression of Medora. She is conforming through love to the role her lord requires, yet, just nascent, is the suggestion of protest implied.

I do not develop this theme further, for Caroline Franklin[2] has already done so, arguing powerfully, and by telling comparison with Scott and Southey, that the Byronic romances show how women are oppressed by a patriarchal order. 'Love is for the free' protests Gulnare, expressing a Byronic *leitmotif*. But it is a freedom not even Gulnare, the patricide, achieves.

Let me compare with Medora another woman to another man, ignoring the context, though the context is well-known:

        And now, sir, I have done, and say no more;
          The little I have said may serve to show
        The guileless heart in silence may grieve o'er

> The wrongs to whose exposure it is slow: –
> I leave you to your conscience as before,
> 'Twill one day ask you *why* you used me so?
> God grant you feel not then the bitterest grief!
> Antonia! where's my pocket-handkerchief?

(Don Juan, I, st. 157)

Like Medora this subservient woman does not 'mean to chide' – indeed the woman's realm is one of inarticulacy:

> The guileless heart in silence may grieve o'er
> The wrongs to whose exposure it is slow . . ..

Out of this silence the voice of the wrongs of woman obtrudes into the masculine narration of Byron's verse, saying 'little', soon relapsing into the speechless wail of female grief as tears stop utterance (so *The Giaour*). She admits her inferiority. She calls her husband 'sir' as a servant might a master. Yet surely the wrongs of women must touch the conscience of the dominant sex at last: 'Twill one day ask you *why* you used me so?' As she writes later to her lover, man has all the resources:

> we but one,
> To love again, and be again undone . . .

> My brain is feminine, nor can forget: –
> To all, except your image, madly blind;
> As turns the needle trembling to the pole
> It ne'er can reach, so turns to you, my soul.

(I, st. 194–5)

So the heroine of romance would run mad, and rush upon 'Death'.

The difference, however, is that the Byronic mode is not now romantic, but satiric. Donna Julia 'in fact' is full of the 'guile' she denies she possesses. She has learnt to use the discourse of the exploited in order to exploit. Her relapse into inarticulacy and silence follows the great tirade of the bedroom scene. Her tears are manipulative. So too is the letter to Juan. The aim is to create a sense of guilt in the man so that he may be controlled. His conscience is her means to power. The silence of inarticulate helplessness in the first canto of *Don Juan* is not that of the woman, but that of the adolescent young man who is her sexual plaything. Although Juan is not plunged into the sea like Leila in *The Giaour*, he is cast away upon it.

The reversal of roles is not quite that simple. The arranged marriage of Julia is offensive – 'Love dwells with . . . the free'[3] – and she is 'in love' with Juan, whatever that means in Byron's poem. But the ultimate power in the first canto of *Don Juan* is in a woman's hands. The controller of the destinies of the cast of the tragi-comedy is Donna Inez – whose influence lies even behind the convenient despatch of Julia to a nunnery (compare the Giaour monastery). That is obvious in terms of plot. But Donna Inez's means to power resides in her expropriation of the discourse of feminine virtue:

> In short, she was a walking calculation,
> Miss Edgeworth's novels stepping from their covers,
> Or Mrs. Trimmer's books on education
> Or 'Coeleb's Wife' set out in search of lovers.

> (I, st. 16)

This matriarch 'perfect past all parallel' uses the language of morality to control as tyrannically as any patriarch of feminist ideology. Her oppressed husband, ruled by her 'magnanimity', like a heroine of romance, dies prematurely.

The gradual emergence of the Byronic heroine both as the central subject of his poetry, and as the manipulator of power, is a problematic issue, and one too large to pursue here.[4] But there is (is there not?) a reversal of earlier motifs in the treatment of the Byronic 'romantic' heroine in *Don Juan*, and that reversal affects certain commonplaces of what we now call 'feminism'. It is a tense matter – tense in the context of our social preoccupations, and a source of tension within the poem.

Consider the Haidée episode, which is in its mode the closest *Don Juan* comes to the early romances, and which is often seen as some form of Byronic ideal. Here, if anywhere in *Don Juan*, is the stereotype of the oppressed woman in a patriarchal (and thus in the cant of the age) a tyrannical society. The sexual politics of the role are explicit, for the poem symbolically relates the heroine to wider structures of political oppression. Haidée is identified with Greece, suffering under the colonial exploitation of the Sultan. Free love and the freedom of Greece are romantically associated (and in a manner not unlike Shelley's *The Revolt of Islam*). Juan and Haidée in one another's arms are 'Half naked, loving, natural and Greek', and Byron's most famous lyric on freedom, 'The Isles of Greece' is sung for them. It begins with a celebration of female sexuality – for Greece is the region where 'Burning Sappho loved and sung', and then proceeds to its nationalist theme.

Here, manifestly, is a heroine of sentimental romance who is also that oppressed figure essential to feminist polemic: 'Can Man be free if Woman be a slave?'[25] Twentieth-century liberal criticism has repeatedly idealised the episode. But are not the ideals set up only to be subverted? The patriarch of the island, Lambro, is supposed dead and the paradisal island to which Juan comes is now a matriarchy. Haidée is absolute ruler, not oppressed woman. It is she who is the seducer, and Juan, naked and helpless on the shore, is first dressed in petticoats, and then in exotic garments perhaps from the dead patriarch's wardrobe. Haidée is associated with the language of masculine power: 'in her air/There was a something which bespoke command'.

The consequences are far from paradisal. Lambro's patriarchy (his dowry for his daughter) is squandered in Sardanapalian feasting, and although Greek freedom is celebrated in sentimental song, no one at the drunken revel has either the will or the power to do anything about it. One might try a feminist reading of Haidée's pregnancy: the woman is not to be married off as a dynastic chattel, but, like a latter-day Duchess of Malfi, has secured control over her own body (and Juan's!) and her sexuality. But the real-world fact of the matter is that her very freedom depends on her expropriation of the wealth won by her father's piracy and slave trading: i.e. her liberty is someone else's enslavement (finally Juan's). The world she lives in is a world at war – the patriarch's world, if one will – and her freely-chosen love for Juan, who is a mere boyish/girlish vagabond, leaves the island utterly unprotected (no one even notices Lambro's return). Her pregnancy blocks the necessary dynastic marriage which would protect family and folk.

It is a mere cant of romanticism to separate the autonomous 'liberation' of the individual from the necessities of social survival. If the world is structured as a series of competing power groups, to survive one must possess or acquire power. Marriage is one such instrument. It is no wonder that the patriarch Lambro, returning home like Ulysses, is angry. Instead of chaste Penelope, he finds a teenage orgy, and his daughter pregnant by a penniless stranger. 'Free love' has destroyed society, and constructed nothing but a conglomeration of dropouts. He has every 'right' to be angry.

The Haidée episode is as close to a celebration of liberated sexuality as a type of political freedom as *Don Juan* gets. It is what Coleridge might call 'sexual Jacobinism'. But the romantic vision is offered only to be shown as wanting, and disappears. Juan is sold from the desert island as a slave, and enters the Sultan's harem as a slave girl. Again the discourse of feminism is implied, for the 'harem' stands in Wollstonecraft (for instance) as a signifier of the general subjection of Woman to Man, as slave to tyrant. Byron might have used this episode, and the Court of Catherine which follows, to explore from a male perspective what it is to be a 'slave' like a woman, and thus extend sympathy to the feminine (if not to feminism):

> ask any woman if she'd choose
> . . . to have been
> Female or male? a school-boy or a Queen?

> (XIV, st. 25)

But the poet who so frequently uses the word 'freedom' does not open an easy doorway to liberation. Women in power are represented as being just as tyrannical as men, and in Catherine's case, just as bloodthirsty. Their motivating force is 'the love of pleasure and the love of sway', and that is Wollstonecraft's own characterisation (out of Pope) of her sex – indeed there are few more persistent and devastating critiques of femininity than *The Rights of Woman*. But it is men's oppression that makes women thus, her feminist argument runs. In Byron, Gulbeyaz, matriarch of her society of enslaved women, is as much a tyrant as the Sultan in her realm, and the Sultana's tyranny – just as much as the Sultan's – is motivated by lust: *libido et dominatio*. The extension of the story to Catherine's Russia would indicate, by an appeal to history, that it is not the haremisation of women that creates this type. It is false to claim that in a world of 'tyrants' and 'slaves' ('exploiters' and 'exploited') the dominant class or sex monopolise vice, and the

slaves who desire liberty are the possessors of virtue. Change
places and it is the oppressed who oppress. Such was one Orwel-
lian lesson even the optimistic Shelley learnt from the French
Revolution. And no one would call Byron optimistic.

It is towards the provocatively bleak view of the sexual politics of
the Revolution that *Don Juan* was headed as the poem approached
its conclusion under the *ancien régime* in England, and the
Revolution in France. When Byron wrote that he did not know
whether to make his protagonist end in marriage, or on the guillotine (destroyed by his own side) in France, he was not choosing
between a sexual or political catastrophe, but between variants
upon the same theme: the obliteration of the masculine 'hero' by
the abuse of feminine power.

Britain, *Don Juan* claims, has evolved from an aristocracy to
petticoat government: the Gynocracy. Byron describes the women:

> You may see such at all the balls and dinners,
> Among the proudest of our Aristocracy,
> So gentle, charming, charitable, chaste –
> And all by having *tact* as well as taste. . .

(XII, st. 66)

That characterisation of the Gynocrats – 'So gentle, charming,
charitable, chaste' – represents an idealised stereotype of women
which the tenor of the lines denies (Byron's rhyme for 'Gynocracy'
is 'hypocrisy'). This is not a gender-typing constructed for women
by men. The suggestion is that this is the kind of language appropriated by women to themselves, so that they appear like the ideal
heroines of their own fictions (the novel), and as all Aurora Rabys:
pure, docile, spiritually *ravissant*. The function of the construction
of this kind of image is to conceal by romanticisation the system of
political power. In Britain, in fact, power depends upon property,
property upon marriage, and marriages are the prerogative of
women, who are the fiercest guardians of the appearances of
Christian institutions.

I have discussed this issue in part in *Byron's Politics* but failed,
myopically, to perceive the implications and context of this sexual
politics. Let me repair the omission.

When Juan lands on English soil he apostrophises not only
British 'liberty' – 'here laws are all inviolate' – but he adds also

'here are chaste wives, pure lives. . .' (XI, st. 10). It is not a fortuitous juxtaposition, for that nexus of ideas: chastity, purity, marriage, 'inviolate' law were at the very heart of the current debate on sexual politics, and the central bastion of the conservative defence of British institutions against the libertinism of revolutionary France.

Political Jacobinism was long since a spent force, discredited by the Terror, and not even the most assiduous efforts of government spies and *agents provocateurs* could dig it up again. The major preoccupation, one might even say obsession, of the intelligentsia was now sexual Jacobinism. It was a charge both Coleridge and Southey threw at Byronism, and it was Coleridge who in the 23rd Chapter of *Biographia Literaria* (1817) had suggested that 'the shocking spirit' of the Mountain had both 'poisoned the taste' and 'directly disorganized the moral principles' of the present age. The major threat to British society still posed by eighteenth-century libertine philosophy after the military defeat of the armies of *liberté* and *egalité* lay in the undermining of that institution of marriage upon which the whole system of legitimate property depended. *Mansfield Park* is the classic instance of the Christian, conservative reaction, but Donna Inez's favoured women writers, Edgeworth, More, Trimmer, would reinforce the position.

It would be false to characterise this as Tory ideology. On the contrary, Jane Austen's heroines already enjoy and take for granted many of the rights for which Wollstonecraft argued, and the novels are not prostitute apologies for things as they are. It was the liberal Sismondi who wrote of British liberty and marriage: '*la constitution britannique . . . nous a appris à considérer la liberté comme une protection du repos, du bonheur, et l'indépendance domestique*'.[6] The enlightened philosophical historians of sexuality, the polymath Meiners, and the popular Ségur, who had lived through the Revolution, both argue that the happiness and proper role for women lies in Christian marriage as a proper *media via* between the atrocious old forms of sexual tyranny (witness the harem) and the evils of that sexual libertinism which Jacobinism released – and Meiners and Ségur were writers Byron would recall as he prepared his poem for its final phase.[7] Meiners writes, provocatively, that Britain is the 'paradise of women', and he makes that claim because under a truly civic Constitution women enjoy as much 'rational liberty' as it is proper for them to possess.[8]

Here is the 'Victorian' ideal of woman as 'the angel in the house' in the making, and, self-evidently, the libertine satire of *Don Juan* attacks this representation as sentimental cant. But this idea is always latent in Byron. If only Medora of *The Corsair* were married – she fulfills her domestic duties so admirably! Aurora Raby is not dissimilar to the ideal – a type of chaste, pious wife denied to Juan – and above the seething sexuality of Norman Abbey, Byron sets a simulacrum of female chastity and motherhood: the Virgin Mary, a sign of a lost faith, and cold as stone.

But although the conservative heroine of the new era may be implied in *Don Juan*, the common practice of the women of English Society is recognisably that of eighteenth-century libertine tradition. Adeline stands to Lord Henry presumably as Julia to Don Alphonso – her sexuality will erupt – and Fitz Fulke's 'liberation' is represented by her dressing as a man. In seducing Juan she acts as if a succuba or vampire. She leaves the man pale, drained, and already, the text suggests, devoted to death.

The *ancien régime* is still in place in England, and it is a characteristic of that régime that women are the engines of social advancement and of political influence. That was a commonplace from the comparative sociology of Montesquieu's *De L'Esprit des Lois*, and accompanied by a deep fear of the pernicious effects of such influence. If women were to acquire despotic control of the state: *'quel est le père de famille qui pourroit être un moment tranquille . . . l'état seroit ébranlé, on verroit couler des flots de sang'.*[9] Every schoolboy knew that one cause of the fall of the empire of Rome was the emergence of emancipated women, and the consequent effeminacy of men.

The commonplaces of Juvenal and Montesquieu became the direct personal experiences of Byron's sexual historians, Meiners and Ségur in the French Revolution. If Byron planned to take Juan to France, there is every probability that the poem, true to its theme of sexual politics, would show that the influence of the Gynocracy upon the *ancien régime* was a prime cause of the Revolution, and its consequence the death of the male hero, his virility chopped short by Madame Guillotine. Thus Ségur, who was present in 1789, explicitly locates the origins of the disaster in the libertine Salons of those aristocratic women 'zealous in their endeavour to overthrow the existing government at the price of any sacrifice; their aim was disorganization; they were directed by the deceitful light of the new philosophy'.[10] Meiners, a more philosophical German, confirmed the interpretation. Under the *ancien régime*, women, by their influence at court, he argued, had attained a 'ruinous ascendancy' over a state thus enervated: 'the weaker . . . the men become . . . the bolder and the more masculine the women'.[11] As the structures of patriarchal power crumbled, the clubs of libertine women multiplied, and Byron's historians see with horror that it is the women who are the instigators and leaders of the bloodthirsty mob – even against their own suffering sex. They swarm about Robespierre, the Tartuffe of Revolution. They even dress like men. It is appropriate, therefore, on this analysis, that the symbol of revolution is Marianne, thirsty for blood: 'Children of the motherland, water the fields with the blood of your enemies'. A remarkable feminist anthem.

While Madame Defarge knitted complacently at the guillotine, Juan died. It was poetic justice. If this were the end to which Byron's tales of sexual politics tended, then it is the polar opposite of the image with which this argument began: Leila drowned by patriarchal tyranny. The wheel has come full circle in the libertine poet, from sympathy for the extreme oppression of women, to fear of the extremity of their power, and it finds no resting place. It was a woman, Lady Blessington, who gave it as Byron's view that all women were 'disposed to be tyrants, and that the moment they know their power they abuse it'.[12] *Tantumne Femina potuit suadere malorum?*

Notes

1. The passage is perceptively discussed by Marina Vitale, 'The Domesticated Heroine in Byron's *Corsair* and William Hone's Prose Adaptation', *Literature and History*, 10 (1984), pp. 72–94.
2. "'At Once Above–Beneath her Sex": The Heroine in Regency Verse Romance', at the time of writing awaiting publication by *MLR*.
3. Gulnare in *The Corsair*, II, 502.
4. In developing the argument I have been especially influenced by Frederick L. Beaty, *Love in British Romantic Literature* (DeKalb, Northern Illinois University Press, 1971); Katherine Kernberger, 'Power and Sex. The Implications of Role Reversal in Catherine's Russia', *Byron Journal*, 8 (1980), pp. 42–9; Peter J. Manning, *Byron and His Fictions*, (Detroit, Wayne State University Press, 1978), Chapter 5; Anthony Paul Vital, 'Lord Byron's Embarrassment: Poesy and the Feminine', *Bulletin of Research in the Humanities*, 86 (1983–5), pp. 269–90 (my thanks to Peter Graham for drawing this to my attention); Susan J. Wolfson, '"Their She Condition": Cross-Dressing and the Politics of Gender in *Don Juan*', *ELH*, 54 (1987), pp. 585–617.

5. Shelley, *The Revolt of Islam*, II, st. xliii.
6. Discussed in *Byron's Politics*, (Brighton: Harvester Press, 1987), p. 187.
7. Sale catalogue of Byron's library (1816) items 226 and 300: C. Meiners, *History of the Female Sex*, 4 vols, 1808; J. A. Ségur, *Women Their Condition and Influence in Society*, 3 vols, 1803. I am indebted to Caroline Franklin for drawing my attention to the importance of these works and their intellectual context. Her interpretative emphasis is different from mine, but this paper is in part both a tribute to our many discussions on Byron and feminism and to the postgraduate work in Romantic studies of the staff and students of the late University College, Cardiff.
8. Meiners, IV, pp. 321ff.
9. Montesquieu, XVI, p. ix.
10. Ségur, III, pp. 19ff.
11. Meiners, I, p. 8 and IV, p. 332.
12. *Lady Blessington's Conversations with Lord Byron*, ed. Ernest J. Lovell, Jr (Princeton: Princeton University Press, 1969), p. 123.

4

Byron and the Empire in the East

MARILYN BUTLER

Byron's 200th birthday on 28 January 1988 was dutifully celebrated in the quality media. It must have been either bad form or too troublesome to tackle the real problem he represents, as an apparently major poet whose poetry has in fact been steadily belittled in the English-speaking world. Unlike most writers, whose lives lack incident and variety, Byron makes wonderful journalistic copy. Personable as Princess Di, action-orientated as Bob Geldof, he really belongs not in the book section but in the gossip column. So it was not to the poetry but to the insider anecdotes that the anniversary's column-inches were devoted. Knowing about Byron meant learning of the good looks, the title, the high living and the low joking; especially of the 'tooling', to use Byron's expression, with Turkish concubines, Venetian laundresses, and the handsome wives of the rich and titled anywhere from Portman Square to Constantinople.

It would be altogether false to blame modern media-men for discovering the interest of Byron's sex-life. During the liberated, gay 1970s, Byron's alleged tastes for boys, buggery and incest contributed significantly to a promising revival of highbrow interest in what he wrote. The word 'alleged' appears here because there is doubt over (for example) the actual incidence of homosexual episodes in Byron's mature career, and the actual currency of rumours of his homosexuality among his contemporaries. Perhaps because a new puritanism is now asserting itself, the academics canvassed on the birthday for quick opinions did not use the sex-life as a way into the poetry. But it functioned just the same, as it generally has since 1820, to frame Byron in a peculiarly middle-class way as a dandy who couldn't be serious about anything that mattered – life, art, love, religion, politics, even himself.

It seemed an ominous symptom that both the BBC External
Services (in particular the German Service) and the *Sunday Times*
took a very pointed interest in the club foot. For it was Byron's
religious opponents in the revivalist 1820s who first seized upon
the wonderful symbolic value of that foot: the Achilles heel, the
cloven hoof, the foot of clay. Frederic Raphael in the *Sunday Times*
gave as much space to the deformed limb and its alleged importance for Byron – would he have written without it? – as he gave to
the two works by Byron he thought we should still be reading,
Beppo and *Don Juan*.[1]

   In attempting to historicise reception-theory, H. R. Jauss has
accepted critical accretions over time as collaborative constructions
that have made literary works as we know them, and have to be
studied as an integral part of their meaning for us.[2] Should one
prefer to think that critical edifices call out for deconstruction quite
as loudly as primary texts do, Byron criticism serves as one of the
classic instances. No critics contemporary with a writer ever inter-
vened so actively to re-mould his reputation; no intervention relied
so heavily on salacious gossip, caricature, and the wilful sup-
pression of what, in the beginning, really explained most of the
critical hostility.

   The concerted campaign against Byron began with Coleridge in
The Courier in August 1816, and continued prolifically until after his
death, led by the two leading journals on the Tory side, the
Quarterly Review and *Blackwood's Magazine*. Most of the critics were
active Anglicans; several were in orders. Their main charge was
that the known immorality of Byron's life was directly reflected in
his poetry; so directly and consciously, indeed, that the poetry
sides with Satan against God. The connection of Byron with the
theme of damnation is, for example, enforced by Coleridge's claim
that Byron reached new modern heights of immorality by failing to
punish his transgressive heroes. Coleridge chose to contrast Byron
on this point with Thomas Shadwell, who in the licentious
Restoration era wrote a play called *The Libertine*. (The example was
presumably chosen because, in the summer of Byron's separation
from his wife, the play's title brought Byron's private life oppor-
tunely to mind.) In licentiously representing the traditional
Spanish story of the rake Don Juan, even Shadwell felt obliged to
give it the proper ending, the hero's punishment in Hell for all
eternity.[3] Coleridge by innuendo was still addressing the character
of Byron, for in 1816 it was not always easy to prove Byron's

programmatic immorality from his poems. After 1819 Byron ironically cooperated with his enemies, by volunteering protagonists
prominently connected with damnation, such as Don Juan himself,
Cain, and Lucifer.

The second charge against Byron from the outset was that he
was a slipshod writer, who often used a weak word or a careless
rhyme. Byron's many twentieth-century demoters, who include
Eliot and for the British Leavis, continue to use these two com-
plaints, but, appropriately in a more professional age, reverse the
order. Byron's self-confessed tendency to corrupt the language
becomes a larger matter: there is felt to be too little feeling for the
concrete in his metaphors, or for the numinous in his symbols, if
indeed his poetry is symbolic at all. Broadly, those linguistic
criticisms seem better grounded than the content-criticism: the
reader of poetry for whom a dense verbal texture comes first is
probably never going to find Byron pre-eminent. On the other
hand, there are different kinds of poetry, and technical qualities
vary considerably according to the kind. There are grounds for
suspecting that most accounts even of Byron's technique remain
bound up in those preconceptions about his thematic content,
what Arnold would deplore as an absence of high seriousness, and
Claude Rawson, thinking of Byron's characterisation of Satan, as
an absence of grandeur.[4] On both sides of the Atlantic, serious
students of literature still return to the notion that the poems are
vapid and concerned with little apart from 'Byronics', the projection of a tawdry, juvenile self-image, Byron coming on not
necessarily as Satan but as the Demon King:

> He stood a stranger in this breathing world,
> An erring spirit from another hurled.[5]

In a recent contribution to this tradition, *Natural Supernaturalism*
(1971), M. H. Abrams wrote a prestigious general study of
Romanticism which omits Byron from its 550 pages, on the
grounds that he ironically opposes the 'vatic stance' allegedly
typical of other Romantics. Abrams centres instead on
Wordsworth, especially on *The Recluse*, justifying this tactic very
simply: 'My rationale is that Wordsworth (as his English contemporaries acknowledged, with whatever qualification) was the great
and exemplary poet of his age.'[6] Now it is not my impression that
poets of the period were quick to cede pre-eminence to one of their

number – literature is a very competitive calling – but the Shelley
circle, Tom Moore and Leigh Hunt more commonly owned to
writing in the shadow of Byron. It was because they feared the
Spirit of the Times was not with them in 1816 that the two
practising critics of the Wordsworth circle, Coleridge and Southey,
joined the 'young fogeys' of the day in the campaign to unseat
Byron.

Let me illustrate the contemporary cases against and for Byron
from the period of his high noon, before the hostile party carried
the day. An early and effective example of the case against is the
review of *Beppo* in 1818 in the new Tory *Blackwood's Magazine* by a
critic calling himself 'Presbyter Anglicanus'. Who is he? The likeliest candidate as author is not a clergyman of the Church of
England, but John Gibson Lockhart, Scott's son-in-law, also
notable for a snobbish and malicious attack in the same year on
Keats, and one of the most effective of the right-wing young Turks
of the day.[7] *Beppo* happens to be a tale of infidelity in contemporary
Italian middle-class life, written in a stanza borrowed from the
Renaissance poet Pulci. The language of the review has little in
common with the language of the poem. It derives from the
discourses of Milton and of the Old Testament:

> Your predecessors, in one word, my Lord, have been the friends
> – you are the enemy of your species . . . . Your poetry need not
> have been greatly different from what it is, although you had
> lived and died in the midst of a generation of heartless, vicious,
> and unbelieving demons. With you, heroism is lunacy,
> philosophy folly, virtue a cheat, and religion a bubble. Your Man
> is a stern, cruel, jealous, revengeful, contemptuous, hopeless,
> solitary savage. Your Woman is a blind, devoted, heedless,
> beautiful minister and victim of lust . . . . In the great struggle
> between the good and the evil principle, you have taken the
> wrong side . . . . [With *Beppo*] you have . . . bought . . . a gaudy
> viol, fit for the fingers of eunuchs, and the ears of court-
> ezans . . . . You have flung off the last remains of the 'regal port';
> you are no longer one of 'the great seraphic lords', that sat even
> in Pandemonium, 'in their own dimensions like themselves' . . . .
> You may resume . . . your giant-height, but we shall not fail to
> recognize, in spite of all your elevation, the swollen features of
> the same pigmy imp whom we have once learned . . . not to
> abhor merely, and execrate, but to *despise*.[8]

What precisely has Presbyter Anglicanus got in his head, since it seems to be something other than *Beppo*? He is giving some kind of selective, exaggerated impression of Byron's earlier manner in the four cantos of *Childe Harold*, in the narrative poems with Eastern settings such as *The Giaour* (1813) and *The Corsair* (1814), and in *Manfred* (1817). Yet in themselves, without knowledge of their author's sex-life, those poems would not have been read as remarkable for their indulgent treatment of female sexuality and male criminality. It is true that adulterous love occurs in their plots, but love-scenes as such are not frequent or overheated in the Turkish tales. In any case lawless passion is generally indulged, if it is sincere, in literary genres such as the ballad, from which these romance plots partly derive. What Presbyter Anglicanus really illustrates is some of the period's familiar displacements of critical discourse – for example, the borrowing of Biblical vocabulary and rhythms – when great transgressions in the poem or in the poet are to be hinted at and introduced rather than shown.

This does not mean that Byron had given no offence with his Turkish tales, merely that the offence was of a kind other than his attackers pretended. Literary critics often react to the chain of ideas a book calls up, not what it specifically says. And Byron's early 'oriental' series of poems had been made to stand for something very specific in the most celebrated favourable review they received. In 1814, Francis Jeffrey, editor of the *Edinburgh Review*, had received *The Corsair* and *The Bride of Abydos* by himself writing a thorough, wide-ranging, intellectually-ambitious review. In the grand Enlightenment historical manner, Jeffrey placed these two poems by Byron in a universal cultural schema: primitive poetry had been crude, passionate, and nationally or tribally significant; advanced poetry had become smooth, rational, decorative and individualised; in the present age, more powerful spirits, with Jeffrey's implied approval, are setting out to recover the vigour but also the large significance of ancient poetry:

This is the stage of society in which fanaticism has its second birth, and political enthusiasm its first true development – when plans of visionary reform, and schemes of boundless ambition are conceived, and almost realized by the energy with which they are pursued – the era of revolutions and projects – of vast performances, and infinite expectations.[9]

This was to imply that in the year of *The Excursion*, of *Waverley* and of *Mansfield Park*, Byron's second and third oriental poems stood out as what Marxists call 'epochal'. For here Jeffrey does not merely say that Byron is now *the* primitivist, tacitly usurping the position of the Lakeists and Lyrical Balladeers. Jeffrey also threatens, or welcomes, a school of new powerful politicised poetry, the subject of which, he seems to imply, is the grandiose public one of revolution and the fall of states. In picking up this notion, Jeffrey may have been prompted by Byron's own dedication and prefatory letter to *The Corsair*, both addressed to Thomas Moore. Here Byron hails Moore as an Irish patriot, and looks forward to the poem set in the east which he is now known to be writing, as likely to be the masterpiece of its type. By the time Presbyter Anglicanus wrote, Moore's *Lalla Rookh* (1817) had indeed proved a great popular success; and Percy Shelley's *Revolt of Islam* (January 1818) seems to be bearing out the prophecy that there was to be a whole series of poems by well-connected liberal poets welcoming the prospect of revolution in the Middle East.

What these works, and plenty more, had in common with Byron's was a setting exactly or approximately suggesting the Ottoman empire. By approximately, I mean that anything from Greece in the west to Moghul Delhi in the east qualified as Turkish. I want to suggest that the extent of this eastern empire, as poets at this time repeatedly draw it, has particular significance – and more explanatory force, in relation to the early nineteenth-century British literary interest in 'orientalism', than the vague notion of visual picturesqueness on which textbooks often fall back. The framework and the four inset stories in *Lalla Rookh*, like Shelley's *Revolt of Islam* (1818), *Prometheus Unbound* (1820), and *Hellas* (1821), together with Mary Shelley's novel *The Last Man* (1824), all describe revolutions, or failed revolutions, directed against an Asiatic old regime that has the same characteristics as European old regimes. In this period of Napoleon's decline and fall, when European old regimes were being reinstated, it was widely expected that the Ottoman empire would soon break up: it appealed to radicals, then, as the likeliest site for a hoped-for replay of the French Revolution. In Shelley's case, as *The Revolt of Islam* proves, the interest of the topic is not what literally happened in France, but the generic structure of revolutions, and thus what was likely to happen again. The willingness of other poets, Byron included, to take a curious geographic licence, and to extend what is Turkish into the Indian sub-continent, gives a more specific and topical application to the theme. For, of course, Britain now had an empire in India which justified the name. It had more than doubled during the current war with France, in local wars fought between 1795 and 1805. Moghul Delhi, historically as much a Mohammedan name to conjure with as Constantinople or Bagdad, had become British. Britain had become an Asiatic power and thus to many of its subjects what the Ottomans were to the Greeks, an alien despotism.

We generally acknowledge that the idea of revolution has a huge presence in English Romantic poetry; not that eastern empire does too, nor that the two themes are indissolubly linked for second-generation poets. The fact is that the transformation of the British state, for which the historical analogue was the transformation of Rome from republic to empire, had been a potent topic in late-eighteenth-century liberal rhetoric. Adam Ferguson and Edmund Burke had memorably warned the British of the corruptions of empire, especially in the east; Gibbon's *Decline and Fall of the Roman Empire* (1776–88) became a great landmark not primarily for antiquarian reasons, but for its contemporary resonance. Thanks to Robert Darnton, we know more of the sociology of literature for France in this period than for Britain. But it is not unreasonable to suppose that in Britain, even more perhaps than in France, literature was an upwardly-mobile profession, which rewarded 'merits', and not (like the established professions) good connections. On the whole written by the middle class and for the middle class, it was bound to deal ambivalently at best with the state; it was the sphere for those who had acquired influence but were still denied power. And Byron, with his misleading rank (misleading because he lacked the inherited wealth and access to patronage of the real Whig oligarch) was doubly alienated, for he identified neither with the centralised state machine, nor with middle-class aspirations to reform that state and join it.

What few adequate accounts there have been of English Romantic oriental poetry suggest that the East exerted a psychic pull on individuals, either for its spiritual values, since German scholars in particular turned India into the home of religious essentialism, or for its sensuous opportunities, the langorous courts and harems the French made of the Arabian Middle East.[10] These various idealisms were not necessarily what the Orient evoked at this time in London, even if they might be in Berlin.

Napoleon visibly aspired to command communications with India: for example, when he invaded Syria and Egypt in 1798, and when he signed the treaty of Tilsit with the Russians in 1808, which extended French influence in Persia and Afghanistan. Both those events were interpreted in Parliament and widely written about in the British press as moves against Britain's interests in India, and both prompted major poems about empires in the East. Byron and Shelley enlist as orientalists in the second wave, post-Tilsit. But any proper account of the literature of empire would have to include those poems of the first wave Byron and Shelley took most note of, Thomas Campbell's *Pleasures of Hope* (1798), Walter Savage Landor's *Gebir* (1798), and Southey's three epics of the first decade of the nineteenth century, *Thalaba* (1801), *Madoc* (1805) and *The Curse of Kehama* (1810).

I mention these titles of celebrated narrative poems about falling empires to combat the modern misconception that the standard Romantic poem is likely to be a lyric, its subject autobiographical. I shall now spare you any more catalogues, and come in at the tail-end of the series Byron joined. Two texts will represent all those to which his oriental narratives implicitly reply. The first is Charles Grant's 'Observations on the State of Society among the Asiatic Subjects of Great Britain', a report on morals and religion originally prepared in 1792 by a servant of the East India Company. Grant's 'Observations' were not printed until 1813, but from the time of writing they had an underground life in manuscript, especially after Grant became Chairman of the Company at its London headquarters in 1805. So much so, that when in July 1811 Byron returned from his eastern Mediterranean travels, he found a vigorous Evangelical campaign in full swing in favour of Christian proselytism in the East. The pressure-group known as the Clapham Sect, to which Grant belonged, was behind it. Their leader William Wilberforce declared that sending missions to India was a cause that even outdid the abolition of slavery as a national moral crusade.

Hitherto the East India Company's policy, which Parliament had always endorsed, was to leave the Indian social structure undisturbed, or if parts were defunct, as was the case with Hindu law, to revive them. This policy was not disinterested, though advocated with the usual high-toned eighteenth-century rhetoric: the Company's small bureaucracy and armed forces relied on collaboration with native rulers and respected the spheres of influence of

Hindu and Moslem religious leaders. But Grant and his friends challenged the old policy of collaboration and religious coexistence not merely on religious but also on moral, social and economic grounds.

Writing in 1792 for Henry Dundas, the minister under Pitt responsible for Indian affairs, Grant argued that Hinduism was not, as the Governor-General, Warren Hastings, and the Orientalist William Jones had argued in the 1770s and 1780s, a social creed rooted in immemorial village customs. Its traditional laws were, Grant asserted, chaotic and in their origins despotic, an imposition on the populace from above. The 'cruel genius' which pervaded them was the ethos of Hinduism, and it encouraged fraud, lying and the exploitation of people of inferior caste.[11] Two civilised systems confronted one another in Bengal, the Christian and the Hindu, and Grant's comprehensive analysis of Hinduism found systemic defects which could be cured by nothing short of a wholesale transformation of society, preceded by religious conversion. In short, Grant in 1792 represented traditionary Indian culture as a classic instance of unreformed despotism, precisely the type of old regime the French were now rationally sweeping away.

It used to be a commonplace that the pro-Hindu policy and enthusiastic orientalist scholarship of the late eighteenth-century British officials in India was the liberal option; the generation that opened up Hindu learning, religion, literature and language to the West was sometimes called enlightened, sometimes romantic. Yet Grant challenged pro-Hindu sentiment from, as it were, the left. Written at the height of the French Revolution, the 'Observations' conducts a strong, almost structuralist argument which breathes the spirit of the revolutionary ideologues. The outlook and terminology is that of a critic of religion such as Constantin Volney, the Foucault of his day, whose *Ruins of Empire* was much read in Britain from its appearance in French and in an English translation in 1791. Grant was in his own way a radical, and his way readily appealed to middle-class radical-Protestant sentiment. His argument reached men like James Mill, the ex-Protestant and Benthamite who began his great demolition-job, *A History of British India* (1817) in 1806; and Robert Southey, the ex-Jacobin poet, who also took up the cause of missions in India from 1802.

Both in journalism and in his epic *Madoc* (1805), Southey began to advocate the mass conversion of native peoples where their own religion was cruel and oppressive. In popularising the case for 'missionizing', which was also a case for imposing Western culture and goals of material progress on colonial populations, Southey joined the well-organised extra-parliamentary lobby which in fact got its way in 1813. The amendment of the East India Act, so that Christian churches were permitted to proselytise in India, was an important symbolic defeat inflicted on the ruling aristocracy by the still-disfranchised middle classes. And it may have been largely as an aristocrat that Byron resented it, as *The Giaour* suggests he did.

To understand the politics of Byron's orientalism, we must know what the Turkish tales are an answer to. Most immediately they react to Southey's epic *The Curse of Kehama* (1810), which illustrates the horrors of Hindu government on lines similar to Grant's, by describing the contest between two Indian peasants, a father and daughter, and their rajah. Kehama is the would-be emperor of the world, an eastern *alter ego* of Napoleon Bonaparte, a despot assisted by a peculiarly non-spiritual religion which functions to serve worldly power. First we meet Kehama at the funeral of his son, a scene which enables Southey to give a graphic description of *sati*, the burning alive of the dead prince's two young wives. Next, after the ceremony, the Rajah curses Ladurlad, the peasant hero of the tale, whose crime was to kill the late prince as he tried to rape Ladurlad's daughter. It is important to remember that cruel fire and that unremitting punishment, for during the next decade the liberal orientalist poets frequently parody them, and invert the ideological values Southey gave them. When translated into other religious circumstances, the human sacrifice and the eternal punishment are made to seem characteristic not just of Hinduism, but of all religious systems, including Christianity. Since religious systems uphold state systems, these become favourite images for the cruelty of state power, which by extension pointedly includes the British. The first of Southey's antagonists and parodists is Byron with *The Giaour* (1813).

Superficially *The Giaour* appears to be a sentimental love story, using clichés of popular romance which are even staler now than in Byron's day. The problem of Byron's genre thus appears here in an acute form: if *The Giaour* is *not* complexly intertextual, *not* a contribution to an already melodramatic and necessarily populist series, it might easily be rubbish. The plot of this so-called 'Turkish tale' addresses Southey's proposition that Christianity (or monotheism, i.e. both Christianity and Islam) brings benefits to the populations that believe, as forms of religion that reflect an

advanced individualism and morality. Byron's method is dialectical, and full of opportunities for irony, since the central action is
given to the representatives of two major religions to narrate. The
first of these interpreters is a devout Turkish fisherman, the second
a simple Christian monk. As a narrative method, this has its own
considerable interest, for its parallelism and laboured duplication
are plainly indebted to Gothic fiction, and indeed seem to anticipate, even to be a model for, Mary Shelley's *Frankenstein* and
Hogg's *Confessions of a Justified Sinner*. In *The Giaour*, both narrators
are led by their religious understandings to misinterpret what they
see. The Turkish fisherman has observed the death of his master,
Hassan, who has been waylaid and assassinated by an infidel, or
Giaour. The fisherman doesn't know the murderer's name – which
indeed we never learn – and is quite uninterested in the motives
for his crime. He finds him guilty anyway because he subscribes to
a false religion, and because Hassan, whose actions and personal
morality the fisherman also doesn't care about, believes in the true
one. So the fisherman rejoices that Hassan is now in Heaven; and
he brings down on the head of the Giaour a terrific curse, the most
dreadful sentence his religion brings to his mind. The fisherman's
curse is the climax of the first, Moslem part of the poem, and the
centrepiece of the poem as a whole:

> But thou, false Infidel! shalt writhe
> Beneath avenging Monkir's scythe . . .
> And fire unquench'd, unquenchable –
> Around – within – thy heart shall dwell,
> Nor ear can hear, nor tongue can tell
> The tortures of that inward hell! –
> But first, on earth as Vampire sent,
> Thy corse shall from its tomb be rent;
> Then ghastly haunt thy native place,
> And suck the blood of all thy race,
> There from thy daughter, sister, wife,
> At midnight drain the stream of life;
> Yet loathe the banquet which perforce
> Must feed thy living livid corse;
> Thy victims ere they yet expire
> Shall know the daemon for their sire,
> As cursing thee, thou cursing them,
> Thy flowers are wither'd on the stem.

> But one that for thy crime must fall –
> The youngest – most belov'd of all,
> Shall bless thee with a *father's* name –
> That word shall wrap thy heart in flame![12]

So the Moslem curse serves as the analogue and the answer to Southey's version of a Hindu curse in *Kehama*. Byron's notes are not unsympathetic to Mohammedanism in comparison with Christianity. It is the most macho of the Hebraic monotheisms, and that he approves of. But, as the curse establishes, Mohammedanism, like all monotheistic structures, gives arbitrary power to a God who has all the attributes of a despot. In the name of the one true God, the pious fisherman calls down a curse of unrelenting savagery, which visits the Giaour's sins on his female progeny in generation after generation.

Monotheistic religions share the habits of cruelty and misogyny, as the reader cannot help noticing when the Christian monk takes up the tale. There is not even a sense of brotherhood in the monastery: the monk superstitiously hates and fears the dying Giaour, and would rather have him thrown out than hear his confession. But there is less confident faith as well: the Giaour either disbelieves in the Christian heaven, or couldn't be cheered by it, since he wants to share eternity with the dead mistress who haunts his dreams. She, Leila, was, it now emerges, Hassan's wife, whom he had sewn in a sack and dumped in the sea when he discovered her infidelity with the Giaour. As a pagan and an adulteress, Leila has no place either in the Christian heaven. And the various afterlives so far proposed by religious minds are all equally useless to the Giaour – Christianity's, Hassan's Moslem paradise of beautiful houris, the fisherman's dreadful notion of an eternity of vampirish pernoctations. Instead the Giaour desperately proposes to Leila's ghost another type of post-mortem sex, it must be said equally cheerless:

> But, shape or shade! – whate'er thou art,
> In mercy, ne'er again depart –
> Or farther with thee bear my soul,
> Than winds can waft – or waters roll! – [13]

This is the first of the plots in which Byron poses the notion of human fidelity – camaraderie, as it were, – against the absolutist notion of a transcendental order. The love story is not, surely, self-sufficient, not even foregrounded. Leila's tragedy provides the human context against which the claims of the great religions are seen, and it is notable that neither religion has a space for her, in this world or the next. Partly because we never see nor hear her directly, Leila retains the mysterious power of her literary ante-cedents. She comes of that line of mourning women in the Bible who, as the eighteenth-century interpreter of Biblical poetry Robert Lowth remarked, stand for defeated cities and fallen peoples; James Macpherson cites the remark when interpreting his own reconstructions of primitive Gaelic epics.[14] In Byron's artfully reconstituted Turkish popular tale, such traditional symbolism has a proper place. Leila stands for the body of the defeated people, the Greeks, and her dealings with her culture's institutional super-structures, the rival religious orthodoxies, are shown to have been far from reassuring.

The sense in which Byron's *Giaour* launches a series of liberal poems on the topic of empire is then this. Written in the year when Parliament was brought to allow 'missionizing' in India, it questions the claims to progressiveness of proselytising Christians. Instead of finding Christian morality necessarily advanced, it likens its backward, despotic tendencies to those of Islam, the other current imperial religion. The similarity is relevant to the Greek question, because there was plainly a danger that the Christian European powers might intervene to 'liberate' their Greek co-religionists from the Turks, and this, Byron implies, would be to exchange one alien despotism for another. But for readers at home the argument becomes more pointed and contro-versial when applied to India, as Byron demonstrates in his very good late play, *Sardanapalus* (1821).

At this point we move on eight years, for five of which Byron had been living abroad, under attack from his critics at home. Apart from the Punjab and the north-west frontier, the subjugation of India was now complete. With the defeat of the surviving group of independent princes in the Third Maratha War, 1817–19, there was no further danger of real resistance or of intervention in Indian affairs by any other European power. Attitudes to empire at home became confident or vainglorious; a rhetoric for which the word 'imperialist' is appropriate now begins to be heard. Indian policy is contested largely between two powerful middle-class lobbies, the evangelising-Christian and the modernising-utilitarian, who have combined to supersede the old gentlemanly orientalists. For the first time, it is widely assumed at home that the British have a mission to rule India for India's good. In *Don Juan*, which begins to appear in 1819, Byron already responds to these pious complacencies, by taking 'cant' to be the appropriate term for the current British mentality. With *Sardanapalus*, written between January and May 1821, he applies himself more specifically to satirising the new notion that the British have a God-given mission to colonise and govern other nations, or that killing people may become in the right circumstances a religious activity.

It is because his contemporaries are fond of citing God's will that Byron in his contrariness becomes literally a devil's advocate. Like certain characters in his subsequent dramas – Cain and Lucifer in *Cain* and the 'gentleman in black' in *The Deformed Transformed* – the character of King Sardanapalus has a whiff of brimstone about it. In his 'Essay on the Devil and Devils', written about 1820, Shelley speculates how the devil came to be called Lucifer, and wonders if a confusion arose from the wording of a verse in Isaiah, which Shelley maintains really refers to an Assyrian king – 'How art thou fallen, Lucifer, King of morning![*sic*]'[15] If Byron had taken note of this observation, it might well have struck him that Sardanapalus, last of the Assyrian line supposedly descended from Baal and Nimrod, could be the historical king whose spectacular fall turned him posthumously into Lucifer.

The play is preoccupied with issues of religious belief. Each act opens with the credo of a different character, from the service to the state of Sardanapalus's loyal general and brother-in-law Salamenes in the first act, to the libertarian Nature-worship of his slave Myrrha in the last. Since Myrrha is a Greek nationalist, all the play's 'religionists' in effect conflate religion with their own political interests; only Sardanapalus, agnostic and hedonist, resists the incessant calls of everyone about him to civic aggression in the national interest. Sardanapalus is known to history for two acts, his fiery suicide when his palace was surrounded by his enemies, and the inscription he had carved on a city he built – 'Eat, drink and love; what can the rest avail us?' Aristotle in his *Ethics* called this the philosophy of a pig, and other ancient moralists thought it made Sardanapalus the type of the sensualist. It is even unclear whether some statues hypothetically of Sardanapalus may not have been meant to represent Bacchus. But when Byron associates Sardanapalus with Bacchus, he impudently has the king propose the link himself, for civilised and quite ethical reasons:

Sardanapalus: Noble kinsman,
 If these barbarian Greeks of the far shores
 And skirts of these our realms lie not, this Bacchus
 Conquered the whole of India, did he not?
Salamenes: He did, and thence was deemed a Deity.
Sardanapalus: Not so:– of all his conquests a few columns,
 Which may be his, and might be mine, if I
 Thought them worth purchase and conveyance, are
 The landmarks of the seas of gore he shed,
 The realms he wasted, and the hearts he broke.
 But here – here in this goblet is his title
 To immortality – the immortal grape
 From which he first expressed the soul, and gave
 To gladden that of man, as some atonement
 For the victorious mischiefs he had done.
 Had it not been for this, he would have been
 A mortal still in name and in his grave;
 And, like my ancestor Semiramis,
 A sort of semi-glorious human monster.[16]

Sardanapalus has adopted the materialism of a nineteenth-century sophisticate. He is a pacifist, an enlightened politician concerned for the health and happiness of the citizenry, a statesman particularly disinclined to go adventuring in the name of religion and patriotism in India. In fact he is blessed or cursed with a post-religious consciousness. Though the site of the Garden of Eden may fall within his dominions, the only Paradise he envisages is the one he can create in his lavish new pavilion. As a dandy, he resembles no prototype from primitive or Biblical literature so much as Britain's own new monarch George IV, whose notorious marital difficulties and flagrant adulteries (also associated with a pavilion) are plainly brought to mind in Act I. With that extraordinary sense of being in dialogue with his readers that he develops in *Don Juan*, Byron, another adulterer, teases the British public for its censoriousness over affairs which are common in high life; as Sardanapalus wryly observes of his queen, 'I loved her as most husbands love their wives.'[17] The play raises the question of whether a public morality dedicated to a politics of war and conquest is not strangely primitive, violent and intolerant for modern conditions, not to speak of its being inconsistent with the religion of the Sermon on the Mount. Though the Turkish tales, especially *The Giaour*, are elegant structures satirising definable targets, they are not wittily written, and the central characters are certainly not wittily perceived. *Sardanapalus* comes from another stage of Byron's development, almost another epoch of theatrical writing, rather as if *The Giaour* and *The Corsair* had been handed over to G. B. Shaw to remodel. The first half at least is a classic comedy of ideas, mockingly holding up for the audience's inspection its own notion of public spirit, tempting it to identify with the sinner rather than the saints.

The conclusion of Byron's play seems all the more surprising. The first surprise is its total unlikeness to Delacroix's celebrated painting, *The Death of Sardanapalus*, which was executed in 1827 after the artist had seen a production of Byron's play in Paris. Delacroix imagines the monarch's deathbed as a barbarous Eastern orgy, in which slavegirls and even a favourite steed are dragged to the bedside to be slaughtered at the feet of the impassive king. In life Delacroix was given to treating his women models as prostitutes; their bodies, supine and nude, give the scene tremendous sexual excitement and turn it into an aggrandising fantasy. The king's indifferent mastery is also the painter's; the Orient becomes what it remained in Western imagination for much of the century, a stage-set for dreams of power.

By contrast, Byron once again characteristically offers a private, lonely and modern act enclosed in a public, barbaric one. 'A problem', is all that he has the king call it in his low-keyed curtain speech, 'A problem few dare imitate, and none /Despise'. (V.i.447–8) There is restraint as well as scepticism in giving this voluntary death-rite, this further reply to Southey's barbaric Hindu pyre, to a modern-minded agnostic to set up for himself. Like the play as a whole, the curtain scene impedes confident readers, and is thus far in line with its satire on the confident readers of divine signals, the men of mission.

But readers who have followed the clever, inventive satire of the earlier acts may also find the dénouement uncertain, ill-prepared and alienating – except as the ultimate instance, perhaps, of Byron's own alienation. In choosing to die as he does, Sardanapalus adopts the sign-language of his ancestors, which is also the language of monotheism, as old in the Hebraic scriptures as the pillar of fire in Exodus. Sardanapalus dies less interested in

his own future, if any, than in the future of his 'sign to lesson ages'
– but lesson them to what? In his curtain speech the king seems to
anticipate only the most conventional judgements of his own
personality; nothing of his high and low potential, whether as a
utopian pacifist or as the prince of darkness; nothing but the poor
opinion of his characer that schoolmaster Aristotle and the other
classical moralists recorded, 'the gross stains of too material
being'.[18] He seems to think his divine ancestors share some of this
materialism, and that they will approve of him for keeping their
treasure and their palace out of the hands of 'usurping bondsmen'
– an important consideration, apparently, for this hitherto com-
radely king suddenly demands the aristocratic prerogative of being
judged by his peers. His last connected remarks are disconcerting
because they entail a sudden reversion to type, which is after all
not much better than the type of Ozymandias:

> the light of this
> Most royal of funereal pyres shall be
> Not a mere pillar formed of cloud and flame,
> A beacon in the horizon for a day,
> And then a mount of ashes – but a light
> To lesson ages, rebel nations, and
> Voluptuous princes. Time shall quench full many
> A people's records, and a hero's acts;
> Sweep empire after empire, like this first
> Of empires, into nothing; but even then
> Shall spare this deed of mine, and hold it up
> A problem few dare imitate, and none
> Despise – but, it may be, avoid the life
> Which led to such a consummation.[19]

This reader cannot be alone, surely, in finding those last two
lines unthinking, suspiciously vainglorious and almost entirely
irrelevant. Byron seems to have been unable to envisage history
except as the record of choices by eminent individuals – essentially
free spirits, the heroes and leaders of primitive, feudal, or otherwise unencumbered times. It is an ending that turns aside from the
play's satire on over-confident government and on the export of
western values, to lose itself in narcissism. Even Myrrha, the Greek
nationalist, subordinates herself and her cause in this crisis by her
decision to share her lover's suicide. Here Byron's fondness for

acts of sexual fidelity doesn't challenge religious systematisation, as so often in his work. For Myrrha's boldness and personal autonomy pose their own challenge to the present order of things, and are tossed away when Byron has her surrender them in the interests of one beleaguered masculine ego.

Byron cannot be turned into an exemplary modern political preacher. His own policies for empire in the East, insofar as his works imply them, appear feudal, nostalgic, and just as surely constructed in the interests of one class within Western society as the policy to Christianise was. It is not clear in the light of history (if indeed it is a light) that Byron had overall the better of his political argument with Southey. And as a polemicist, especially in his personal attacks on Southey in *The Vision of Judgement* and *Don Juan*, he repeats the vices of his own early critics, of whom Southey was one: he obscures his enemy's seriousness and travesties his case.

On the other hand, we would surely achieve something for Byron's reputation if we could clear away certain long-held critical assumptions about his work, such as the easy dismissal of the Turkish tales as private fantasies or self-advertisements, and the equation of his assaults on religion with flippancy. At his best, for example in the late play *Sardanapalus*, he is witty in the truest sense. Even much earlier in *The Giaour*, his materialism relates not only to the flesh, especially to the sins of, but also to the physical worlds of time and space; Caesar's sphere rather than God's; the matters of the world as well as of worldliness.

Notes

1. Frederic Raphael, *The Sunday Times*, 24 January 1988.
2. H. R. Jauss, *Toward an Aesthetic of Reception* (Minneapolis: University of Minnesota Press, 1978).
3. S. T. Coleridge, *The Courier*, September 1816 and *Biographia Literaria*, (1817), ch. XXIII; ed. W. J. Bate and J. Edgell (Princeton, 1984), II, p. 208. The double appearance of this attack on Byron, in a newspaper as well as in an expensive book, greatly increased its circulation, and must help to explain Byron's decision to reply – with a poem about Don Juan which shows no sign of satisfying Coleridge's requirements.
4. See chapter 5 below, by Claude Rawson.
5. *Lara*, 1, ll. 315–16.
6. M. H. Abrams, *Natural Supernaturalism* (New York: Norton, 1971), p. 14.

7. The grounds for the identification of Presbyter Anglicanus as Lockhart are given by A. L. Strout, *Bibliography of Articles in Blackwood's, 1817–25*, (London, 1959).

8. 'A Letter to the Author of *Beppo'*, *Blackwood's Edinburgh Magazine*, 3 (June 1818), 323–9; partly reprinted by Andrew Rutherford, *Byron: the Critical Heritage* (London: Routledge, 1970), pp. 125–9.

9. [F. Jeffrey], *'The Corsair'*, etc., *Edinburgh Review* 23 (1814); reprinted in Rutherford, op. cit., p. 55.

10. For an account of nineteenth-century western orientalism angled towards French and British sources, see Edward Said, *Orientalism* (London: Routledge, 1978). B. Feldman and R. D. Richardson supply an anthology relatively strong in German materials in *The Rise of Modern Mythology, 1680–1860* (Bloomington: Indiana University Press, 1972). The quotation here comes from their extract (p. 356) from Friedrich Majer, *Allgemeines Mythologie Lexicon* (Weimar, 1803), p. 240.

11. Charles Grant, 'Observations on the State of Society among the Asiatic Subjects of Great Britain, particularly with respect to Morals, and on the means of Improving It. Written chiefly in the Year 1792.' *Parliamentary Papers*, 1812–13, 10, Paper 282, p. 66.

12. *The Giaour*, ll. 747–70.

13. Ibid., ll. 1315–18.

14. R. Lowth, *Lectures on Hebrew Poetry* (Latin edn 1753), trans. into English by G. Gregory (London, 1787), II, 138–9.

15. P. B. Shelley, 'On the Devil and Devils', *Shelley's Prose*, ed. D. L. Clark (Albuquerque: University of Mexico Press, 1954), p. 274.

16. Byron, *Sardanapalus*, I, ii, 163–81 (*The Works of Lord Byron: Poetry*, ed. E. H. Coleridge 2nd edn (London, 1904–5), V, 21).

17. Ibid., I, ii, 214.

18. Ibid., V, i, 425.

19. Ibid., V, i, 436–49.

5

Byron Augustan: Mutations of the Mock-Heroic in *Don Juan* and Shelley's *Peter Bell the Third*[1]

CLAUDE RAWSON

Byron's Augustanism is a large subject. There are certain aspects of it which I shall take for granted, mainly (1) that it is more authentically evident in the great *ottava rima* poems, which have no formal models in the English Augustan writers, than in such formally Popeian compositions as *English Bards and Scotch Reviewers* or *Hints from Horace* (the relative poverty of the couplet poems may itself imply a certain weakness in the post-Augustan transmission); and (2) that for all his celebrated championship of Pope, it is from an alternative Augustanism of Butler, Prior and Swift that Byron derived his most successful styles[2] – a fact that he was himself predicting as early as *Hints from Horace* in the Popeian couplets he was gradually to disengage himself from:

> Peace to Swift's faults, his Wit hath made them pass,
> Unmatched by all save matchless Hudibras,
> Whose Author is perhaps the first we meet
> Who from our couplet lopped two final feet,

whose 'measure moves a favourite of the Nine . . . And varied skilfully [as by Scott] surpasses far/Heroic rhyme' (ll. 397ff.). (3) Perhaps more controversially, but not unconnectedly, that Byron's famous letters on Pope, with the exception of a handful of eloquent

or amusing utterances (that Pope was 'the moral poet of all civilisation; and as such . . . [may] one day be the national poet of
mankind'; or that it was 'of no very great consequence whether
Martha Blount was or was not Pope's mistress, though I could
have wished him a better'), are not very interesting or
distinguished documents, more preoccupied with a tedious and
self-important wrangle with Bowles than with a genuine understanding of Pope;[3] and (4) that the self-conscious or Shandean
dimension, though derived like *Tristram Shandy* itself from old
traditions of 'learned wit' and the parodic fooleries of Swift's *Tale of
a Tub*, is either a corrupted or debased Augustanism or something
else altogether.

I shall talk principally of *Don Juan* and the *Vision of Judgment*, and
also of Shelley's *Peter Bell the Third*, from a perspective, and in the
context of a tradition, which seem to me crucial to any understanding of the Augustan complex in Byron: namely the tradition of epic
and mock-heroic. It is the tradition which Byron invoked when he
wrote in *Don Juan*:

> Thou shalt believe in Milton, Dryden, Pope;
> Thou shalt not set up Wordsworth, Coleridge, Southey;

(I, st. 205)

identifying in the first list the last great author of classical epic in
Europe and the two greatest English practitioners of mock-heroic;
and in the second list a group of poets notable in his eyes for their
possession of undeserved official honours, chiefly Southey's
Laureateship, or for the epic pretensions in their work, or both.
Even Coleridge, the least official and least epic of the three, is
conceived as 'the Laureat of the long-ear'd kind' (*English Bards*,
l. 264), braying like a poor man's version of sonorous Blackmore's
strain. In this sense, these poets occupied the place which
Shadwell, Blackmore, or Cibber had in the work of Dryden and
Pope. I shall argue that there is a pervasive fixation on epic or
mock-heroic in *Don Juan* especially; that the preoccupation runs
very deep, as a catalyst for important acts of poetic, social, and
political self-definition; but that this is paradoxically manifested
through a sustained, insolently brilliant feat of trivialisation,
through the formal underminings of inspired persiflage, through

deflation, and ultimately through a ringing denial of the epic's moral worth.

In the Augustan cultural code, with its anguished broodings on the relation of past and present, no issue was so centrally problematic as that of the 'epic', still potently celebrated in the words of Dryden, Pope and many others, as 'the greatest work which the soul of man is capable to perform',[4] yet clearly no longer writable by good poets: its military morality unacceptable, its social ethos unreal, its language out of line with a lowered sense of reality. Of all the 'ancient altars' that still stood green, it was the most tarnished, official denials merely confirming the fact. By one of the many contradictions of the ancient–modern tug-of-war, it was the Ancient faction that proclaimed the virtues of epic while failing to deliver epics of its own (except by proxy, in translations of Homer or Virgil, or in ironic guise in mock-heroic); while the Moderns, Blackmore or the French biblical poets who had dismayed Boileau, went on writing to the ancient prototype without inhibition. This is how Byron often viewed Southey, supplier of 'an epic . . . every spring' (Don Juan, III, st. 97); though, as Marilyn Butler has recently suggested, he may have taken more from Southey than he would have wished to admit.[5]

It was frequently in mock-heroic idiom, or in the context of heroic pretension, that the forms of Augustan scorn, the gestures of patrician loftiness, the putdowns of cits by wits, expressed themselves. And the epic gestures of Don Juan, the Vision of Judgment and Peter Bell the Third, with their obsession with the laureate and proto-laureate figures of Southey and Wordsworth, and their identification of the Laureateship and the poetic establishment with a debased form of the epic muse (laurels were traditionally the rewards of martial as well as poetic prowess, and appear in both roles in Don Juan, sometimes with a specific epic allusion: see, for example, I, st. 209; VII, st. 68), derive closely from Augustan models.

This may have harked back to an obsolete idiom. But in so far as it expressed patrician superiority, the ironic fact is that Shelley and Byron actually possessed a patrician status that Dryden, Swift and Pope all lacked. The lordly accents of the latter were partly mimicked from the mob of gentlemen who wrote with ease, sometimes at the expense of Dryden or of Pope themselves. Byron's putdowns of Lake or Cockney poets and related riffraff, the would-be wits and can't-be gentlemen, thus partly derive from authors who were sometimes themselves the victims of such putdowns. When Byron said of Southey in *Don Juan*:

> because you soar too high, Bob,
> And fall, for lack of moisture, quite adry, Bob!

(Dedication, st. 3)

he was evoking the Drydenian nickname of Drybob, found not only in the low Shadwell, whom Dryden scorned, but in the lordly Rochester, who scorned Dryden, and who spoke famously, in his 'Allusion to Horace' (whose very title seems to prefigure Byron's 'Hints') of Dryden's 'dry bawdy bobs' (l. 75), signifying Dryden to be a non-event, socially, sexually and poetically, in interchangeable and interconnected order.[6]

When Pope and his contemporaries wrote mock-epics, then, straight epic no longer seemed possible to good poets. And the high standing of epic which Dryden and Pope proclaimed was in practice manifested only (as I said) in the great mock-heroics, in which epic grandeurs are filtered through irony, and survive not as primary expressions of contemporary aspirations, but as a standard from which the modern world can be shown to have lapsed. Hence the mushrooming majesties of Pope's *Dunciad*, and even the delicate ballooning of the *Rape of the Lock*. You sense in them the surviving importance of the lost model, just as you sense it in a lower key in the coarse couplets of seventeenth-century travesties of Virgil where the high is treated in low language instead of the other way round, as in the opening of Charles Cotton's *Scarronides* (1664): 'I *Sing the Man* (read it who list,/ A *Trojan* true, as ever pist,) . . .'.[7] Coarse and demotic, admittedly, but unthinkable even in, or especially in, popular culture, unless a live awareness of the significance of epic originals is taken for granted even among those who didn't or couldn't read them. Scarron, Butler, Cotton are not demotic authors in a simple sense: but they wittily play with an idiom which would not be out of place in popular farces and drolls and puppet shows at Bartholomew and Southwark fairs. In the eighteenth century such shows sometimes dealt specifically with ancient heroic themes, including the siege of Troy.[8]

Now compare Byron 150 years or so later announcing in *Don Juan*,

> My poem's epic, and is meant to be
>   Divided in twelve books; each book containing,
> With love, and war, a heavy gale at sea,
>   A list of ships, and captains, and kings reigning,
> New characters: the episodes are three:
>   A panorama view of hell's in training,
> After the style of Virgil and of Homer,
> So that my name of Epic's no misnomer,

(I, st. 200)

This is not demotic. It is as witty and allusive and exclusive as Pope. But I shall argue that as far as any real relationship to epic might be concerned, it is no more than a debonair flourish.[9] Epic has ceased to be more than a topic for intertextual jokerie, though there is a lot of this in *Don Juan*. But I shall first talk about Shelley.

Shelley and Byron are the two major Romantic poets who are closest to the Augustan 'aristocratic' sensibility, and both of them treat the epic with a frivolity and a lightness that would be unthinkable in Pope. *Peter Bell the Third*, a poem roughly contemporaneous with *Don Juan*, can be thought of in some ways as a low-key *Dunciad*. It mocks Wordsworth's *Peter Bell*, which Shelley may not have read at the time, a poem dedicated to Southey in 1819 and also guyed in *Don Juan*.[10] It thus has, like *Don Juan* and the *Vision of Judgment*, an honorary connection with the Laureateship, though not so direct as the *Dunciad*'s (but the *Dunciad* itself only came to the Laureateship second time round). In this poem, in which Peter, alias Wordsworth, goes to Hell, one of the Devil's guises is said to be that of 'a bard bartering rhymes/For sack' (II, st. ii). There is jeering at Wordsworth's increasing alignment with the respectable (that is, tyrannical and warmongering) establishment, which culminates in "odes to the Devil" (VI, st. xxxvi). His consequent 'promotion' to a genteel sinecure (VII, st. i–viii) refers to the distributorship of stamps for Westmorland which Wordsworth obtained in 1813 (cf. *Don Juan*, Dedication, st. 6) but seems almost to hint, with prophetic accuracy, at a 'poetic justice' which was to make Wordsworth a suitable Laureate in the future.

As in the *Dunciad* the elevation is intimately bound up with Dulness:

> Peter was dull – he was at first
> Dull – Oh, so dull – so very dull!
> Whether he talked, wrote, or rehearsed –
> Still with this dulness was he cursed –
> Dull – beyond all conception – dull.

(VII, st. xi)

What has disappeared is the vast misshapen majesty of the Popeian Mighty Mother. Dulness is no longer an engulfing force of Miltonic dimensions, Daughter of Chaos and eternal Night, but reduced to chatty drawing-room proportions: 'Dull – Oh, so dull – so very dull!'. If an Augustan analogy must be sought, it would be in the low-key idiom of Swift's conversational travesties, and the cheeky rhyming of 'rehearsed/he cursed' is out of Swift by Byron. Byron took it from Swift (Swift, said Byron, 'beats us all hollow, his rhymes are wonderful').[11] Other Swiftian strains (not necessarily direct influences) in the poem include the portrayal of Peter as a canting dissenter, with 'eyes turned up' and 'a nasal twang' (I, st. ii):

> Turned to a formal Puritan,
> A solemn and unsexual man, –
> He half believed *White Obi*.

(VI, st. xix)

Swift didn't think puritans unsexual, though he exposed their pretences that way; and '*White Obi*' (or what Leigh Hunt spoke of as the 'methodistical nightmare' of Wordsworth's hero)[12] evokes that traditional satire of sectarian enthusiasts which Swift brought to its wittiest culmination in the *Mechanical Operation of the Spirit*. Swift is mentioned in the stanza after the one about Peter's Dulness, when Peter is compared to a Struldbrug:

> No one could read his books – no mortal,
> But a few natural friends, would hear him: –
> The parson came not near his portal; –
> His state was like that of the immortal
> Described by Swift – no man could bear him.

(VII, st. xii)

The mystifying pseudonymous 'Dedication' by Miching Mallecho, with its Grub-Street-garret-joking, recalls *A Tale of a Tub* and its later avatars: 'Pray excuse the date of place; so soon as the profits of this publication come in, I mean to hire lodgings in a more respectable street.' The words come, moreover, in a mock-nervous postscript in a genre familiar from the *Tale*'s 'Apology' or the ending of the *Mechanical Operation*, and there is some mock-learned footnoting in the style broadly associated with Tubbaean or Dunciadic exercises.

Such generically Scriblerian routines don't call for particular source-seeking. As with Eliot's *Waste Land*, which had its origins in an attempt to write mock-heroic couplets in the style of the *Rape of the Lock*, and whose whole portrayal of cultural chaos has a Dunciadic scope, there is behind Shelley's ostensibly Popeian structure a whole system of local effects that are in a lower key and more specifically traceable to Swift.[13] In Eliot it is a matter of satiric tone and of scabrous detail, the 'drying combinations . . . Stockings, slippers, camisoles, and stays' (ll. 225–7), which come more from 'The Lady's Dressing Room' (ll. 11ff.) than from *The Rape of the Lock* (the common source, in its way, of both Swift *and* Eliot). In Shelley, the scope is also Dunciadic (the section 'Hell is a city much like London' [III, st. i] is followed, as in the *Dunciad*, by a satirical array of dunces from the political and literary world), and the ostensible pretensions are epic: 'a *very heroic* poem' was how Shelley described it to Leigh Hunt in a letter (2 November 1819).[14] Shelley supplies the 'panorama view of hell' which Byron promised in *Don Juan* and didn't get round to, offering instead the London cantos of *Don Juan*. But the more local evocations are often of Swift, and it is consistent with Shelley's as well as Byron's low-key conception of epic resonance that the Swift who rejected the 'lofty style' should act as a catalyst in the use by both poets of a mock-heroic idiom whose conceptual and to some extent formal character is more readily associated with Pope.

Shelley is hardly a poet whom one would compare closely with Eliot, who disliked him. But both poets in their mock-heroic enterprises belong to stages in cultural history when mock-heroic could no longer act, as in Pope, in majestic and respectful homage to the heroic original. Shelley's way is to trivialise the epic connection: not nervously, like Cowper singing the sofa with eulogium due, but with a confidence which (like Byron's) suffers from few or no residual epic longings. If Pope is confident in his loyalty to epic, Shelley (and Byron) seem confident the opposite way, where poor Cowper remains stuck in between, coyly protesting both his seriousness and his unseriousness, not with a bang but a whimper. When Shelley speaks in the Dedication of the 'scene of my epic', though concerned with 'Hell and the Devil', as being 'in "this world which is"', deriding Wordsworth's claims to have avoided 'supernatural machinery'; or when he refers to his poem about Peter, the third treatment (after Wordsworth and John Hamilton Reynolds) of this hero and as being 'like the *Iliad*' part of a 'series of cyclic poems'; or when he speaks of 'the full stop which closes the poem . . . [as] being, like the full stops at the end of the *Iliad* and *Odyssey*, a full stop of a very qualified import', we are in a world of epic joking which is totally relaxed in its signalling that no part of the mock-heroic idiom is anything but an act of persiflage. When Garth or Pope ridiculed Blackmore writing epics, the joke was at the idea of a puny modern age pretending to grandeurs no longer available. But when Shelley, in Hell the 'city much like London', reports on 'suppers of epic poets', it is a passing glimpse of frivolous nonsense closer to *Beppo*'s Venice than to the *Dunciad*'s bloated metropolis:

> And all these meet at levees;–
> > Dinners convivial and political;–
> Suppers of epic poets;– teas,
> Where small talk dies in agonies;–
> > Breakfasts professional and critical;
>
> Lunches and snacks so aldermanic
> > That one would furnish forth ten dinners . . .

> > > > > > > (III, sts. 12–13)

Even that last item, with its Dunciadic vision of aldermanic binges, lacks, as the references to aldermanic feasts and their Homeric prototypes in *Don Juan* lack, the enormity of Pope's gluttonous Lethe of City-dignitaries, and the cosmic torpor which they spread over the culture:

> Now May'rs and Shrieves all hush'd and satiate lay,
> Yet eat, in dreams, the custard of the day.

> > > > > > (*Dunciad* I, 91–2)

Even the protracted account of a widespread onset of sleep at the
end of Shelley's poem comes over merely as a 'drear ennui' (VII,
st. 13), with none of the massiveness of this single couplet, let
alone Pope's larger orchestrations of the great yawn of gods and
men (*Dunciad*, IV, 605–6).

Nevertheless, Shelley's hellscape should not be underestimated
because of the surface frivolity, the mock-lyrical-ballad flatness of
its stanza, or whatever. The theme of the great city as Hell receives
at times an eloquent and laconic astringency which makes Pope's
couplet seem almost genial by comparison:

> Hell is a city much like London –
> A populous and a smoky city;
> There are all sorts of people undone,
> And there is little or no fun done;
> Small justice shewn, and still less pity.

> (III, st. 1)

The passage takes its place not only among the classic satirical
accounts of the city, Juvenal's third and Boileau's sixth satires,
Swift's 'Description' poems, Johnson's *Londòn*, but specifically
with those visions of a metropolitan inferno which we identify
with Milton and Pope and Baudelaire and Eliot, in whose unreal
city,

> Under the brown fog of a winter dawn,
> A crowd flowed over London Bridge, so many,
> I had not thought death had undone so many.

> (*Waste Land*, ll. 60ff.)

Eliot, like Pope, used images of Hell to bring out the urban
nightmare, Pope mainly from Milton, Eliot mainly from Dante.
'Undone' reverberates, fortuitously or otherwise, from Shelley's
poem, but Eliot's passage as a whole derives from Dante's *città
dolente* in *Inferno*, III, 55–7:

> sì lunga tratta
> di gente, ch'io non averei creduto
> che morte tanta n'avesse disfatta.

Pope's Dunciadic London similarly gains its infernal resonances and its monstrous shapes from Milton's Hell and Milton's Chaos. But if Pope and Eliot drew on Hell to portray the city, Milton and Shelley proceed the other way round: the city is instead used to portray Hell. In *Paradise Lost* the comparison is both memorable and oddly brief. Satan, after prolonged exile in Hell, visits Eden:

> As one who long in populous City pent,
> Where Houses thick and Sewers annoy the Air,
> Forth issuing on a Summers Morn to breathe
> Among the pleasant Villages and Farms
> Adjoind, from each thing met conceives delight,
> The smell of Grain, or tedded Grass or Kine
> Or Dairie, each rural sight, each rural sound.

> (IX, 445ff.)

It is a traditional country–city opposition, remarkable here mainly because the image of the city presented itself as an immediately available analogy for what Satan had been experiencing in Hell. It is so taken-for-granted as to be almost perfunctory. Milton doesn't offer much detail as to how a city might be like Hell, beyond noting populousness, confinement ('pent'), and bad atmospheric conditions: 'Where Houses thick and Sewers annoy the Air'. Shelley's 'populous and smoky city', though its phrasing echoes Milton's, is much more particularised. It is evident that Shelley is more concerned with cities than with Hell, while Milton, unlike Pope, or Shelley, or Eliot, is not much concerned with cities at all.

A feature of Milton's passage has perhaps been unremarked, however. If you want to describe the horrors of the city, Hell may offer some useful support. If you want to describe Hell, cities might be a bit of let-down, unless you raise the power of the city to the supercharged levels of apprehension which we variously encounter in the *Dunciad* or in Baudelaire or in Eliot, in whom the whole analogy is viewed (as I began by saying) from the other end of the telescope anyway. Milton could, like Shelley, have given more detail. He could in principle have gone the way of Pope: the argument that this would have been anachronistic in Milton's story must be set against the fact that Milton allowed himself all the prophetic incursions into the future he chose. The germ of city-horror which helped him momentarily to actualise a sense of infernal unpleasantness was not developed, perhaps because that was not what seemed to Milton the most telling example of horror, but it was a beginning.

If there is any sense in Milton's glimpse of the city that the horrors of Hell invited secularisation, this might be consistent both with Milton's more generally awkward treatment of ineffable and superhuman phenomena in temporal and humanised terms, and with the persistent feeling we get in *Paradise Lost* that Milton was engaged in a critique of the heroic at the same time as writing the last distinguished European poem in the older epic mode. *Paradise Lost* is full of secularising elements, and full of uncertainty too as to whether Hell is to be conceived as a geographical place or a mental state (an issue Shelley addressed with Miltonic reminders, but with a radically trivialised reduction of scope). It is also a poem which many readers have seen as tantalisingly poised between transcendent sublimity and some brilliantly contained comic effects, often embodied in combination in the character of Satan, titanic villain-hero and comic butt. It is the only full-scale epic that includes mock-heroic resonances which prefigure the *Dunciad* not only in reverse, as we should expect, but also directly, as when:

> So eagerly the Fiend
> O'er bog or steep, through strait, rough, dense, or rare,
> With head, hands, wings or feet persues his way,
> And swims or sinks, or wades, or creeps, or flies,

> (II, 947ff.)

which Pope imitated and cited at *Dunciad* II, 63ff., describing Lintot who like 'a dab-chick waddles thro' the copse/On feet and wings, and flies, and wades, and hops' (II, 63–4).

Such ambivalences were a major issue for Milton, in whom mock-heroic was a minor strand, and they were a major issue for Pope, in whom mock-heroic was the *major* element. But when we compare Shelley's comparison of Hell to a city (not overtly of a city to Hell, though that may be the effect) we sense this ambivalence in a greater degree. Where Milton's comparison is 'perfunctory' in the sense that it gives little city detail, Shelley's is perfunctory in spite of a great deal of detail. In Shelley, as against Milton, the reversal of expectation (saying Hell is like London) comes over as a way of saying London is like Hell, just as in Pope (or in Eliot). But unlike Pope, Shelley shows no obvious interest in actualising the analogy, no real concern with an active play of infernal resonance, only a focus on the city in its specific secular unpleasantness, so that his reverse comparison functions as an extended rhetorical turn rather than as a fully-realised epic fiction.

Shelley won't lightly let the Miltonic echoes and connections disappear, however. London evidently brought the anxiety of influence to the surface of his mind (though perhaps only the surface). In another poem which contains some of his pithiest literary–satirical formulations, the Horation epistle known as the 'Letter to Maria Gisborne' (1820), Shelley wrote, a year later:

> You are now
> In London, that great sea whose ebb and flow
> At once is deaf and loud, and on the shore
> Vomits its wrecks, and still howls on for more.
> Yet in its depth what treasures! You will see
> That which was Godwin, – greater none than he
> Though fallen – and fallen on evil times – to stand
> Among the spirits of our age and land
> Before the dread Tribunal of *to come*
> The foremost . . . while Rebuke cowers pale and dumb.
> You will see Coleridge – he who sits obscure
> In the exceeding lustre and the pure
> Intense irradiation of a mind
> Which, with its own internal lightning blind,
> Flags wearily through darkness and despair –
> A cloud-encircled meteor of the air,
> A hooded eagle among blinking owls.

(ll. 193ff.)

The portraits, affectionate, not uncritical, finely ironic and studiedly charged with Miltonic evocations, occur in a work which, like *Peter Bell the Third*, is memorable for its literary portraits, in both poems more fastidiously exact than the mushrooming fantastications of the *Dunciad*. Here more than in *Peter Bell the Third* a residue of grandeur is allowed to show itself, but the Miltonic resonances strike one as loose mythologising gestures, not deeply integrated into the fabric of the poem.

When in *Peter Bell the Third* Shelley secularised and desublimated

Hell, his immediate point, as we saw, was to joke about the
Wordsworthian renunciation of the 'supernatural' in poetry, a
renunciation Wordsworth makes a point of in the original *Peter Bell*
(and related to what Coleridge reports on their respective roles in
the *Lyrical Ballads* in Chapter xiv of *Biographia Literaria*). And so
when the poem gets to the Devil we have the following
disclaimers:

> The Devil, I safely can aver,
> 　　Has neither hoof, nor tail, nor sting;
> Nor is he, as some sages swear,
> A spirit, neither here nor there,
> 　　In nothing – yet in every thing.
>
> He is – what we are; for sometimes
> 　　The Devil is a gentleman;
> At others a bard bartering rhymes
> For sack; a statesman spinning crimes;
> 　　A swindler, living as he can;
>
> A thief, who cometh in the night,
> 　　With whole boots and net pantaloons,
> Like some one whom it were not right
> To mention; or the luckless wight,
> 　　From whom he steals nine silver spoons.
>
> But in this case he did appear
> 　　Like a slop-merchant from Wapping,[15]
> And with smug face, and eye severe
> On every side did perk and peer
> 　　Till he saw Peter dead or napping.

> > (II, sts i–iv)

It is a graceful patrician putdown, of the sort Byron also liked to
make against Lake or Cockney poets: the last stanza belongs to a
tradition which includes Swift's jibes at Dissenters or Fielding's at
Richardson. (Shelley also capped his jeering by making Peter 'A
footman in the Devil's service!' IV, st. i).

In the entire list of the Devil's guises, each a disreputable real-
world type, there is one about whom nothing specific is said:

'sometimes/The Devil is a gentleman'. This is left dangling, where all the other types are specified in more or less contemptible *doings*: 'a statesman spinning crimes', 'A thief, who cometh in the night'. One may speculate that the gentleman is unscathed because, while disreputable in context and in company, there is an ironic hint of what we might call poetic class-loyalty to the type, as though Shelley would not willingly traduce gentlemen when addressing a vulgarian like Wordsworth. There is, moreover, an amusing tendency, seen also in Byron's *Vision of Judgment*, to give comic glimpses of the Devil as a figure of patrician grace. The meeting between the Archangel Michael and Satan in Byron's *Vision* is perhaps the *locus classicus*:

> Yet still between his Darkness and his Brightness
> There passed a mutual glance of great politeness.
>
> The Archangel bowed, not like a modern beau,
>   But with a graceful oriental bend, . . .
> He turned as to an equal, not too low,
>   But kindly; Satan met his ancient friend
> With more hauteur, as might an old Castilian
> Poor Noble meet a mushroom rich civilian.

> (st. xxxv–xxxvi)

Such effects include an odd Augustan lordliness, but they are not wholly accounted for as putdowns for the lower poetic orders. There is a disengagement from the kind of harshly targeted hostility you find in the *hauteurs* of Swift or of Pope, and this probably is due not only to the fact that Shelley and Byron are more secure in their patrician standing and more relaxed in their gestures of lordliness. It is partly that they don't take their satirical purposes quite so seriously as Swift and Pope did, because the standard of gentlemanly morality in whose name the lordly accents are mustered have become less absolute. Thus the lordly superiority to turpitude and folly has become culturally less, not more, secure as an instrument of moral judgement: the uppish urgencies of Swift and Pope are higher in their cultural and lower in their personal sense of lordly certitude.

Notice, meanwhile, what has become of Satan. He is now neither a titanic villain as in Milton, nor, as in both Milton and

Pope, a grovelling 'familiar Toad' (*Epistle to Dr. Arbuthnot*, l. 319), but an easy, lordly charmer, cousin to Don Juan the 'inveterate Patrician' (XI, st. 45) with his noble Castilian pride (V, st. 104) and his 'very graceful bow' (IX, st. 83) and also to Lambro, the pirate who had 'such true breeding of a gentleman,/You never could divine his real thought' (III, st. 41). This will seem surprising to those who recall the Satanising heroes whom we witness in sublime rebellion in some other works by Shelley or Byron: Prometheus, Cain, Lara, and that whole array of romantic villain-heroes whose creators were labelled the Satanic school by the Laureate Southey.[16] It has often been said that such heroes of Romantic rebellion derive from Milton's Satan, and build on the perception (especially evident in some Romantic readers including Blake as well as both Shelley and Byron), of a secret Miltonic sympathy for the fallen angel, seen as a courageous and defiant adversary to authority.[17]

If this perception has substance (Dryden's view that Satan was the hero of *Paradise Lost* suggests that it wasn't wholly a Romantic aberration, though Dryden was probably insisting on Satan's centrality as a protagonist rather than on his moral attraction),[18] the blend of attitudes in Milton is finely balanced, not only between sublimity and mock-heroic ridicule but also between derogation and approval, hatred and admiration. Neither Shelley nor Byron could absorb such a mix. Their rebellious villain-heroes become simplified and unironic projections of the nobility of heroic defiance, including the readiness to carry guilt and endure punishment. They are not touched by humour, which is present in the Miltonic treatment and is radical to the Popeian version. What Shelley and Byron cannot do (I think) is regard evil as simultaneously comic and deadly, or as simultaneously comic and noble, so that while their serious treatments tend to be solemn, their comic treatments hive off into the domain of brilliant hard-edged frivolity which is represented by *Peter Bell the Third*, *Don Juan* and the *Vision of Judgment*. If Pope's culture precluded a new Miltonic epic, it nevertheless took that epic seriously enough to adapt it to massive urgencies of satiric perception. Shelley and Byron not only didn't take it seriously enough to risk the mixture. They transvaluated Milton's structure of moral authority, and created adversarial counterparts that do not move with enough certainty to contain their own critiques within them, let alone the sense of fun. Fun was to be had, if at all, elsewhere, in contexts where seriousness (whether of the Miltonic or the Dunciadic kind) could not be overtly accommodated.

So Satanic figures in Shelley or Byron can only become sublime rebels or comic charmers, never any genuine blend. This shows strikingly in the one possible exception, that domain of heroic suffering psychologised, where Milton's Satan understands that the limitless geography of Hell is in part at least a function of his own mind:

> Which way I flie is Hell; my self am Hell;
> And in the lowest deep a lower deep
> Still threat'ning to devour me opens wide,
> To which the Hell I suffer seems a Heav'n

(IV, 75–8)

and especially:

> The mind is its own place, and in it self
> Can make a Heav'n of Hell, a Hell of Heav'n.

(I, 254–5)

This is the kind of utterance which we expect to find in Shelleyan or Byronic heroes of the non-satiric kind, and which we would suppose both poets likely to be especially moved by. It is, of all items in the Miltonic inheritance, the one closest to a frame of mind which both poets could readily internalise, and has been shown to be particularly active in the Byron of *Cain* and *Manfred*.[19] But what Milton had presented as the inescapable ubiquity of damnation, and as a predicament of suffering on a cosmic scale, turns in *Peter Bell the Third* to a narrowed state of mind, confined by parodic purposes and chiefly insisted on in order to harp on Wordsworth's have-it-both-ways anti-supernaturalism and one or two other items of Wordsworthian rhetoric. The idea that Hell is everywhere, for example, turns up in the secularising stanzas about the Devil having no 'hoof, nor tail' and being embodied in common human types (II, st. iff.).

A more interesting quasi-sympathetic projection of the idea of turning a Hell into Heaven occurs in a stanza about Coleridge which may be set beside the Miltonising phrases of the 'Letter to

Maria Gisborne':

> This was a man who might have turned
>   Hell into Heaven – and so in gladness
> A Heaven unto himself had earned;
>   But he in shadows undiscerned
>   Trusted, – and damned himself to madness.

(V, st. iii)

If the satire seems to turn sentimental and unfocused, this is not mainly because of Shelley's obviously ambivalent feelings about Coleridge. His feelings about Wordsworth were just as ambivalent, but the stanzas about Wordsworth's poems which follow (V, st. viff.) show an acute sense of strengths and weaknesses in Wordsworth's writings and are literary criticism of a high order. A likelier cause is that the language used about Coleridge here picks up precisely that area in Milton's presentation of Satan to which Shelley (and Byron) would be disposed to respond with particular self-implication. Indeed, an earlier stanza honorifically applies the same Satanic phrases to Shelley himself and the idealistic reformers who were his friends:

> And some few, like we know who,
>   Damned – but God alone knows why –
> To believe their minds are given
> To make this ugly Hell a Heaven;
>   In which faith they live and die.

(III, st. xx)

The appropriation of Satan's predicament teeters between an exalted self-pity and derision of a directionless sort, and 'like we know who' is simperingly sub-Shandean. A fussy gravity invades a satiric idiom whose normal effects tend to be laconic and flattening, and strengthens the suspicion that Shelley, more than Byron, can only be satirical in a wholly externalised mode: where anything of himself is introduced, the result has to be total seriousness or awkward muddle. In *Peter Bell the Third* he generally avoided both, but it is interesting that his collapse into the latter occurs in the one area of Miltonising mock-heroic where the original language of

Satan might have felt particularly close to ideals of his own, whether of introspective heroism or of ardour to change the world. For once Milton can't be confidently joked about, while the immediate context precludes an easy retreat into the high mode of *Prometheus Unbound* or of Byron's non-satiric poems.

To students of mock-heroic it is a further paradox worth pondering that Shelley's critique of Wordsworth as a poet has few moments of grandeur, or mock-grandeur, in the mode of Pope's treatment of Cibber or Blackmore. Unlike Shelley, Pope is never appreciative of his Dunciadic victims. But nothing Shelley says in praise or blame of Wordsworth has the resonance of Pope's majestic tonalities of celebrative rejection, of Cibber's 'brazen, brainless brother' or 'sonorous Blackmore's strain', let alone the orchestrated Miltonic reverberation of Dulness's universal darkness burying all. Shelley's treatment, even at its most jeering, is more complimentary than anything Pope says about these. Mixed feelings come over not as grandeurs collapsing into bathos, but in flip low-key diminutions:

> And these obscure remembrances
>   Stirred such harmony in Peter,
> That, whensoever he should please,
> He could speak of rocks and trees
>   In poetic metre.

> (V, st. x)

It is partly, and only partly, a matter of Wordsworth's constant insistence on humble subjects and ordinary language, and if he protested that sublimity might be achieved through these, Shelley's tactic is not so much to mimic this through an inverse grandeur of bombast, as Pope might have done, but instead to flatten it to a muddled banality:

> He had also dim recollections
>   Of pedlars tramping on their rounds,
> Milk-pans and pails, and odd collections
> Of saws, and proverbs, and reflexions
>   Old parsons make in burying-grounds.

> (V, st. xii)

Shelley is jeering at Wordsworth's bids to make the prosaic sublime. It is one of the oddities of literary history that such details only became sublime again much later by what almost seems like an unparodying of the parody, as in the last stanza of Yeats's 'Circus Animals' Desertion', where 'masterful images' begin in low places:

> Those masterful images because complete
> Grew in pure mind, but out of what began?
> A mound of refuse or the sweepings of a street,
> Old kettles, old bottles, and a broken can,
> Old iron, old bones, old rags, that raving slut
> Who keeps the till. Now that my ladder's gone,
> I must lie down where all the ladders start,
> In the foul rag-and-bone shop of the heart,

or in Wallace Stevens's 'Large Red Man Reading':

> There were those that returned to hear him read
>   from the poem of life,
> Of the pans above the stove, the pots on the
>   table, the tulips among them . . .
>
> *Poesis, poesis,* the literal characters, the
>   vatic lines . . . .

It is almost as though Yeats or Stevens had taken Shelley's lines and written in defiance of them. It is unlikely that this happened, but Yeats especially has been known overtly to pick up an idiom of derision or parody, and *un*parody or rewrite it upwards.

It is instructive in this connection to note that both Byron and Yeats did their own versions of Dryden's famous portrait of Zimri in *Absalom and Achitophel*:

> A man so various, that he seem'd to be
> Not one, but all Mankinds Epitome.
> ....
> Was Chymist, Fidler, States-Man, and Buffoon:
> Then all for Women, Painting, Rhyming, Drinking;
> Besides ten thousand freaks that dy'd in thinking.

(ll. 545ff.)

By coincidence, Dryden's lines have here a peculiarly Byronic cadence, and Byron seems to have remembered the passage, in his portrait of Suwarrow:

> For the man was, we safely may assert,
>   A thing to wonder at beyond most wondering;
> Hero, buffoon, half-demon, and half-dirt,
>   Praying, instructing, desolating, plundering.[20]

(Don Juan VII, st. 55)

Byron retains Dryden's derision but not the ideal of the Renaissance complete man against which the derision had been played off. When Yeats picked up the passage in 'In Memory of Major Robert Gregory', he discarded derision altogether, and restored the heroic ideal, resublimating Dryden's mockery into the portrait of Gregory, 'Our Sidney and our perfect man':

> Soldier, scholar, horseman, he,
> As 'twere all life's epitome.

This is one of the strangest and least-studied mutations of mock-heroic. It begins in the mock-majesties which were valued because they retained a residue of original grandeurs: the classic fruition of this phase is the *Dunciad*. It has connections with the Shandean enterprise of taking Swift's mockery of moderns in *A Tale of a Tub* and outfacing it in self-assertive mimicry. But the Yeatsian form to which I drew attention is less commonly noted. In this development original grandeurs are not preserved, but restored, and original derisions are not outfaced but discarded. A revaluation has taken place, not as in mock-heroic, downwards, but in the opposite direction, upwards, in a species of mock-mock-heroic. The two mocks cancel out, as two negatives do in logic, but as seldom happens in poetry: for if Drydenian or *Dunciadic* mock-heroic preserved elements of the old heroic, the Yeatsian mock-version does not preserve the mockery, but resublimates the whole effect. It is an extension, perhaps, of that Shelleyan or Byronic inability to sustain a live and serious ambivalence in those domains where the heroic and the derisive might interact. It took a later age, further removed than they were from Augustan inhibition, to reactivate heroic idiom on unheroic subjects, in the teeth of an accumulated tradition of mockery. In the readiness to assume heroic accents straight, if in nothing else, this may be thought to stretch back before Dryden to Milton himself.

But there is a shorter and more immediate leap to be made, from Milton to Shelley and Byron, where Pope and his generation differ in their own ways from earlier and later ones. This is the area occupied by the subject of war, in two of its guises: the heroic ethos of martial prowess, held up for admiration in traditional military epic, and the awkward fact of war in history, past or present. It is, as I have argued elsewhere, a peculiarity of Augustan mock-heroic that one hardly ever sees any kind of warfare in the major or distinguished examples.[21] This is surprising because the principal heroic originals, and in particular the *Iliad* and the *Aeneid*, have war as their central subject-matter. In Boileau's *Lutrin*, or Garth's *Dispensary*, or Swift's *Battle of the Books*, or Pope's *Rape of the Lock*, there are formal simulacra of an unsanguinary kind: learned quarrels among divines, or medics, or men of letters, and a comic battle of the sexes among the flirty *jeunesse dorée* of the Catholic gentry. The *Dunciad* is even more remarkable, since it lacks even this element of ghostly imitation. The poem uses every rhetorical routine associated with classical or Miltonic epics, including an Odyssean or Aenean journey from East to West, a visit to the Underworld, and a parody of heroic sports. But there is no fighting. I suspect that this military *pudeur* proceeds from an inverse anxiety of influence, timorous of allowing the revered heroic poems to be contaminated by their traditional subject-matter, now increasingly felt to be disreputable. Pope declaimed against the shocking spirit of cruelty in Homer's battles, and he suppressed much of the gory material in his translation. The mock-heroic mode purported not to attack the epic but to pay it homage, by playing its grandeurs off against a lapsed or subheroic modern world. But in pursuing this aim it continually risked self-subversion from reminders of epic's martial values: and especially so in a context of prevailing irony or derision, where cherished positives might pick up a secondary infection from the low-life whose company they are made to keep.

The problem of epic and war had already, as is well known, troubled Milton. He was writing not a mock-epic but a full-scale original, and he was not only the last author of a great classical epic, but also (and the facts are connected) the first major epic writer to have to reconcile his prosecution of a martial genre with a strongly felt dislike of war and of the celebration of war. He met the problem not by omission (as the Augustan mock-heroic writers did), but by a continuous and overt critique of the martial ethos from within: asserting that *his* subject is 'Not less but more heroic' than those of combative epics, than 'the wrauth/ Of stern *Achilles* . . . or rage/Of *Turnus* for *Lavinia* disespous'd' (IX, 14–17), and declaring his poor opinion of 'Warrs, hitherto the onely Argument/ Heroic deemd' (IX, 28–9). But Milton also (unlike the later, mock-heroic writers) offered a major martial episode at the centre of his poem. The War in Heaven is by definition one not open to censure like human wars. But Milton courted difficulties by presenting the military business insistently and graphically, and simultaneously circumvented some of the awkwardness by making sure no one was killed, since the participants were immortal (VI, 434). Even Satan's spectacular wound releases not blood but a 'Nectarous humor' (VI, 332: an idea Byron played with in *Vision of Judgment*, xxv) and, like Aphrodite's wound in the prototype passage in *Iliad*, V, 339ff., 416ff., is immediately healed anyway.[22] Both these items of Miltonic precaution were amusingly appropriated in the *Rape of the Lock*, the first at V, 43–4, when the battle in which no one will die except in the sexual sense is about to begin:

> No common Weapons in their Hands are found,
> Like Gods they fight, nor dread a mortal Wound,

and the second at III, 151–2, when the Sylph guarding Belinda's lock is cut 'in twain,/(But Airy Substance soon unites again)'.

Milton thus has it both ways, presenting traditional epic subject-matter and structure while simultaneously condemning previous treatments; and offering a grim battle that is 'unreal' in human terms and free of the disreputability that normally attends warfare in his eyes. The unrealising effects of this treatment are compounded in the account of gunpowder combat. The spectacular anachronism involved in the portrayal of modern technological warfare in a pre-human battle among celestial beings rests partly on a traditional notion that gunpowder was the invention of the Devil. But the portrayal has a graphic particularity, and a species of military realism, which are in dramatic and pictorial effect bizarre beyond Disneyan fantasy. It is paradoxical features of this kind that animate Milton's treatment of war, enabling him to retain the military business and even the martial partisanships of heroic poetry while mounting a massive onslaught on the morality of war and the traditional values of epic. He not only reports on the evil technology where he need not have done, rather than avoiding it as the mock-heroic writers were to do (with minor exceptions, including a passing mention in the *Battle of the Books*),[23] but rubs it in anachronistically and revels in the portrayal. In this sense, though he is writing a straight epic, Milton is less protective of that genre than are the authors of the mock-form. (The more extended discussion of gunpowder in *Gulliver's Travels* is held outside the epic's range of associations, and thus does not arise as a problem.) There is no gunpowder combat in the *Rape of the Lock* or the *Dunciad*, or in the *Dispensary* or *Le Lutrin*. But it re-emerges in a Miltonic allusion in Byron's *Vision of Judgment*:

> Infernal thunder shook both sea and land
>   In all the planets – and Hell's batteries
> Let off the artillery, which Milton mentions   .
>   As one of Satan's most sublime inventions.

> (lii)

The reminder is jokey, like some of Shelley's flip Miltonisms. But despite the relatively genial satiric context, there are in Byron's poem and also in Shelley's some very harsh reminders of modern war: the military disreputability of George III's reign erupts as early as in Stanza v, with its report of thousands of daily deaths culminating in the 'crowning carnage, Waterloo'. And just as Byron reminded the Poet Laureate Southey of the ugly realities of the reign of the monarch he has been celebrating, so Shelley in *Peter Bell the Third* attacks Wordsworth and specifically his celebration of Waterloo in the 'Thanksgiving Ode':

> Then Peter wrote Odes to the Devil; –
>   In one of which he meekly said: –
> 'May Carnage and Slaughter,
> Thy niece and thy daughter,
> May Rapine and Famine,
> Thy gorge ever cramming,
>   Glut thee with living and dead!'

> (VI, st. xxxxvi)

Wordsworth had written rather sanctimoniously of righteous slaughter in God's name: 'Yea, Carnage is thy daughter'. Byron, like Shelley, picked up the phrase in *Don Juan* VIII, st. 9: '"Carnage" (so Wordsworth tells you) "is God's daughter"'. Wordsworth eventually removed the line in 1845.

The fact that some mealy-mouthed texts by Southey or Wordsworth existed to trigger these reactions is almost beside the point. Such a hostile reminder of contemporaneous warfare would be unthinkable in the Augustan mock-heroists, whose only historically-attested fights are the clerical or medical or learned or flirty imbroglios which are allegorised in their mock-epics. Milton had indeed mentioned gunpowder war, but on an unreal and unsanguinary plane, with no strong specific applications from human history past or present. There is an overwhelming sense of 'war-in-general' about the sequence, quite as much as in Gulliver's generalised war-descriptions in Books II and IV. But in the work of Shelley and of Byron it is an insistent theme, very closely interwoven with mock-epic gesturing.

The siege of Ismail is the *locus classicus* in *Don Juan*, with Suwarrow the Russian general 'lecturing on the noble art of killing' (VII, st. 58), and with Jonathan-Wild-like ironies about heroes, as when Suwarrow feels a momentary stirring of pity:

however habit sears
Men's hearts against whole millions, when their trade
Is butchery, sometimes a single sorrow
Will touch even Heroes, and such was Suwarrow.

(VII, st. 69)

There is a comic list of combatants, which imitates Homeric enumerations, including Russians with unpronounceable names of 'twelve consonants a-piece' (VII, st. 14–17) and 'several Englishmen of pith,/Sixteen called Thomson, and nineteen named Smith' (VII, st. 18). When the fighting gets started, there is more Homeric reminder, as when the battle is compared to what it might have been in the *Iliad* had gunpowder been available:

The work of Glory still went on
In preparations for a cannonade

As terrible as that of Ilion,
     If Homer had found mortars ready made;
But now, instead of slaying Priam's son,
     We only can but talk of escalade,
Bombs, drums, guns, bastions, batteries, bayonets, bullets,
Hard words, which stick in the soft Muses' gullets.

(VII, st. 78)

It is a type of entranced listing which we may associate with Gulliver boasting about war-technology to the King of Brobdingnag or Master Houyhnhnm, but there studiously avoiding all epic reminder while Byron rubs it in. The two next stanzas repeatedly apostrophise 'eternal Homer' (VII, sts. 79–80):

Oh, thou eternal Homer! I have now
     To paint a siege, wherein more men were slain,
With deadlier engines and a speedier blow,
     Than in thy Greek gazette of that campaign;
And yet, like all men else, I must allow,
     To vie with thee would be about as vain
As for a brook to cope with Ocean's flood;
But still we Moderns equal you in blood.

(VII, st. 80)

There is a handsome compliment to Homer, but no mere question of a hushed elevation ('thy Greek gazette of that campaign' more or less affectionately downgrades Homer, whereas Swift's parallel piece of mock-heroic and mock-journalese, 'the Full and True Account of the Battel Fought last Friday', is meant to mock newspapers and protect Homer).

'Gazette' comes over with reverberations of Scriblerian scorn of journalists: see, for example, *Dunciad* II, 314 and the notes of both Scriblerus and Pope. It is a frequent word in *Don Juan*, particularly obsessive in the siege cantos, where Byron accentuates the official Gazettes' special role as necrologies of war. Byron is playfully, but I think insultingly, assimilating Homer to the shoddy ephemera of 'daily scribes', not separating him from these in Swift's manner. It is interesting in this connection that Samuel Johnson thought Joseph Warton's description of Addison's poem *The Campaign* as a

'Gazette in Rhyme' was particularly contemptuous, 'with harshness not often used by the good-nature of his criticism'.[24]

In the same place, Johnson describes Addison's poem as a departure from the epic habit of celebrating 'personal prowess, and "mighty bone"', and concentrating instead on Marlborough's virtues of cool judgement and tactical generalship. Scott later said 'Addison was the first poet who ventured to celebrate a victorious general for skill and conduct' rather than dealing with the old kind of individual heroic prowess,[25] a procedure held by some to be radically contrary to epic (Goldsmith, for example, is said to have believed modern war to be unsuitable for epic treatment precisely because its technologies make strategic expertise more important than personal heroism).[26]

It is interesting at all events to see Addison the Whig celebrant demystifying the heroic in this fashion, while the Tory mock-heroic writers tried to omit mention of war altogether. Steele, in *Tatler* No. 6, amused himself by 'putting the Actions of *Homer's Iliad* into an exact Journal', very much in a contrary spirit to the mock-journalese of Swift's *Battle* five years before.[27] It is of a piece with this kind of readiness to speak of heroic warfare in everyday or journalistic terms that Steele also made a point of noting the military actions performed in the current war 'by Men of private Characters, or Officers of lower Stations' (*Tatler*, No. 56).[28] Byron cheerfully extends this unheroic practice to his epic, with its jeering replacement of Homeric lists of leaders by his own famous lists of common soldiers' names, including the unpronounceable Russian ones and the British Thomsons and Smiths, until he is defeated by sheer numbers. These 'Would form a lengthy lexicon of glory,/And what is worse still, a much longer story' (VIII, st. 17), so that the matter has to be resolved journalistally:

> And therefore we must give the greater number
> To the Gazette – which doubtless fairly dealt
> By the deceased, who lie in famous slumber
> In ditches, fields, or wheresoe'er . . ..

> (VIII, st. 18)

There is no attempt here to protect the hallowed forms of epic from association with the military squalors you read of in the papers, nor any sign of the common Augustan project of separ-

ating Homer from history. Homer may not have had the advantage
of gunpowder, but when Byron boasts that 'still we Moderns equal
you in blood', it is part of his point that Homer was very gory too.
As the reflections on the siege continue, we see a readiness not to
distinguish between epic deeds and historical horrors, ancient and
modern:

> Oh, ye great bulletins of Bonaparte!
>   Oh, ye less grand long lists of killed and wounded!
> Shade of Leonidas, who fought so hearty,
>   When my poor Greece was once, as now, surrounded!
> Oh, Caesar's Commentaries! now impart ye,
>   Shadows of glory! (lest I be confounded)
> A portion of your fading twilight hues,
> So beautiful, so fleeting, to the Muse.
>
> When I call 'fading' martial immortality,
>   I mean, that every age and every year,
> And almost every day, in sad reality,
>   Some sucking hero is compelled to rear,
> Who, when we come to sum up the totality
>   Of deeds to human happiness most dear,
> Turns out to be a butcher in great business,
> Afflicting young folks with a sort of dizziness.
>
>   (VII, sts 82–3)

Byron's peculiar brand of jokeyness is painful. But its pain is
over human suffering, not the status of epic. Byron may have any
amount of affection for Homer's poem, and of acceptance that 'to
vie with [him] would be about as vain/ As for a brook to cope with
Ocean's flood'. But harsh exposures of war are harsh exposures of
Homer, and the joking bruises Homeric dignity without blunting
the disparagement of carnage.

Again and again Byron goes out of his way to jeer at sentimental
disconnections in which epics are supposed to be one thing and
slaughter another:

> Yet I love Glory; – glory's a great thing; –
>   Think what it is to be in your old age
> Maintained at the expense of your good king:
>   A moderate pension shakes full many a sage,

And heroes are but made for bards to sing,
   Which is still better; thus in verse to wage
Your wars eternally, besides enjoying
Half-pay for life, make mankind worth destroying.

                              (VIII, st. 14)

        these rhymes
   A little scorched at present with the blaze
Of conquest and its consequences, which
Make Epic poesy so rare and rich

                              (VIII, st. 90)

The claim which had been made in the cheerful nonsense of Canto I ('My poem's epic, and is meant to be') is taken up here and at the end of VIII, with all the grim business of the siege ringing in our ears:

Reader! I have kept my word, – at least so far
   As the first Canto promised. You have now
Had sketches of love, tempest, travel, war –
   All very accurate, you must allow,
And *Epic*, if plain truth should prove no bar;
   For I have drawn much less with a long bow
Than my forerunners. Carelessly I sing,
But Phoebus lends me now and then a string.

                            (VIII, st. 138)

The carelessness, the easy surface, is, like Shelley's, very insulting where it wants to be, and the Muse of Epic surely ends up with her reputation in tatters, while no intelligent reader would ever be taken in by Byron's protestation that he is courting her. He is not attacking her in the ordinary sense, and he doubtless goes on loving his Homer. But History, ancient and modern, has been allowed to demonstrate that heroic fables are not pretty.

   History and fact have played a dual, complementary role in this context. In Milton and more especially in Swift and in Pope, epic is partly kept insulated from the brute facts which would impair its standing. Addison's remark about Homer's Achilles, that he was

'Morally Vicious, and only Poetically Good' (*Spectator*, No. 548), reminds us that the supremacy of epic resided in a distinction between works of art and real-life deeds, and the essential project (for which Byron and Shelley had no use, but which was vital to Swift, Pope or Fielding), was to shield the former from the latter. Hence the silence about war in mock-heroic, or the silence about epic in Swift's attacks on war.

But if history could release disturbing suspicions of epic, it could also be used to allay them. This is not much in evidence in the time of Byron or Shelley, when the need to shield the standing of epic from disrepute no longer existed, but it is powerfully evident in the work of Pope and Fielding. It springs not only from perceptions like Addison's about Achilles or like Cowley's comment as early as 1656 that 'a warlike, various, and a tragical age is best to *write of*, but worst to *write in*'.[29] A large part of the Homer debate in Pope's day was concerned with the barbarity of the age in which Homer wrote, or that which he depicted, and with the saving distinctions that might be made between the greatness of the poetry and the disreputability of the material. This is not quite the simple distinction between the order of art and the order of fact which it may seem. For history is a loose concept which may refer both to events, facts, *and* to the writing which records them. And among those who expressed the deep, uneasy admiration of epic which lies at the heart of Pope's Homeric translations or the *Dunciad* or Fielding's *Jonathan Wild*, both these notions of history could be used as lightning conductors, absorbing and diverting disparagements which would otherwise strike mortally (as came to happen in Byron) at the edifice of a cherished loyalty.

Aristotle's famous distinction between poetry and history, according to which poetry was of more universal import than history (*Poetics*, ix; 1451b), offered a traditional formula for downgrading history which Fielding made use of in *Joseph Andrews*, III, i, and to which Wordsworth alluded in grander and cloudier terms in the Preface to the *Lyrical Ballads*.[30] A related distinction, which Wordsworth also voiced, was between 'Poetry and Matter of Fact, or Science'. Although there is a logical extension which would, as W. J. B. Owen expresses it, include 'in general truth . . . what is factually true, merely because it is true', the impulse to assert the distinction is sustained by a traditional contempt for mere particulars, and for types of utterance that aim or are content to report facts for no other reason than that they are facts.[31]

This partly accounts for the tendency, especially strongly marked among such Augustan humanists as Swift, Pope and Fielding, to despise mere chroniclers and journalists, historians of ephemeral and day-to-day facts (Byron's 'daily scribes'), and even to identify them with the essential ephemerality of any historical fact, and therefore of history as the written record of such things. Byron turned the tables on this, as we saw, by speaking of Homer's *Iliad* as a gazette and thus downgrading epic writers themselves to gazetteers. A similar irony in inverse form was to say that the claim that *Don Juan* was epic could stand only 'if plain truth should prove no bar' (VIII, st. 87).

Feeding into this and cutting across the distinction between the order of fact and the order of art is a habit of not distinguishing, linguistically, between history and story (as in Latin *historia*, or French *histoire*): a convergence which C. S. Lewis spoke of as surviving into the Middle Ages, when, he said, 'the very words *story* and *history* had not yet been desynonymised',[32] but which surely lasted longer than that, and which still leads, in our own time, to Lucian's most famous work being translated variously as *True History* or *True Story*, an ironic phenomenon apt to an ironic title.

'Medieval' confusion on such a point is more or less an Augustan synonym for barbarism, directly assimilable to modern duncery, and the full reverberation of scorn for a benighted age occurs in Pope's note in the *Dunciad* on Caxton, one of 'The Classics of an Age that heard of none' (I, 148). Caxton's 'rude' English is part of the Gothick decor, but the essential point is that Caxton is identified as 'A Printer [who] . . . translated into prose *Virgil's Aeneid* as a History; of which he speaks in his Proeme in a very singular manner, as of a book hardly known'.'A Printer' recalls Horace Walpole on Richardson's novels: 'pictures of high life as conceived by a bookseller' (to Sir Horace Mann, 20 December 1764). Translating epic into prose, as a 'history', a daily or journalistic history, is what Swift had done in the *Battle of the Books*, 'A Full and True Account of the Battel Fought last Friday', protectively deflecting parody of epic into parody of journalism. The burden of Pope's charge is that low-class 'medieval' Caxton joins modern dunces in pulling down cherished majesties, which include the drop into prose, the miscellaneous alleged ignorance of the nature of the *Aeneid*, and the conversion of it into 'history' – whether as fact or fiction who can tell, both being in their way disreputable.

The issue becomes further complicated when in Pope's and in Fielding's time novels start to call themselves 'histories', in straight bids for verisimilitude or as ironic travesties of such bids, and when 'history' pretending to truth was therefore openly used to advertise fiction or lies (*histoire*, the history/story confusion, re-entering by the back door of a coy self-awareness). Fielding's practice is to downgrade 'history' in the name of 'epic' or 'comic epic'; to scorn mere chroniclers (in fact or fiction) as 'daily and weekly Historians' (*Tom Jones*, III, i); and yet to put *History* on the title pages of the very novels in which all these takes and double-takes are taking place.

Part of Fielding's subtext is concerned to strike against the phoney authentications of fiction, the lies that pass for fact in Grub Street as much as the 'to the moment' immediacies and the pretence of documentary integrity in the Richardsonian novel in letters. If 'history' can't even guarantee to be truthful, what is left? But if it is true, it is even worse. A nasty fact like mass killing is nastier than a poem on the subject. You may say there is inconsistency or even confusion in this cauldron of strongly-held views (often held by the same person in varying combinations), but the history of ideas has never been strong on logic. If the siege of Ismail is like Homer, as Byron said, you could, as Byron did, leave it unnervingly at that. But if you wished to shield Homer from the disrepute, you could attribute the badness to the times or whatever, with Homer's art transcending history. But if this proved hard to sustain in practice, you could divert the focus on heroic deeds from epic to history, from Achilles to Alexander or Aeneas to Caesar.

In the last stages of Augustan mock-heroic, history came to the aid of epic in this way. In Fielding's *Jonathan Wild*, heroic reminder shifts constantly from epic heroes and 'heroic' assertions to the historical Alexander and Caesar, and from the poets Homer and Virgil to historians like Plutarch. The most striking example, which I have cited elsewhere, occurs in Fielding's *Jonathan Wild*, where, for example, Fireblood is ironically described as Wild's *fidus Achates*, but where as soon as this Virgilian association is made, Fielding also makes the decisive correction: 'or rather the Hephaestion of our Alexander' (III, iv).[33] By this time, however, there are forces which work to collapse the distinction. When we read that Jonathan Wild 'was a passionate admirer of heroes, particularly of Alexander the Great' (I, iii), we may think we know where we stand. But in the same chapter we also learn that as a schoolboy he loved to hear the epic poets translated and was, for example, 'wonderfully pleased with that passage in the eleventh *Iliad* where Achilles is said to have bound two sons of Priam upon a mountain, and afterwards to have released them for a sum of money. This was, he said, alone sufficient to refute those who affected a contempt for the wisdom of the ancients' (I, iii). Here, the rot has been allowed in. Wild's love of Homer is not the same as Fielding's, but if Wild can love Homer, there must be something wrong: the episodes he admired are after all present in the epic poets.

That removal of the difference between ill deeds in epic and in history which is so harpingly evident in Byron is already in Fielding rearing its head as a ghastly possibility, and within a few years Fielding was announcing in the Preface to the *Voyage to Lisbon* that 'I must confess I should have honoured and loved Homer more had he written a *true history of his own times in humble prose*, than those noble poems that have so justly collected the praise of all ages' (my italics). Contrast Swift's or Pope's view of the offensiveness of reducing epic to either history *or* humble prose, in the *Battle of the Books* or the note on Caxton, and also Pope's scorn of the indistinguishability of poetry and prose in the work of the dunces (*Dunciad*, I, 189–90, 274): a species of Augustan *hauteur* which survives in Byron's comment on Wordsworth 'Who, both by precept and example, shows/ That prose is verse, and verse is merely prose.' (*English Bards*, ll. 241–2). But Byron is also ready as Pope or Fielding could not be to jeer at epic expectation by contaminating it systematically with the 'plain truth' of modern warfare, and *Don Juan* opens with a roll-call of heroes who are precisely of the historical sort, 'the butcher Cumberland' or 'Buonaparté and Dumourier/ Recorded in the Moniteur and Courier' (I, st. 2), the ruling or conquering thugs who are the modern counterparts of Alexander or Caesar and who regularly come in and out, 'cloying the gazettes with cant' (I, st. 1). Nothing stands in the way of identifying them with epic heroes or of suggesting that the latter differ only in having been lucky enough to get into poems, a distinction which seemed as trivial to Byron as it was important to Pope: 'Brave men were living before Agamemnon/ And since, . . ./ But then they shone not on the poet's page' (I, st. 5).

It would be amusing to think that in Fielding's yearnings for a 'true history . . . in humble prose', Clio was getting some retribution for the humiliations which he and other Augustan writers had been inflicting on her in the great years of mock-heroic. In *Jonathan Wild* we are not only on the way to Byron. We are also half-way to the *Waste Land*'s pervasive suggestion both that the older poems were grander than modern times, *and* also not so very different from them after all. And in *Amelia*, that low-key transposition of the *Aeneid* to modern life, we are, as many have noted, half-way to Joyce.

Pope didn't quite lose his nerve about epic in the way that the Fielding of the *Voyage to Lisbon* did, though he persistently worried about the 'shocking . . . Spirit of Cruelty',[34] and was, like other of his contemporaries, more or less studiously concerned to let military disrepute rub off on historical rather than poetic targets. In Fielding's *Jonathan Wild*, however, an epic and a historical model are more insistently juxtaposed, registering both an unheroic decline *into* history and the all-too-'heroic' continuities *of* history. The distinction between heroic poetry and historical massacres is beginning to wear thin, but Fielding probably never wholly abandoned it, not even in the *Voyage to Lisbon*. Byron did. If Milton retained epic forms and majesties to criticise the heroic from within, Byron effected a radical travesty of this procedure. His 'epic' tells you enough about epics to ensure that no sorrow is felt at the fact that (flaunted assertions notwithstanding) it isn't one at all.

Notes

1. Quotations from Byron's poems are from the *Complete Poetical Works*, ed. Jerome J. McGann (Oxford, 1980–), with the exception of the *Vision of Judgment*, which is cited from the *Works of Lord Byron: Poetry*, Vol. IV, ed. E. H. Coleridge (London, 1901). Shelley's poems are cited from his *Poetry and Prose*, ed. Donald H. Reiman and Sharon B. Powers (New York, 1977). This edition has been chosen because it provides the only complete text of *Peter Bell the Third* to have been based on the Bodleian press-copy manuscript (see *The Bodleian Shelley Manuscripts*, Vol. I, ed. Donald H. Reiman (New York, 1986), p. 13). In referring to particular passages in the poem, however, I have departed from Reiman's and Powers's continuous lineation, in favour of the more traditional stanzaic numeration.
2. The fullest discussion of this matter is in A. B. England, *Byron's Don Juan and Eighteenth-Century Literature* (Lewisburg, 1975), esp. pp. 68, 80ff.

3. *Works of Lord Byron: Letters and Journals*, Vol. V, ed. R. E. Prothero, 1901, pp. 560, 571.
4. John Dryden, *Of Dramatic Poesy and other Critical Essays*, ed. George Watson (London, 1962), II, 223.
5. Marilyn Butler, 'Revising the Canon', *The Times Literary Supplement*, 4–10 December 1987, p. 1360.
6. Thomas Shadwell, *The Humorists* (1671); Rochester, *Complete Poems*, ed. David M. Vieth (New Haven, 1968), p. 124.
7. Charles Cotton, *The Genuine Poetical Works*, 3rd edn, 1734, p. 1.
8. See Sybil Rosenfeld, *The Theatre of the London Fairs in the 18th Century* (Cambridge, 1960), and a brief discussion in my *Henry Fielding and the Augustan Ideal Under Stress* (London, 1972), pp. 213–14, 226.
9. Byron's frequently-quoted protestations to Thomas Medwin about the epic nature of *Don Juan* seem to me to be in the same spirit of jokey bravado (*Medwin's Conversations of Lord Byron*, ed. Ernest J. Lovell, Jr. (Princeton, 1966), pp. 164–5).
10. Shelley probably wrote his parody on the basis of reviews of Wordsworth's poem. An earlier parody, John Hamilton Reynolds's *Peter Bell, A Lyrical Ballad*, actually appeared before Wordsworth's *Peter Bell* (see Reiman's discussion in *The Bodleian Shelley Manuscripts*, I, 6–16.) Shelley's poem, which was not published until 1839, is sometimes seen as being in a similar spirit to Byron's *ottava rima* satires, and Mary Shelley felt impelled to deny an early reviewer's supposition that Byron had had a hand in it (ibid., pp. 12, 16n.28). Byron himself derided *Peter Bell* in *Don Juan*, III, st. 100, and in an 'Epilogue' written on the margins of the first page of a copy sent to him by Murray (see *Works: Poetry*, VII, 63–4; A. E. H. Swaen, 'Peter Bell', *Anglia*, XLVII (1923), 146ff.; Leslie A. Marchand, *Byron: A Biography* (London, 1957), II. 873 and notes p. 95).
11. *His Very Self and Voice: Collected Conversations of Lord Byron*, ed. Ernest J. Lovell, Jr. (New York, 1954), p. 268.
12. Swaen, op. cit., p. 161. Hunt's review of Wordsworth's poem (*Examiner*, 3 May 1819) is reprinted in Swaen, op. cit., pp. 159–62.
13. For further evidence on this point, see my *Order from Confusion Sprung: Studies in Eighteenth-Century Literature* (London, 1985), pp. 154ff., esp. 187–8n.23.
14. *Letters of Percy Bysshe Shelley*, ed. Frederick L. Jones (Oxford, 1964), II, 134.
15. For the significance to Augustan satirists of Wapping as a sleazy district with sectarian associations, see John Arbuthnot, *The History of John Bull*, ed. Alan W. Bower and Robert A. Erickson (Oxford, 1976), p. 169n.35.
16. Robert Southey, Preface to *A Vision of Judgment*, *Poetical Works* (Longman, London, n.d.), X, 205–6.
17. On Milton's influence on Byron's poems, see the good discussion in Jerome J. McGann, *Don Juan in Context* (London, 1976), Chapters 2 and 3. For Byron on Milton's Satan, *Letters and Journals*, ed. Leslie A. Marchand (Cambridge, Mass., 1978), VIII, 115, and Medwin,

Conversations, pp. 77–8, both cited by McGann at pp. 24–5; Shelley on Satan, *Defence of Poetry*, in *Poetry and Prose*, p. 498; Blake, *Marriage of Heaven and Hell*, Plate 6.

18. Dryden, *Of Dramatic Poesy and other Critical Essays*, II, 233.
19. For Byron's exploitation of Milton's lines in *Cain* and *Manfred*, see McGann, *Don Juan in Context*, op. cit., pp. 32–3, 36–7.
20. See the discussion in A. B. England, *Byron's Don Juan*, op. cit., pp. 53–5. For another use by Byron of the portrait of Zimri, see Rawson, '"Beppo" and "Absalom and Achitophel": A Parallel', *Notes and Queries*, CCIX (1964), 25.
21. *Order from Confusion Sprung*, pp. 205–6.
22. See Rawson, 'Byron's *Vision of Judgment*, XXV, Pope, and Hobbes's Homer', *Byron Journal*, XI (1983), 48–51, and *Order from Confusion Sprung*, p. 206.
23. See *Battle of the Books*, in *A Tale of a Tub*, ed. A. C. Guthkelch and D. Nichol Smith, 2nd edn (Oxford, 1958), p. 236 and n.6; there is a chemical explosion in Garth's *Dispensary* (1699), III, 232 (*Poems on Affairs of State. Volume 6: 1697–1704*, ed. Frank H. Ellis (New Haven, 1970), p. 91).
24. Samuel Johnson, 'Addison', in *Lives of the English Poets*, ed. G. Birkbeck Hill (Oxford, 1905), II, 128–9. See Joseph Warton, *An Essay on the Genius and Writings of Pope*, 4th edn, 1782, I, 30.
25. *The Works of John Dryden*, ed. Walter Scott, 1808, IV, 3.
26. See Dustin Griffin, *Regaining Paradise: Milton and the Eighteenth Century* (Cambridge, 1986), p. 50.
27. *Tatler*, ed. Donald F. Bond (Oxford, 1987), I, 56.
28. *Tatler*, I, 395; cf. also no. 87, II, 48ff.
29. Abraham Cowley, *Poems*, ed. A. R. Waller (Cambridge, 1905), p. 7.
30. See *Prose Works of William Wordsworth*, ed. W. J. B. Owen and Jane Worthington Smyser (Oxford, 1974), I, 139, 179; W. J. B. Owen, *Wordsworth as Critic* (Toronto, 1969), pp. 88ff.
31. *Prose Works*, I, 135, 140–41, 174, 181–2; Owen, *Wordsworth as Critic*, op. cit., p. 96.
32. C. S. Lewis, *The Discarded Image* (Cambridge, 1964), p. 179.
33. Rawson, *Henry Fielding and the Augustan Ideal Under Stress*, pp. 153–4.
34. Pope, note to translation of *Iliad*, XIII, 471, Twickenham Edition, ed. Maynard Mack, Vol. VIII, p. 129n.

6

Continuities and Discontinuities of Language and Voice in Dryden, Pope, and Byron

BERNARD BEATTY

Skill'd by a touch to deepen scandal's tints
With all the kind mendacity of hints,
While mingling truth with falsehood – sneers with smiles –
A thread of candour with a web of wiles;
A plain blunt show of briefly-spoken seeming,
To hide her bloodless heart's soul-harden'd scheming;
A lip of lies – a face formed to conceal;
And, without feeling, mock at all who feel:
With a vile mask the Gorgon would disown;
A cheek of parchment – and an eye of stone.
Mark, how the channels of her yellow blood
Ooze to her skin, and stagnate there to mud,
Cased like the centipede in saffron mail,
Or darker greenness of the scorpion's scale –

('A Sketch from Private Life', ll. 55–67)

These lines, written at the height of the Separation scandal in 1816 and addressed to Mrs Clermont, his wife's former governess, are perhaps the closest in all Byron's corpus to satire in the manner of Pope and Dryden. Wordsworth did not like them. He wrote to John Scott (18 April 1816):

> The man is insane . . . . The verses on his private affairs excite in
> me less indignation than pity. The latter copy [i.e. 'A Sketch'] is
> the Billingsgate of Bedlam.

Wordsworth's comment is cogent. The first thing we notice about
these lines is that they have an 'over the top' quality which makes
the voice unPopeian.

Nevertheless, verse such as this is directly based on Pope's
practice in, for instance, the *Epistle to Dr. Arbuthnot*. Byron himself
draws this to our attention by the deliberate allusion to Pope's
famous lines on Addison ('And without sneering teach the rest to
sneer') in his 'And, without feeling, mock at all who feel'. Many of
the lines here are adroit and well-managed. They stand comparison with Pope:

> With all the kind mendacity of hints . . .
>
> A thread of candour with a web of wiles . . .
>
> Cased like the centipede in saffron mail.

We could make a collection of lines as good as or better than these
from *English Bards, The Age of Bronze* and other couplet poems in
which we would find an accomplished use of the major operating
principles of the closed couplet as perfected by Pope. Byron,
however, uses Pope's habit of inversion less frequently than Pope
does. We do not get many lines like Pope's 'eternal smiles his
emptiness betray'. This detail may be instructive. Pope can put the
object before its governing verb because he knows, or appears to
know, in advance what he is going to say. Doubtless this has much
to do with the constant revising and polishing of his phrases.
Byron on the other hand writes forwards, revising as he goes
along, and thus prefers a less regulated syntax than Pope. Dryden
is somewhere in the middle here. Roughly speaking, we can say
that Byron's syntax is Romantic in that it is exploratory. He does
not know or appear to know in advance what he is going to say.
Byron is as careful to preserve this effect in the final form of his
verse as Pope is to suggest the opposite. For the same reason,
Byron's syntax more usually discloses and exhibits a current mode
of consciousness than a judgement. This is true in comparison with
Pope, but we might want to qualify it if we compared Byron with
Shelley, for instance. For this reason, the momentum of Byron's

verse – and Yeats in a letter to H. J. C. Grierson (21 February 1926) praised Byron for constantly seeking a 'natural momentum' in his syntax – is significantly different from Pope's. In the lines above, for instance, we do not anticipate, as we do in Pope's sketch of Atticus or Dryden's of Zimri, a stunning conclusion which will confirm the astonishing poise of the couplets which have led up to it ('Who would not weep if Atticus were he', and 'He left not Faction but of that was left'). If we ask how Byron's lines continue we discover that they modulate into a curse:

> The time shall come, nor long remote, when thou
> Shalt feel far more than thou inflictest now . . ..
>
> May the strong curse of crush'd affections light
> Back on thy bosom with reflected blight!

We can find plenty of satiric predecessors for such a curse – satire may indeed have originated in ritual cursing – nevertheless in a curse we are more interested in the power rather than the poise of the one who is cursing and a curse obliquely testifies to the corresponding fear of the one who is cursed. There is no point in cursing them otherwise. It is this fear, the disruption of the speaker's poise, which leads Byron to retaliate as viciously as he can. Wordsworth spots this in his epigram 'the Billingsgate of Bedlam' and it leads him to 'pity' for the poet. Who would ever pity the author of the Atticus or Sporus portraits, though Pope suffered more than enough to make him an object of pity? Pope is at great pains to fend this off.

This perceptible lack of poise in Byron's poised couplets has its, perhaps surprising, origin in Byron's lack of hatred. So far Pope has been coming out rather better than Byron, but we must recall Byron's disapproval of literary hatred. In *Hints from Horace* he wrote originally

> Satiric rhyme first sprang from selfish spleen.
> You doubt – see Dryden, Pope, St. Patrick's dean.[1]

Whenever Byron does write out of 'selfish spleen' himself he nearly always does something to retract it. In the last lines of 'A Sketch' he says that he will not name Mrs Clermont. If he were to do so then

> Thy name – thy human name – to every eye
> The climax of all scorn should hang on high,

The poem will not terminate in this 'climax of all scorn' because of his love for his wife:

> But for the love I bore, and still must bear,
> To her thy malice from all ties would tear.

The opening of the poem is indeed dominated by praise of Annabella who has not been corrupted by her exposure to Mrs Clermont and could not be, because she is

> Serenely purest of her sex that live,
> But wanting one sweet weakness – to forgive.

Byron is so much taken up with this that he has to remind himself that the object of his poem is satirical hatred and scorn and so, almost in the manner of *Childe Harold*, he says

> But to the theme: – now laid aside too long,
> The baleful burthen of this honest song.

We might comment on this that a good hater does not need to prod himself back into concentration upon the hated object. It offers itself. Byron has to generate his hatred not out of the object but out of his own feelings. This is why the modification of Pope's line into 'And, without feeling, mock at all who feel', is so revealing and why the curse heaped upon Mrs Clermont is a redirection of his own 'crush'd affections'. Even when he has generated hatred in this way, Byron becomes uncertain in his stance and wants to redirect the curse into some kind of suspension or withholding of a 'climax of scorn' that he would otherwise give. This, of course, is what he does in stanza 35 of Canto IV of *Childe Harold* ('That Curse shall be forgiveness') and what he makes Dante do in his *Prophecy of Dante* (I, 118–20).

Again we can see this difference in a detail. The last two lines of the extract from 'A Sketch' –

> Cased like the centipede in saffron mail,
> Or darker greenness of the scorpion's scale –

appear to do something quintessentially Popeian. They diminish in scale, they associate human life with that of insects, accordingly they disgust and yet, at the same time, in some curious way, they beautify.

Byron does not normally do any of these things. It must be by a conscious effort of will that he reproduces these effects so closely here. Normally, his imagination enlarges. The experience of walking into and through St Peter's is always, and quite rightly, seen as a paradigm here. Only Byron would see the great circle of the Colosseum with its then circumambient culture of shrubs and weeds as resembling Julius Caesar's head – 'Like laurels on the bald first Caesar's head'[2] – where our shock is not at the diminution of a giant building to a man's head but wholly the other way round. The surreal expansion of head-space here, as in St Peter's, echoes the way in which Byron's consciousness fills and overflows the circle of the Colosseum in which he stands. Nothing could be farther from Pope. Pope uses the couplet to diminish. Byron uses stanzas to expand. In the same way, Byron can never write out of physical disgust as Pope, Dryden, and Swift do, so regularly. The closest he comes to it is in almost any lines on Castlereagh (who is his Achitophel), Southey (who is his Colley Cibber), and Mrs Clermont. Southey falls 'for lack of moisture, quite adry, Bob'[3] and Castlereagh is an 'intellectual eunuch'[4] just as Sporus speaks 'in florid impotence' and Achitophel's 'pigmy body' is pictured making love with 'huddled notions', begetting the 'Shapeless Lump' of his son.[5] Byron's detestation of Castlereagh is real but odd. Why did he hate him *that* much? The lines addressed to him reveal the dislike but do not focus on its occasioning. We feel Byron's hatred but find it embarrassing because we are not given a clear view of the detested object. Hence, unlike Lord Hervey or Shaftesbury or Titus Oates in *Epistle to Dr. Arbuthnot* or *Absalom and Achitophel* we do not see and loathe the satirised object in exactly the same way as the author does. We are simply caught up in the loathing itself by infection. In Pope and Dryden's verse we are pleased to share in Pope and Dryden's 'selfish spleen' because we are delighted by its exuberance, poise, and accuracy. In this fashion, disgust turns into beauty. Disorder becomes an aesthetically realised property.

Byron attempts exactly this effect in

> Cased like the centipede in saffron mail
> Or darker greenness of the scorpion's scale.

This, it seems clear, is meant to be equivalent in effect to the butterfly and carnation section of Book IV of *The Dunciad* or to those remarkable lines from *Epistle to Dr. Arbuthnot* on the critics and editors who hope to become famous through their pedantic editing of great poets:

> Ev'n such small Critics some regard may claim,
> Preserv'd in *Milton's* or in *Shakespeare's* name.
> Pretty! in amber to observe the forms
> Of hairs, or straws, or dirt, or grubs, or worms!
> The things, we know, are neither rich nor rare,
> But wonder how the Devil they got there.

(Epistle to Dr. Arbuthnot, ll. 167–72)

In these lines, disgust is real. The critics are 'industrious bugs' digging their way into and contaminating the great living forms of Milton and Shakespeare. More generally, in the association of 'hairs' with straw, dirt, grubs, and worms (all preserved in amber) we are reminded first of the preservation of human hair as a delicate keepsake (much as Belinda's lock of hair might have been kept by the Baron), but then of straw (dead grass), and so to dirt, grubs, worms. These, fused with straw and hair, make us think of hair as animal. The fur on our bodies hides, as straw does, dirt and innumerable creepy-crawlies. Thus we are momentarily alienated from our own surface of skin as we so frequently are in Swift. This physical disgust at bodily life and function or, as in impotence and old age, at the failure of bodily function, nearly always, perhaps always, lies at the root of satirical attack. As Byron comments in *Observations upon 'Observations'* that you can call anybody anything but 'look him steadily and quietly in the face, and say – "Upon my word, I think you are the *ugliest fellow* I ever saw in my life"' – and it will produce spectacular results. 'So much easier it is to *provoke* – and therefore to vindicate – (for Passion punishes him who *feels* it more than those whom the passionate would excruciate) – by a few quiet words the aggressor, than by retorting violently.'[6]

But this is exactly what Byron cannot do, with Lord Castlereagh and Mrs Clermont. We never look them steadily in the face and thereby have a focus both for disgust and beauty. Beauty is present because Pope's lines, 'Pretty! in amber to observe the forms', are indeed, and precisely, 'pretty'. We are not overcome by the disgust we feel because the disgust is encased by the amber of the lines themselves; hence, unlike in Swift, we simultaneously experience delight and disgust, movement towards and recoil from. It is exactly this effect that Byron is after in the 'saffron mail of the centipede' and the 'darker greenness of the scorpion's scale' which are juxtaposed with 'Ooze to her skin, and stagnate there to mud'. Theoretically Mrs Clermont is a Gorgon with a cheek of parchment and an eye of stone. Her yellow blood (age and bile) has dried up and stagnates on to the surface of her discoloured skin where it turns into mud like the exposed banks of dried-up rivers. Byron is interested in this imagery because any description of persistence in aridity always attracts him and the imagery itself is like that of the wonderfully mixed-up metaphors of stanza 111 of *Childe Harold*, Canto III ('The furrows of long thought, and dried-up tears'). Here, however, openly obedient to Pope's example, Byron turns this disgust in a different direction. Yellow blood/mud becomes the saffron mail of the centipede or darker greenness of the scorpion's scale. As so often in Pope the attack is conducted by a brilliantly-mixed diction from plain 'mud' to periphrastic 'saffron mail'. The focus remains coherent, however, at least in theory. The changes of colour from yellow to saffron to green are unifying. So too is the concentration on unpleasant skin which is like parchment, like mud, and like that of insects or reptiles. In addition, there is the separate disgust of comparing someone to a centipede (one of Pope's grubs in amber) and to a scorpion which lies in wait and stings like Mrs Clermont. The centipede and scorpion couplet in itself, in diction and cadence, could belong in a non-satiric poem, in Pope's *Messiah* or Dryden's version of Virgil's *Georgics* or Thomson's *Seasons*.[7] Theoretically therefore beauty and disgust should be associated into pleasing satire. Despite Byron's considerable effort, however, the intended effect does not quite materialise. Exactly why is hard to say but it must have to do with the failure to look at Mrs Clermont steadily and quietly in the face and tell her that she is the ugliest thing alive. If we switched the focus, for example, and applied some of these lines to Conrad in *The Corsair* or to Lara or to Manfred (some of the vocabulary is very close to that of the Incantation verses which Byron inserted into *Manfred*), or even applied it to Fletcher Christian in *The Island*, we would know that Byron's eye, and therefore our eye, was much more trained on the object than it is here. The reason for this will be examined later.

For the moment we can simply say, what has so often been said, that this very precise imitation of Pope's manner does not function in the same way as Pope himself though the relationship is not a superficial one. Should we simply agree with Donald Davie then?

Fragments from Pope gleam, like spars from a ship-wrecked world, all about the tumultuous sea of Byron's verse, a criterion acknowledged but no longer to the point.[8]

Dr Leavis said something very similar.[9] Are they right?

It is this question which underlies the present essay. An answer to it should be possible. We can pose the question more precisely by instancing a stanza from *Don Juan*:

> They are young, but know not youth – it is anticipated;
>   Handsome but wasted, rich without a sou;
> Their vigour in a thousand arms is dissipated;
>   Their cash comes *from*, their wealth goes *to* a Jew;
> Both senates see their nightly votes participated
>   Between the tyrant's and the tribunes' crew;
> And having voted, dined, drank, gamed, and whored,
> The family vault receives another lord.

(*Don Juan* XI, st. 75)

A. B. England has some good close comment on these lines which he compares in detail with examples from Pope:

In the stanza as a whole, an undirected and mechanical process of drift has been defined by a noticeably purposeful and disciplined verbal pattern . . ..[10]

That is exactly true. Indeed the 'purposeful and disciplined verbal pattern' is such that here, unlike the sketch of Mrs Clermont, we both anticipate and find a climax of scorn in the final couplet. The accommodation of Pope's couplets into the different momentum of Byron's *ottava rima* is masterly, wholly successful, and without any trace of pastiche. Indeed Byron is able to use a sequence of bravura four-syllable rhymes (anticipated, dissipated, participated) that Pope would never have used, so as to increase the force and finality of his concluding couplet. Or, to put it the other way round, the customary ingenuity of Byron's rhyming ('participated' is a brilliant way out of an apparently insuperable difficulty) is not offered to us *as* ingenuity or daring as it normally is in *Don Juan* but is subordinated to the noticeably purposeful and disciplined verbal pattern.

It may be relevant to make an apparently tangential point here. We could say that Pope offers us masterly couplets but suppresses the process which has led to this mastery. He cannot share with us therefore a kind of glee at his own inspired practice. But Crashaw, from whom Pope learnt a great deal and who can, amazingly, place words better than Pope himself, communicates precisely his own self-conscious delight in his judicious daring and somehow refers this across to his subject-matter (i.e. rapture). Byron, who had no kind thoughts of Crashaw, nevertheless in stanzas such as this from *Don Juan* restores and recovers a trait in the couplet that Pope has suppressed.

If we want an example of continuity of language and voice from Pope to Byron, this stanza is as good as we will get. But England's larger point, lucidly reiterated, is not much different from Donald Davie's. Though such coincidences of manner and viewpoint exist, yet Byron is only half-committed, so we are told, to the moral order which Pope's artistic order serves and therefore the resemblance is only intermittent. This is certainly true as far as it goes, but are we saying any more than 'Pope is orderly and Augustan, Byron is wild and Romantic? However, Byron admires Pope and Order so there are bits of Order knocking about. Really he's wild and Romantic?' Or, if that is in too colloquial mode for an English review of a half-Scotch bard, we could say more decorously that 'Byron is haunted by the moral order represented by Pope's verse but can only reproduce the appearance of that order in his own verse. His Augustan idiom, detached from the context which should support it, is not an Augustan idiom at all.' The contrary of that account is clearly not true but we should certainly contradict it. 'Yea', up to a point but also, everlastingly 'No'!

The next stanza to *Don Juan* XI, st. 75 is instructive here:

> 'Where is the world?' cries Young, 'at *eighty*. Where
> The world in which a man was born?' Alas!
> Where is the world of *eight* years past? '*Twas there –*
> I look for it – 'tis gone, a Globe of Glass!
> Cracked, shivered, vanished, scarcely gazed on, ere

A silent change dissolves the glittering mass.
Statesman, chiefs, orators, queens, patriots, kings,
And dandies, all are gone on the wind's wings.

(XI, st. 76)

These lines at first seem to confirm England's argument. Byron
has abandoned the controlled cadence set up in the previous
stanza. Only line 6 exists as a balanced metrical entity. ('A silent
change dissolves the glittering mass').[11] Apart from this line, all
the others spill over into anacoluthon and enjambement. Contrast
the metrically contained list in stanza 75 ('And having voted,
dined, drank, gamed, and whored') with the two metrically uncon-
tained lists in stanza 76, lines 5 and 7. Clearly 'whored' (the last
word in its list) functions as a climax of sense and line, whereas
'And Dandies' (the last phrase in its list) does not function as a
climax or as bathos (cf. 'bibles, billets doux') but adds a note of
pathos which is quite hard to pin down. Indeed having three sets
of lists so close together removes the kind of effectiveness they
would have in Pope's more sparing use. The metrical and gram-
matical shift in stanza 76 is bound up with a shift of voice and
viewpoint. The viewpoint now identifies with the pain of the
world whose mutability is ridiculed in the previous stanza. What
was there moral criticism of a particular style of life, as based on
vice and illusion, is here an evocation – crazed, elegiac, religious,
witty, improvised yet pondered – of the illusory character of all life.
From such a standpoint the life-style reprobated in stanza 75 ceases
to be particularly reprehensible. Correspondingly, the voice, morally poised, unimplicated in the situation which it explicates (let us
say 'Popeian') in 75, now lets itself appear as rooted in the inexplicable disappearances which it cannot order:

> '*Twas there* –
> I look for it – '*tis gone.*'

Where the first stanza works to its climax of scorn, the second, like
the glittering mass which it tries to catch, dissolves away into 'all
are gone on the wind's wings'. Pope can be fey about his own
mutability and insists that 'In Man, the judgement shoots at
flying game',[12] but Pope would never give us so oddly staged a
dissolution.

This is familiar terrain. Byron is scarcely consistent. How else could he show things existent? Hence Byron's Popeian stanza 75 is framed. It is meant and it works. It is not pastiche. But it works only within a context that will reinterpret rather than reinforce it. And in this way, it is not at all like Pope. At this point, however, our sense of impasse which leads to distinction – Pope is not Byron – can be turned quite easily into a pleasing deconstruction which leads to reunion and paradox – Pope is Byron after all. How can we perform this trick and is it worth performing? The first route is esoteric but lies at hand. Absence reveals presence. Discontinuity reveals continuity. Texts breed from texts in obscure and paradoxical fashion rather than through the perspicuous and consciously acknowledged influences which we have been tracking so far.

Another starting point, less fashionably opaque, may help us to perform the trick of reuniting Pope and Byron. We can set it out quite soberly.

If we take any case of influence or continuity of any kind, what we will notice first and most easily demonstrate is local and manifest continuity. Newstead Abbey has spatial and historical continuity with Byron and his ancestors in an obvious way. Anyone strongly attracted to Byron's personality will always want to visit it. We seek this limited continuity out as a starting point. Byron translated Horace's *De Arte Poetica* in couplets that immediately recall Pope's manner. Parts of Beethoven's Eighth Symphony sound as if they could have been written by Haydn.

But it must be the case that there are some real kinds of continuity which are much less apparent than this. After all, if Beethoven was profoundly influenced by Haydn, then the bits of Haydn in Beethoven that come out sounding like Beethoven suggest a deeper and more pervasive influence than the bits which come out still sounding like Haydn. If we can easily detect the difference then the influence is comparatively superficial. The most obvious example here is the relationship of Herbert and Vaughan. Vaughan's direct debt to Herbert and his desire to imitate him is unquestionable; what emerges, however, is quite different, yet Herbert is working within that difference.

These two starting-points invite us to relaunch our enquiry into continuity and discontinuity beyond the point which we reached. The first of these is more likely to produce a very general intertextuality rather than the specific continuities suggested in the title of this essay. The second starting-point, less irridescent, may take us further. How then could we demonstrate that there is some continuity between Byron's language and voice and those of Pope and Dryden even, and indeed especially, where that continuity is hidden or less manifest than in the lines to Mrs Clermont or stanza 75 of Canto XI?

An example that might readily be granted is Julia's letter to Juan in Canto I. It does not seem special pleading to find the influence of Pope's Eloisa here, though Julia is Byron's Julia and not Pope's Eloisa. Similarly, the impassioned speech which Sigismonda makes to her father in Dryden's version of Boccaccio's 'Sigismonda and Guiscardo'[13] surely underlies Hugo's great speech in *Parisina*, and perhaps surfaces again in the force and character of Marina's utterances in *The Two Foscari*. Peter Vassallo has argued that there is a direct influence from Boccaccio[14], but it seems more plausible that it comes via Dryden. We can attempt a larger focus. What happens to antithesis in Byron's verse? Donald Davie is again to the point:

> The couplet in fact, at least as used by Dryden and by Pope is capable of rendering only one sort of movement through the mind; it is committed by its very nature to a syntax of antitheses and razor-sharp distinctions. That may be one reason why all the Romantic poets, except Byron, eschewed it.[15]

Byron would probably have agreed with this. In *Hints from Horace* he praises the verse of Scott's octosyllabic couplets which, he says,

> . . . varied skilfully, surpasses far
> Heroic rhyme, but most in Love and War,
> Whose fluctuations, tender or sublime,
> Are curbed too much by long recurring rhyme.

(ll. 407–10)

Don Juan is concerned with the fluctuations of love and war, 'Fierce loves and faithless wars' (VII, st. 8, misquoting Spenser) and therefore is not suited to heroic couplets. But what if Byron's fluctuations were to include, miraculously, the habit of antithesis? Then we would be producing an accurate description of Byron's *ottava rima* – which is a form at once fluctuating and curbed. But we need not confine ourselves to *ottava rima*. Manfred's instability is founded on antithesis:

> How beautiful is all this visible world!
> How glorious in its action and itself;
> But we, who name ourselves its sovereigns, we,
> Half dust, half deity, alike unfit
> To sink or soar, with our mix'd essence make
> A conflict of its elements, and breathe
> The breath of degradation and of pride,
> Contending with low wants and lofty will,
> Till our mortality predominates,
> And men are – what they name not to themselves,
> And trust not to each other.

Manfred I, ii, 37–47

The antitheses in these lines (dust/deity, sink/soar, degradation/ pride, low wants/lofty will, to themselves/to each other) recall the pattern of heroic couplets and inevitably recall the opening of Epistle II of the *Essay on Man*. Byron's analysis of Man's position on the *confinio* between God and Beast, dust and deity, is the same as Pope's, but Pope's antitheses have been shifted so that the metre and grammar do not coincide as they do in Pope. The antitheses still operate but they have been dislodged and put out of step with the verse. This is a characteristic device in *Don Juan*. The effect here in *Manfred* is to refer the antithetical analysis back to the speaker rather than to what he diagnoses. Correspondingly, the antitheses now reinforce disturbance and suffering rather than the poise Pope maintains even when he insists that we are 'Chaos of Thought and Passion, all confus'd'. (*Essay on Man*, II, 13) In these lines from *Manfred* the fluctuations of his thought escape from and yet at the same time fret against the curbing antitheses which give them their form and energy.

The effect is exactly the same in Byron's brilliant portraits of Rousseau and Napoleon in Canto III of *Childe Harold*.[16] These two portraits, far more than those of Southey or Castlereagh, are Byron's true equivalent to Zimri, Achitophel, and Sporus. Here, if anywhere, Haydn comes out sounding like Beethoven. Byron's Rousseau and Napoleon could not have been fashioned without Pope and Dryden's example (though, of course, other influences shaped them too, including Milton's Satan, Johnson's Charles XII and Cardinal Wolsey). Sporus, indeed, is 'himself one vile Antithesis'.[17] Pope castigates Lord Hervey, as G. Wilson Knight used to insist in his Byronic reading of Pope, for his failure to make a synthesis out of his discordant elements.[18] Byron's Napoleon on the other hand has a spirit 'antithetically mixt'[19] and this understanding, though it is both diagnosis and criticism, is primarily not so. Primarily, once again, we are directed towards disturbance, towards the 'fever' at Napoleon's fluctuating centre (his breath is 'agitation') just as Rousseau's 'phrenzied' condition is only glossed by him in a 'show' of reasoning.[20] For he, in Pope's phrase that could be so differently carried by Byron's voice, is also a 'Chaos of Thought and Passion all confused'. Dryden would present such fluctuations, in Zimri for instance, with energetically poised distaste. Byron redirects the same analysis, with its accompanying and still-preserved moral perspective, into the experience of antithetical fluctuation itself. In this way we are caught up in an emblem of suffering, intensity, and folly rather than standing back and judging it, though judgement remains relevant.

This, we can now see, is the reason why Byron cannot hold his eye steadily on Mrs Clermont or on Castlereagh simply as detested objects. It does not interest him sufficiently to do so. Nor can he use the antitheses which he derives from Pope and Dryden (and his constant practice in their idiom from *English Bards* to *The Age of Bronze*) to categorise and lessen the human characters about whom he most wants to talk. The antitheses are present but dislodged and refer directly back into suffering and puzzlement. Byron will terminate in these rather than see through them. The simplest and most persuasive example is from almost the last poem that he wrote:

> I am a fool of passion, and a frown
>   Of thine to me is as an adder's eye
> To the poor bird whose pinion fluttering down
>   Wafts unto death the breast it bore so high;
> Such is this maddening fascination grown,
>   So strong thy magic or so weak am I.
>
> ('Last Words on Greece', ll. 5–10)[21]

The antitheses of controlling snake/fluttering bird, ascent/descent, strong thy magic/weak am I, do not clarify. We do not even notice them as antitheses as we read because we are taken directly to the person who generates, suffers, and is bewildered by them. Yet within that peculiarly Byronic voice and timbre (who else could have written those sublime, assured, yet awkwardly exposed lines?) we can still detect, startlingly transformed, Augustan habits of mind and feeling, the tender excess of Pope and the rhetorical excess of Dryden. It is perhaps worthwhile remaking this central point *via* a different vocabulary and concluding with it.

In *The Island*, Byron has a splendid description of one of the mutineers Jack Skyscrape who, with Christian Fletcher, is waiting for the end but has, as we all have according to Pope and Byron, a little time to spare before that arrives.[22] The mutineer passes this time by half-whistling a tune, picking up a pebble and letting it drop –

> And then his former movements would redouble
> With something between carelessness and trouble

(III, 115–16. *Poetry*, ed. E. H. Coleridge, V, 621.)

Byron holds on to, endures, and illumines that 'something between carelessness and trouble' more, perhaps, than any other writer. He matches his verse very finely to what we might now designate 'the unbearable lightness of Being'.[23] Here, Skyscrape, of all people, is momentarily compared to Manfred. 'But yet *what minutes*' says Byron of him as Manfred says of himself that he is 'Plough'd by moments'.[24] In general, half of Byron's verse is directed to the 'unbearable' character of Being (*Childe Harold, Manfred, Cain*) and the other half is directed to its 'lightness' (*Don Juan, Beppo*, etc.) with *Mazeppa* as a transition point (not simply chronologically). But both halves form part of a single antithetical perspective terminating in puzzlement, mirth, horror, wonder, and (to use Ruskin's word) 'reverence'.[25] We may distinguish but should not separate these out as Augustan and Romantic or on the other hand, patronise them simply as an incoherent jumble. Neither Pope nor Dryden could have kept their eye so steadily on Skyscrape's prolonged moments as Byron does here.

The stylistic question, however, is whether within Byron's ostentatious carelessness of manner – in the Oriental Tales for instance, and, in a different sense, in *Don Juan* and *Beppo* – there lurks a carefulness. It is odd, after all, that the most careless of great poets (Byron) should so much admire the most careful (Pope). And it won't do to explain this away as the attraction of opposites. The answer to this question (is there carefulness within carelessness?) must be simply 'Yes'. Byron's calculation of careless-ness ('Hail muse etc', 'I write down what's uppermost' or three lists within two stanzas of *Don Juan*) depends upon a fidelity to what is being said that is as much Augustan in its inspiration as it is Romantic. Moreover the calculation and constant adjustment of idiom, though specifically Byron's, has its most obvious prototype in Pope.[26] Pope's adjustments of diction (in *The Rape of the Lock*, the *Imitations of Horace* and the *Dunciad* rather than in his *Iliad* or the *Essay on Man*) exist for different purposes and in different contexts but Pope's manner re-emerges in Byron's verse. *The Vision of Judgment* is Byron's closest linguistic equivalent to Pope's *Rape of the Lock* here. Heaven's Gate, for instance, is described twice, first in low key with rusty hinges by a comic St Peter and then with resplendent flashes of light in elevated idiom when Michael bursts through.[27] Dryden, and especially Pope, were sometimes anxious in a melancholy way that all they could do to surpass Milton, Spenser and Shakespeare was to write more correctly, more care-fully, in diction, syntax and metre. And yet within the exquisite surface that Pope and Dryden produced we re-encounter Milton and Spenser in *Absalom and Achitophel*, the *Fables*, the *Dunciad*. Byron's case was the opposite. All he could do to surpass Pope and Dryden whilst, unlike his famous contemporaries, remaining in declared contact and continuity with them, was to take their manner up into a spectacular carelessness. Samuel Rogers tried to surpass Pope in carefulness and laboriously did so. But it does not seem worth the candle. What Byron aimed at, however, was not any old carelessness but a 'something between carelessness and trouble', between curb and fluctuation which, obliquely, acknowl-edges its parentage in Augustan idiom.

    Thus if we re-read Canto XI, sts 75–6, it is not enough simply to notice the Popeian symmetry of stanza 75 and its abandonment in 76. The adjustment of idiom between the two, though peculiarly Byronic and, doubtless, Italian too, derives from Pope. Moreover the effect of framing that thus settles round stanza 75 – an effect so frequently reduplicated that every utterance in the poem becomes framed in some sense – now can be recognised as profoundly Popeian. The difficulty of reading Pope's *Imitations of Horace* aloud or *Don Juan* aloud (they always seem to come out in too arch and sneery a voice) derives from the same source. Further, Byron's ability to snatch a direct speaking voice ('And if my voice break forth'), out of a juxtaposition of equally framed voices, an effect that seems impossible, is based, surely, on Pope who can suddenly change register and produce a voice which, though rhetorically deployed, is presented as pure emergence: 'Oh let me live my own, and die so too'.[28]

It is not only Pope's voice that Byron sometimes catches or incorporates then, it is the mimicking of emergence itself. Byron takes this vastly further than Pope so that it ceases to be recognisable. Voices rise up out of nowhere – unbearably in *Childe Harold*, lightly in *Don Juan* – in poems that Pope couldn't have written, and oddly transformed from the curb of the couplet to the fluctuations of the stanza, but Pope is inside both Byron's curbs and his fluctuations.

If we think of Wordsworth writing 'An Evening Walk' and 'Descriptive Sketches' in accomplished Augustan couplets and then moving on to very different things, or recall Keats, in *Lamia*, setting himself to unlearn *via* Dryden's better example what he had learnt from Leigh Hunt's collapsed couplets, or remember Gifford (and earlier Churchill) writing only in the manner of Pope, then Byron is not like any of these. Romantic poetry and Romantic art in general, unlike Augustan poetry, has no specific style of its own. Byron himself is a relentless experimenter in style. *The Deformed Transformed* and *Heaven and Earth* are experiments in idiom as is the loose blank verse of the Venetian plays and *Sardanapalus* or *Don Juan* itself. *Don Juan*, as it were, institutionalises and foregrounds the habitually experimental character of Byron's idiom. At the same time, Byron declares openly his tutelage by Pope and sets himself publicly to defend him. Sometimes he writes in direct transcriptions of Pope's idiom and never simply puts this aside as Wordsworth does. *Don Juan* may be seen as the mean between these two drives and, as such, suggests that they have a single origin. Pope and Dryden's language and voice are not merely the keepers and curbers of Byron's stylistic conscience. They are the guarantors of his remarkable fluctuations and the 'something' between his carelessness and trouble.

Notes

1. It is ironic and characteristic that Byron in 1821 eventually decided that these lines on Pope, Dryden, and Swift should themselves be withdrawn for a new edition of *Hints from Horace* which never appeared. J. J. McGann therefore omits them from his new text of the poem but quotes Byron's original note to the lines: '*MacFlecknoe*, and the *Dunciad*, and all Swift's lampooning ballads. Whatever their other works may be, these originated in personal feelings, and angry retorts on unworthy rivals; and though the ability of these satires elevates the poetical, their poignancy detracts from the personal character of the writers.' *Complete Poetical Works*, I, 432. I quote therefore from E. H. Coleridge's *Poetical Works* I, 397 (lines 115–16). Whatever the rights and wrongs of editorial practice it would be unfortunate if these important lines disappeared from standard editions of the poem.
2. *Childe Harold's Pilgrimage* IV, st. 144.
3. *Don Juan*, Dedication, st. 3.
4. *Don Juan*, Dedication, st. 11.
5. Pope, *Epistle to Dr. Arbuthnot*, l. 317; Dryden, *Absalom and Achitophel*, ll. 170–72.
6. *Byron's Letters and Journals*, ed. R. E. Prothero, V, 580.
7. Pope's *Messiah*, for instance, offers cognate lines such as 'Pleas'd the green lustre of the scales survey' (l. 82).
8. Donald Davie, *Purity of Diction in English Verse* (London, 1952). I quote from the paperback edition (1967), p. 131.
9. 'The eighteenth century element in him is essential to his success, and yet at the same time has the effect of bringing out how completely the Augustan order has disintegrated.' F. R. Leavis, *Revaluation* (London, 1936), p. 153.
10. A. B. England, *Byron's Don Juan and Eighteenth-Century Literature* (New Jersey/London, 1975), p. 53.
11. The imagery here seems to involve us in taking the globe as both glass ('Cracked') and ice ('A silent change dissolves').
12. Pope, *Moral Essays* I, 95.
13. Ll. 390–581.
14. Peter Vassallo, *Byron: The Italian Literary Influence* (London, 1984), pp. 7–8.
15. Donald Davie, *Articulate Energy: An Enquiry into the Syntax of English Poetry* (London, 1955), p. 79.
16. Wordsworth makes an acute comment on Byron's preservation of antithesis in apparently 'Wordsworthian' passages in *Childe Harold*. Commenting on II, sts 25–6, in a letter to R. P. Gillies, he writes: 'But the sentiment by being expressed in an *antithetical* manner, is taken out of the Region of high and imaginative feeling, to be placed in that of point and epigram. To illustrate my meaning and for no other purpose I refer to my own lines on the Wye, where you will find the same sentiment not formally put as it is here, but ejaculated as it were fortuitously in the musical succession of preconceived feeling.'

(9 June 1817) The distinction he makes is shrewd and valid here. It is less obvious that we can so easily distinguish between '*antithetical manner*' and 'high and imaginative feeling' in Manfred's lines or the descriptions of Rousseau and Napoleon (or for that matter Sporus and Achitophel).

17. *Epistle to Dr. Arbuthnot*, l. 325.
18. G. Wilson Knight, *The Poetry of Alexander Pope* (London, 1955), p. 68.
19. *Childe Harold* III, st. 36.
20. Ibid., st. 80.
21. *The Works of Lord Byron: Poetry*, ed. E. H. Coleridge, 2nd edn, 1904–5, VII, 85–6.
22. For example,

> ' . . . (Since life can little more supply
> Than just to look about us and to die)'

Essay on Man I, 3–4.

> 'All things that have been born were born to die,
> ....
> So thank your stars that matters are no worse
> And read your Bible, sir, and mind your purse'.

Don Juan, I, st. 220.

23. Milan Kundera's novel *The Unbearable Lightness of Being* was published in 1984. Philip Davis in ' "I leave the thing a problem, like all things": On trying to catch up on Byron', in *Byron and the Limits of Fiction*, ed. Bernard Beatty and Vincent Newey (Liverpool, 1988), pp. 242–83, compares Byron to Kundera and to the practice of other modern novelists.
24. *Manfred* I, ii, 72. Byron applied the same metaphor to himself as late as 1823 in 'To the Countess of Blessington': 'There are *moments* which act as a plough' (line 14).
25. J. Ruskin, *Fiction, Fair and Foul, The Works of John Ruskin*, ed. E. T. Cook and A. Wedderburn (London, 1908), XXXIV, p. 333. The original MS reading here, given in a note, talks of Byron's 'reverence for the laws of God and pity for the creatures of the earth'.
26. Geoffrey Tillotson's loving demonstration of Pope's intricate habits here in *On the Poetry of Pope* (Oxford , 1950), remains unsurpassed and, within its limited compass, unsurpassable.
27. *The Vision of Judgment* I, 16; 27–8.
28. *Epistle to Dr. Arbuthnot*, l. 261.

7

Augustan Satires and Panegyrics on London and Byron's Image of the City

MICHAEL GASSENMEIER

Having described the journey of his hero from Russia to Holland where 'he embarked . . . for the island of the free' (X, st. 64) the narrator eventually leads Don Juan over Shooter's Hill from where he first espies the 'great city':

> . . . Juan now was borne,
> Just as the day began to wane and darken,
>   O'er the high hill which looks with *pride* or *scorn*
> Toward the great city . . .

> (X, st. 80; *italics mine*)

It is unusual, even in *Don Juan*, to find two rarely compatible perspectives or attitudes like 'pride' and 'scorn' attributed to a hill. But it may be felt to make sense if we bear in mind that Shooter's Hill, situated on the Dover Road eight miles from London, is possessed of a remarkably ambiguous fame both in literature and in history. In the former it is praised as offering one of the most magnificent views of London, and censured in connection with highway robbery. In the latter it is mentioned as a battlefield of consequence in the Civil War from which the triumphant Roundheads hailed and the desponding Cavaliers cursed the city of London which had supported the Great Rebellion.[1] In key with this literary and historical ambiguity, here, at the very beginning of the London passage of *Don Juan*, the 'hill which looks with *pride* or *scorn*/Toward the great city' figures as a metaphor for Byron's

narrative conception, for presenting London from two rarely compatible perspectives. This becomes very evident in the following
stanza:

> The sun went down, the smoke rose up, as from
>   A half-unquenched volcano, o'er a space
> Which well beseemed the 'Devil's drawing-room,'
>   As some have qualified that wondrous place.
> But Juan felt, though not approaching home,
>   As one who, though he were not of the race,
> Revered the soil, of those true sons the mother,
> Who butchered half the earth, and bullied t'other.

> (X, st. 81)

And a few lines later, after just such another juxtaposition of
dissimilar views

> A mighty mass of brick, and smoke, and shipping,
>   Dirty and dusky . . .

> (X, st. 82)

> But Juan saw not this: each wreath of smoke
>   Appeared to him but as the magic vapour
> Of some alchymic furnace, from whence broke
>   The wealth of worlds . . .

> (X, st. 83)

the narrator ends his first contemplation of London from this
vantage-point with the phrase: 'He paused – and so will I' (X, st.
84) Thus the contradictory views of the city are explained explicitly
as those of the poem's protagonist and the poem's narrator.

Byron, the real author of the poem, plays a sophisticated dialectical game with these two contrary voices. By allowing the narrator
to play with the naiveté of the protagonist, the views of the latter
are undermined ironically and the readers are led to accept the
views of the former which are, if not identical, closely akin to those
of the real Byron's 'riper mind'.[2]

It is the aim of this chapter to show that in playing this dialectical

game of the two voices and elaborating his double-focus illumination of London in *Don Juan*, Byron employs both the poetical
models mentioned in my title: the more familiar satirical and the
widely-forgotten panegyrical genres of Augustan city poetry.

To start off, I shall give a brief account of these two genres of
neo-classical city poetry, their interrelation, and their respective
political and ideological affiliations and functions. The analysis of
the London stanzas in *Don Juan* that will follow is intended to
throw some new light upon the make-up of Byron's image of the
city, its unprecedented fusing and telescoping of rivalling genres of
urban poetry, its poetic achievement and its political connotations.

THE TWO GENRES OF AUGUSTAN CITY-POETRY

While classical scholars are familiar with two genres of urban
poetry, the *laudes urbis* and the *denuntiationes urbis*, which are
known to have flourished and been interrelated with one another
since the Roman Augustan Age[3], writers on the English Augustan
age have failed to see the city poetry of the period as part of a once-
vivid double tradition of panegyrics and satires on London in
which the eminent literary, social and political controversies of the
age of revolutions were debated. This state of affairs may be
explained partly by the splendid isolation of literary scholars, by
their policy of non-involvement in extra-literary issues and controversies, which has consigned to oblivion – or, should I say,
deconstruction – more texts and contexts than the historicists of
former times and our own days[4] were able to restore. Of the
innumerable city poems of the later seventeenth and eighteenth
centuries, as a matter of fact, only a small number has retained a
certain degree of popularity. Simplifying the case, one might say
that what descended to us in some more or less recent anthologies[5]
is little more than a round dozen of city poems which survived in
the standard editions of their major authors. So we are, to take an
example, familiar with Swift's city pieces. But outside their literary
and extra-literary contexts, Swift's city poems are regarded as little
more than fine achievements in the lightweight genre of mock-
Georgic pastiche written for the enjoyment of a learned
aristocracy.[6]

In my *Poetry and Politics, Texts and Contexts of London Poetry from
the Restoration to the End of the Walpole Era*[7] I have tried to investigate

the literary and extra-literary context of the urban poetry of the period. The result of this research has been the rediscovery of a double tradition of London poetry which throws new light on the poetic strategies and the political and ideological functions of canonical and non-canonical texts. The date and the causes for the formation of this double tradition of satires and panegyrics on London, it was found, can be determined with unusual exactness. Polemics against the City were first heard in poetry after London's support for the Parliamentary opposition in the Civil War had become manifest. Thus already in Cowley's poem *The Civil War* of 1643, London is denounced as the 'seed of rebellion' or as 'Lud's seditious town'[8], and Alexander Browne imputes to the City 'Rebellions . . . both to the King above and him below' and, as early as 1648, conjures up a devastating judgement upon the disloyal town, a 'deluge' to flood her or a 'raging fire [that] shall burn [her] stately towers down.'[9] Earlier and even more overtly partisan is the London passage in John Denham's *Cooper's Hill* (1642), the first major example of local or topographical poetry in English:

13   Exalted to this height, I first looke downe
    On *Pauls*, as men from thence upon the towne . . .

17   Now shalt thou stand, though Time, or Sword, or Fire,
    Or *Zeale* (more fierce than they) thy fall conspire,
    Secure, while thee the best of Poets sings,
    Preserv'd from ruine by the best of Kings . . .

27   So rais'd above the tumult and the crowd
    I see the City in a thicker cloud
    Of businesse, then of smoake; where men like Ants
30   Toyle to prevent *imaginarie wants;*

    Yet all in vaine, increasing with their store,
    Their vast desires but make their wants the more.
    As food to unsound bodies, though it please
    The Appetite, feeds onely the disease;
35   Where with like haste, though severall waies they runne
    Some to undoe, and some to be undone:
    While Luxurie, and wealth, like Warre and Peace,
    Are each the others ruine, and increase,
    As Rivers lost in Seas some secret veine

40   Thence reconveies, there to be lost againe.
      Some study *plots*, and some those *plots* t'undoe,
      Others to make 'em, and undoe 'em too,
      False to their hopes, affraid to be secure,
      Those *mischiefes* onely which they make, endure,
45   Blinded with light, and sicke of being well,
      In *tumults* seeke their peace, their *heaven* in *hell*.[10]

For Denham – whom we may imagine as actually looking down
from Cooper's Hill with the aid of a telescope or as equating the
physical elevation of the ridge with a superior point of view from
which to judge the capital – for the loyal supporter of his monarch
all through the Civil War, the city is a place of horror in which an
unscrupulous commercial class victimises its citizens with ever
new 'imaginary wants' (l. 30) not unlike the criminal traffickers of
dependence-causing drugs. With its 'Zeale' (l. 18) and 'plots'
(l. 41), moreover – terms which for royalists like Denham were
synonymous with the puritans' rebellion against 'the best of Kings'
(l. 20), the Anglican Church (ll. 14ff.) and the manor-house based
nobility (l. 47) – London is regarded as the subverter of the
sacrosanct hierarchic society and the Devil's ally that 'In tumults
seeke their peace, their heaven in hell' (l. 46).

    In many variations this odium of being the traitor, the rebel and
the destroyer of worldly and heavenly order figured for more than
a century as the central *topos* in London satires written by royalists
or, later, by Tory authors. More than ever before, the genre
flourished after the Plague and the Great Fire. Dryden and
numberless of his imitators interpreted the disasters as judgements
of an angry God against the 'rebellious city which was always an
enemy to the crown'.[11] And the poets proclaimed that the rebuild-
ing and recuperation of the devastated city was not to be suffered
unless, once and for all, London eradicated rebels and zealots in
her walls and surrendered to her king in unquestioning loyalty and
obedience.[12]

    But London would not surrender. The hope of Charles II to seize
control of the city – which was reflected in the stanzas of Dryden
and other royalists and seemingly well-founded in the years after
the Great Fire – proved to be wishful thinking. With the restoration
of her traditional administration – her own trainbands and
treasury, her elective Lord Mayor and sheriffs, and her representative institutions with a fairly wide franchise – the post-fire City

again embodied principles of government diametrically opposed to those represented by the King, the court, and his ministers with absolutist tendencies.[13] And in the years before the Glorious Revolution, when London once more developed into the stronghold of another generation of rebels, the Whig-Exclusionists, and was threatened with the *Quo Warranto* which eventually forfeited her charters and privileges into the hands of the King and his court, the city was again the target of Dryden and his numerous fellow Tory satirists. In *Absalom and Achitophel*, for example, the city is denounced as harbouring the 'Sons of Belial' (l. 598) and his 'Factious Friends' (1. 606);[14] and in *The Medall* Dryden cursed London as the irreclaimable breeding ground of 'Sedition' (l. 175) and the wrestling place of 'Monsters' (1. 173) whose 'ordures neither Plague nor Fire can purge' (l. 188) and who, as in the 1640s, force the crowd to 'Arbitrary sway' (l. 302) and to the dethronement of their monarchs 'for God's cause' (l. 199).[15]

The founders of the complementary genre of London verse, the panegyric on the city, were nonconformists and republicans, in later decades committed or hired Whigs who, after the Restoration, the Great Fire, and the Exclusion Crisis, countered the severe accusations against the capital. Starting as cautious poetic apologies and carefully encoded rejoinders in times of rigid censorship, the genre soon developed into unreserved panegyric. Here the descriptions of metropolitan life were fraught with slogans and concepts of political and religious dissent. And here the political, economic and sacramental clichés of the emerging 'Whig myth' were first projected on the increasingly idealised images and impressions of the 'Blest City':

> Blest City whose commodious and sweet site
> Invites the Eye to wonder, and delight:
> 120 Thou being cram'd with blessings in such store,
> That Heaven could not well give, or Earth ask more.
> Oh! With what splendor, and prodigious state
> Doth she the Eyes invite! and yet amate
> Them, dazled with her luster, where the port
> 125 Of every brave built house doth seem a Court . . .
>
> Thrice happy London . . . how should I praise thee then . . .
> [With] thy renowned Guild-Hall? Where the Law
> Well executed keeps bad men in awe.

265   Here Justice like a Queen inthron'd doth sit
      To whom for love all good men do submit,
      The Bad for fear; for regent wisdom here
      Sitteth possest, in her own Orb and Sphere.

                                        (ll. 118ff.; 262ff.)

Londinum: Or, the Renowned City of London (1670)[16] is one of the
earliest examples of numerous panegyrics, and already, by means
of its narrative design, it implies London's unique liberalism and
constitutionalism. As in many later *encomia* of this type, the
speaker in *Londinum* is not a Londoner or an Englishman. He is a
'banish't' foreigner (l. 71) who, being denied fundamental human
rights in his 'Own Home' (l. 16), flies into the 'safe armes [of]
London' (l. 17). What encouraged him to do so is the 'Fame of
[London's] Beauty, [her] great Bounty' (l. 21) and her 'most liberal
kindness' (l. 24) that is praised by 'such Exile strangers' (l. 22) as
him all over the world.

          To thy safe armes London we are hurld
          London the great *Emporeum* of the world,
          Whose benigne Soule still ready is to bless
          And succour strangers in their most distress.
          Fame of thy Beauty, and great Bounty too
          Extended to such Exile strangers, who

          Profess the same Religion, which combin'd
          With thy most liberal kindness, hath enclin'd
          Me to believe blest *England* doth alone
          Comprize the blessings of the spacious Zone:

                  . . . O may Heavens Sun still shine
          On thee the Granary of the world, and Mine
          Of golden Oare. Indulger of just truth
          And known Integrity! . . .

                                        (ll. 17ff.; 29ff.)

   While thus the enthusiastic praise the stranger utters when he
first espies the city is not yet founded on his own experience but
merely based on London's universal fame, the following sight-

seeing tour which he undertakes under the guidance of a local
Muse not only confirms but greatly excels his expectations.
London, he realises, is indeed the fascinating bustling centre of
trade and commerce (ll. 234ff.), the 'sole domain' of liberalism
(l. 24), 'Justice' (l. 270), 'Integrity' (l. 32), 'Charity and Love' (l. 74),
and the 'illustrious Seat' of the 'liberal arts' and the sciences
'which/Like a great wealthy store-house doth enrich/The minds of
men' (ll. 82; 86ff.). At the same time, however, London is felt to be
much more. With her 'proud situation', her innumerable
'Trophies' (l. 285), her architectural 'beauties [that] are/Beyond my
Pen, or mortal mans compare' (l. 264), and with the multiplicity of
'fine and gay structures, as now this City here and there/Presents
the Eye and suggests to the Ear' (ll. 130f.), the metropolis virtually
overwhelms the observer and evokes in him an unprecedented
intensity of perception which is described in terms reminiscent of
the so-called *perturbationes animi et oculorum*, familiar *topoi* of some
encomia romae aeternae.[16a]

Here, as in some Latin panegyrics on ancient Rome, formulae
like the following:

Whilst I do advance . . . I seemed in a trance

(ll. 234f.)

With what splendour, and prodigious state
Doth she the Eyes invite! and yet amate
Them, dazled with her luster . . .

(ll. 122ff.)

Wondring at such variety of things,
My mind was taken captive, and her wings
Were imp't, not suffering her for to ascend
Those heights to which this stately town doth tend

(ll. 122ff.)

are not meant to expose the dialectics of short-lived fascination and
lasting irritation that some Romantic poets believed to be the
hazardous characteristics of the urban experience.[17] Here, rather,
the perturbations of mind and eye are hyperbolic figures meant to

suggest the grandiosity of the capital, which, the speaker claims, can be praised adequately only as the 'Blest City' (l. 118) and 'the wonder of the Skie' (l. 70), that is, as a kind of *civitas dei* which *qua definitione* transcends man's power of perception and conception.

The golden age of London panegyrics, however, was yet to come. It began immediately after the Glorious Revolution, when James II, who had enslaved the city and deprived her of her charter, fled to St Germain, when the Tories and their concept of divine right disintegrated as a political force, and their powerful poet-laureate had to quit the arena. And it lasted a whole century, if we disregard some minor irritations during the later years of Queen Anne's reign.

To the aforementioned panegyrical elements and conventions the post-revolutionary encomiasts added the two major aspects of Whig ideology: the praise of London both as the political and as the economic pioneer of the empire.

In poems written by Taubman, Tutchin, or Shadwell, Dryden's successor in the positions of laureate and historiographer royal, London is hailed as the 'bulwark to the people's liberty' and as the liberator of the whole kingdom. So we read in John Tutchin's *Civitas Militaris* (1689):[18]

> The *Roman* Gallantry long since retir'd,
> Its City Valour in its Flames expir'd;
> But *London's* Fame Immortal Glory bears,
> Preserv'd from wasting age, and Flames, and Wars . . .
>
> Though loss of Charters might deject the mind,
> Yet ev'n when Slaves, we could true Courage find;
> And when a Papist had forsook the Throne,
> *We gave a Juster Monarch the lost Crown.*
> With Generous Rage, and Manly Virtue Arm'd,
> With Kingly Goodness, and the Souldier Charm'd,
> We sit securely underneath his Shade,
> And *prop the Righteous King our Hands have made.*
>
> (ll. 1ff., 71ff.)

In breaking the yoke of a despot who 'devour'd the Peoples Law' (l. 36) and in re-establishing her republican principles within her own walls, the City, at the same time, freed the whole nation from 'the Holds of *Hell* and *Rome*' (l. 131), restored its constitutional basis and founded a new era of 'Liberty', 'Plenty and Peace' in which 'Defunct Tyrants shall be seen no more' (ll. 133–4)

A paradigm for the praise of London as the economic pioneer of the empire is Elkanah Settle's *Augusta Triumphans* (1707)[19]:

25   Here in the midst, thy central Gresham [i.e. Royal Exchange] stands
     Ready, when Pow'rs least Exigence demands,
     On either side t'extend his succouring Hands.
     Such then AUGUSTA, such thy radiant Brow,
     Not only Great Britannia's Honour Thou;
30   From thy Auxiliary Smiles we view,
     In thee no less her Patriot City too.
     From kind Britannia then prepare to take
     The just Return her Gratitude shall make.

(ll. 25ff.)

Here, for the first time, a London panegyric focuses on the Royal Exchange as the holiest of places and the very *genius loci* of the city that with its 'succouring hands' (l. 27) and 'Auxiliary Smiles' (l. 30) symbolises her financial resources and her unreserved bounty, and justifies her title as the 'Patriot City' (l. 31). While up to the Glorious Revolution the term 'Patriot' was associated with the Whigs' policy of resistance against Stuart despotism, these political connotations are neglected here in favour of the central economic ideas of Whiggism:

     Who, fair Augusta, but thy Sons of TRADE
     Have great Britannia's rich Foundation laid? . . .
     O COMMERCE, what a Task did the Divine
     Dispenser to thy potent Hand assign!
50   Here fair Augusta, claim thy Honour's due,
     This beauteous Scene presented to thy View,
     From the rich Product of this Field behold
     The glorious Harvest from thy Seeds of GOLD . . .
     Oh Industry! bright Industry to Thee,
55   Here let my Muses venerating knee
     Her awful homage pay. For, oh, to raise
     The Pyramide to thy immortal Praise . . .

60   Oh Industry! when did thy Reign commence
     Thou eldest Favourite of Omnipotence!

     Thou greatest, First-borne Virtue, Industry,
     The God his First Command dispens'd to Thee . . .
     Thus, great AUGUSTA, with industrious Toyl,
65   Make the wide Universe thy fruitful Soyl.
     Plant, cultivate fair Nature's spacious Field:
     And from the Product thy rich Crop shall yeild;
     Around the World thy Conquering Heroes led
     Thy Garden ne'er shall want a Laurel Bed.

                                        (ll. 42ff.)

By identifying London's 'Wealth, Grandeur, Power' (l. 3) with
the expansion of 'Trade' (l. 42), 'Commerce' (l. 48) and 'Industry'
(l. 54) and by glorifying these activities as the tools or 'potent
Hands' (l. 49) to which God dispensed the execution of his divine
'Task' (l. 48) and 'Command' (l. 63), Settle sacramentalises the
bourgeois centre of rising capitalism as a man-made means of
individual and national salvation.

Panegyrics written, like Voltaire's 'Ô Londre! heureuse terre', by
continental authors demonstrate that in the following decades the
universal fame of the British metropolis was no longer – as in the
'exile stranger-type' of the genre – merely a poetic fiction.

37   O rivale d'Athène! Ô Londre! heureuse terre!
     Ainsi que les tyrans vous avez su chasser
     Les préjugés honteux qui vous livraient la guerre.
40   C'est là qu'on sait tout dire et tout récompenser;
     Nul art n'est méprisé, tout succès, à sa gloire.

     Le vainqueur de Tallard, le fils de la Victoire,
     Le sublime Dryden, et le sage Addison,
     Et la charmante Ophils, et l'immortel Newton,
45   On part au temple de mémoire:

48   Quiconque a des talens à Londre est un grand homme.
     L'abondance et la liberté

Ont, après deux mille ans, chez vous ressuscité
L'esprit de la Grèce et de Rome.

(ll. 37ff.)[20]

Voltaire wrote this poem shortly after his return from his exile in England where he at first allowed himself to be patronised by Tory critics of the metropolis under rising capitalism such as Pope, Swift and Bolingbroke, but later turned to Sir Robert Walpole and the liberal Whigs. As a matter of fact, the correspondence of Voltaire's apotheosis of London with Whig panegyrics on the City or Addison's enthusiastic essays on the urban experience is striking. For Voltaire the City owes her fame as 'rivale d'Athène' and 'heureuse terre' (l. 37) to her successful struggles against despotism (l. 38) and to her policy of toleration (l. 39) which promoted creativity in commerce, in the arts, and in the sciences, and re-established peace in a nation formerly haunted by 'préjugés honteux', and afflicted with ever-new internal conflicts and wars. And in summarising the achievements of London in the formula 'L'abondance et la liberté/Ont . . . ressuscité/L'esprit de la Grèce et de Rome' (ll. 49f.), which blends the Whig slogan 'liberty and property'[21] with his lifelong appreciation of the classical taste, Voltaire presents London as a model to his compatriots, believing, as he did, that his comprehensive ideal of progress could be materialised only in an 'heureuse terre' of *laissez-faire* like London, whose commercial classes produce the prerequisite atmosphere and economic advantages.

After the victory of the Whig cause in 1688 the older royalist and Tory satire that had portrayed London as the rebellious subverter of wordly and heavenly order ceased to be produced or listened to. Only twenty years later, however, from the end of the first decade of the eighteenth century, the increasing popularity of London panegyrics provoked new poetic refutations that exposed and discredited the Whig poets' unqualified enthusiasm for the City and the historical *laissez-faire* urban capitalism she stands for. Seen in that context, the classification of the above-mentioned city-poems of Swift as lightweight parodies of pastoral models appears to be less than they deserve. They can be re-appreciated as poems with a profound social message, a message which may be said to be decorated but not cloaked by the conventional garment of burlesque imitation. This applies already to 'A Description of the Morning' (1709), Swift's first mock-poem on the city. By focusing on conspicuous aspects of the shabbiness and corruption of Augustan London, the poem exposes the social and moral changes in the early phase of *laissez-faire*:

> The Turnkey now his Flock returning sees,
> Duly let out a Nights to Steal for Fees.

(ll. 15f.)[22]

By transforming the central image of pastoral poetry, the shepherd guarding his flock, into a jailor who – letting out his flock to steal for fees – exploits the starving inmates of his prison and, at the same time, throws the property and security of the citizens to the wolves, Swift suggests that perversion and corruption are predominant features of urban capitalism.

A similar sophisticated tightrope-walk between literary mockery and aggressive social criticism can be recognised in 'A Description of a City Shower' (1710). Here, too, at first sight, the urban evil that provokes the violent flood in the city seems to be little more than a sequence of pardonable human faults, weaknesses, vanities and hypocrisies. But the details accumulate. They add up to a contracted impression – rich in contemptuous allusions and innuendos – of social and political mismanagement and depravity. And they culminate in a vision of the *'Devoted* Town' (l. 32) that is about to be submerged by an excremental 'Deluge' of its own making:

> Now in contiguous Drops the Flood comes down,
> Threat'ning with Deluge this *Devoted* Town . . .
> Now from all Parts the swelling Kennels flow,
> And bear their Trophies with them as they go:
> Filth of all Hues and Odours seem to tell
> What Street they sail'd from, by their Sight and Smell.
> They, as each Torrent drives, with rapid Force
> From *Smithfield*, or St. *Pulchre*'s shape their Course,
> And in huge Confluent join at *Snow-Hill* Ridge,
> Fall from the *Conduit* prone to *Holborn-Bridge*.
> Sweepings from Butchers Stalls, Dung, Guts, and Blood,

Drown'd Puppies, stinking Sprats, all drench'd in Mud,
Dead Cats and Turnip-Tops come tumbling down the Flood.

(ll. 31f.; 53ff.)[22a]

Gay, Pope and Dr Johnson each fell in with Swift's scatological vision of London life and helped to popularise it by bringing its social, its cultural, or its more exclusively political connotations into prominence in their own city poems.

With the *Cloacina* episode, a genealogical myth narrating the fateful love-affair of the Goddess of the Fleet-ditch with a mortal Scavenger in a dark alley of the town, John Gay inserted a sociological rebus in his *Trivia* which explains the birth of the fourth estate out of the very scum of early bourgeois metropolitan life that is flooding London in Swift's 'City Shower'.

> Then *Cloacina* (Goddess of the tide
> Whose sable Streams beneath the City glide)
> Indulg'd the modish Flame; the Town she rov'd,
> A mortal Scavenger she saw, she lov'd . . .
>   . . . Swift the Goddess rose
> And through the Streets pursu'd the distant Noise,
> Her Bosom panting with expected Joys.
> With the Night-wandring Harlot's Airs she past,
> Brush'd near his Side, and wanton Glances cast;
> In the black Form of Cinder-Wench she came,
> When Love, the Hour, the Place had banish'd Shame;
> To the dark Alley Arm in Arm they move:
> O may no Link-Boy interrupt their Love![23]

Thirteen years later in his *Dunciad* Pope helps to aggrandise the symbolic aspects of London's *cloaca maxima* by making it the setting of cultural activities in the city. In the course of her triumphant and riotous peregrination from Guildhall to Westminster the 'Queen of Dulness' arranges high heroic games in the 'King of Dykes' (II, l. 261) which provide an opportunity for her 'Smithfield Muses' to 'prove who best can dash thro' thick and thin' (II, l. 264):

> This labour past, by Bridewell all descend,
> (As morning-pray'r and flagellation end.)

To where Fleet-ditch with disemboguing streams
Rolls the large tribute of dead dogs to Thames,
The King of Dykes! than whom, no sluice of mud
With deeper sable blots the silver flood.
"Here strip my children! here at once leap in!
"Here prove who best can dash thro' thick and thin,
"And who the most in love of dirt excel,
"Or dark dexterity of groping well.
"Who flings most filth, and wide pollutes around
"The stream, be his the Weekly Journals, bound.
"A pig of lead to him who dives the best.
"A peck of coals a-piece shall glad the rest."
In naked majesty great Dennis stands . . .
Next Smedley div'd; slow circles dimpled o'er
The quaking mud, that clos'd, and ope'd no more.
All look, all sigh, and call on Smedley lost;
Smedley in vain resounds thro' all the coast . . .
Sudden, a burst of thunder shook the flood.
Lo Smedley rose, in majesty of mud!
Shaking the horrors of his ample brows,
And each ferocious feature grim with ooze.
Greater he looks, and more than mortal stares;
Then thus the wonders of the Deep declares.
First he relates, how sinking to the chin,
Smit with his mien, the Mud-nymphs suck'd him in:
How young Lutetia, softer than the down,
Nigrina black, and Merdamante brown,
Vy'd for his love in jetty bow'rs below;
As Hylas fair was ravish'd long ago.
Then sung . . .
How to the banks where bards departed doze,
They led him soft; how all the bards arose;
Taylor, sweet bird of Thames, majestic bows,
And Shadwell nods the poppy on his brows;

(II, ll. 257ff.; 279ff.; 301ff.; 321ff.)[24]

A decade after the publication of Pope's bitter and obscene satire on the ragged city-bards who, indulging in the polluted floods produced by the commercial and political Whig gang, pave the way for the restoration of 'great Anarch's ancient reign' (III, l. 339),

Samuel Johnson emphasises the more exclusively political aspects
of Swift's scatological vision of London:

> London! the needy villains's gen'ral home,
> The common sewer of Paris and of Rome;
> With eager thirst, by folly or by fate,
> Sucks in the dregs of each corrupted state.
> Forgive my transports, on a theme like this,
> I cannot bear a French metropolis.

(ll. 93ff.)[25]

THE IMAGE OF THE CITY IN BYRON'S *DON JUAN*

Having familiarised ourselves with the double tradition of
Augustan city poetry we can, for the sake of analysis, disentangle
Byron's appropriation and transformation of the two genres.

As far as the general layout and the protagonist's perspective
and attitude are concerned, the London passage in *Don Juan* may
be said to be an imitation of what we called the 'exile-stranger type'
of London panegyrics. Don Juan, the continual sport of arbitrary
conditions, approaches the city with feelings and expectations that
bear a striking resemblance to those of the victimised and banished
protagonist of poems like *Londinum*. And the Byronic *persona* takes
considerable pains to emphasise Don Juan's enthusiasm for the
'island of the free' (X, st. 64) and its 'great city' (X, st. 80). In doing
so he attributes to Don Juan, or makes him mouth in direct speech,
those very feelings and figures of praise, veneration and pride the
Whig panegyrics employed to illustrate the political, economic,
and moral accomplishments of the capital. Thus he is presented as
revering London's 'soil' as 'the mother' (X, st. 81) of the architects
of the Empire, and as feeling a 'kind of pride that he should be
among/Those haughty shop-keepers, who sternly dealt/Their
goods and edicts out from pole to pole' (X, st. 65). And when we
see him 'lost in wonder of so great a nation' and 'wrapt in
contemplation' of the great city, and hear him rhapsodise on
'Freedom's chosen station' (XI, st. 9), Juan's metropolitan fervour
does not lag behind the most zealous glorifications of London as
the chosen city and the permanent abode of liberty, property,
constitutionalism and morality:

I say, Don Juan, wrapt in contemplation,
  Walked on behind his carriage, o'er the summit,
And lost in wonder of so great a nation,
  Gave way to't, since he could not overcome it.
'And here,' he cried, 'is Freedom's chosen station;
  Here peals the people's voice, nor can entomb it
Racks, prisons, inquisitions; resurrection
Awaits it, each new meeting or election.

'Here are chaste wives, pure lives; here people pay
  But what they please; and if that things be dear,
'Tis only that they love to throw away
  Their cash, to show how much they have a-year.
Here laws are all inviolate; none lay
  Traps for the traveller; every highway's clear:
Here' – he was interrupted by a knife,
With 'Damn your eyes! your money or your life!'

(XI, sts. 9–10)

Nevertheless, my initial contention needs qualification. Though in his enthusiasm for the city Juan reflects various poetic versions of the 'Whig dream', his function is not so much to imitate but, more Augustan in spirit, to mock-imitate that genre. While the exile-strangers' hymns to the city are rendered as solo-parts or occasionally accompanied by a second narrative voice that reaffirms and reinforces the protagonist's views, Juan's praise of the capital is, from the very outset, placed in juxtaposition with the dissimilar perspective and attitude of the Byronic *persona*, or, to be more exact, Juan's praise of the city is, from the very beginning, ridiculed, distorted, and deranged, as it were, by the narrator:

    . . . and Don Juan felt . . .,
A kind of pride that he should be among
  Those *haughty* shop-keepers, who *sternly* dealt
Their goods and *edicts* out from pole to pole,
And made the very billows pay them toll.

(X, st. 65)

But Juan felt, though not approaching *home*,
  As one who, though he were not of the race,
Revered the soil, of those true sons the mother,
  Who butchered half the earth, and bullied t'other.

(X, st. 81)

In neither of the statements that begin with the phrase 'Juan felt', does the narrator really care to communicate what Juan felt. By coupling Don Juan's topics of praise and admiration with derogatory adjectives or adverbs (*'haughty* shopkeepers'; *'sternly* dealt'), with semantically interfering nouns ('goods and *edicts'*), or with whole lines of sardonic comments (as in the last line of both stanzas), i.e. with notions that are completely incompatible with those of the protagonist, the narrator intimates that his real aim is not a double perspective illumination of the city but the exposing and discrediting of Juan's praise of London and the bringing into prominence of his own rather sardonic views.

It is Don Juan's encounter with the highway robbers on Shooter's Hill that interrupts his rhapsodising on the 'chaste wives' and 'pure lives' of the town, and precipitates him from the heights of his enthusiasm for 'Freedom's chosen station' into the depressions of uneasiness and meditation:

Don Juan, having done the best he could
  In all the circumstances of the case,
As soon as 'Crowner's 'quest' allowed, pursued
  His travels to the capital apace; –
Esteeming it a little hard he should
  In twelve hours' time, and very little space,
Have been obliged to slay a freeborn native
In self-defence: – *this made him meditative.*

(XI, st. 18)

And it is that very encounter which serves the Byronic *persona* as a turning-point with respect both to his depiction of Don Juan and to his narrative technique.

The narrator cancels the shortlived and fairly unequal interplay of 'He' and 'I' (X, st. 84). And showing himself pretty unconcerned, he remarks on the further development of Don Juan's attitude towards England and the city, at the most, in empty paranthetical phrases like 'Howe'er he might esteem this moral nation' (XII, st. 68). Moreover, he devaluates Don Juan's perspective and attitude by calling him 'a hero [who] like other slaves of course must pay his ransom' (XI, st. 74). While the interplay of 'He' and 'I' is discontinued and the voice of the Byronic *persona* comes to the fore, we perceive also a change in the time-scheme of the London passage, a shift from the protagonist's present in the early 1790s to the *persona's* retrospective point of view which we associate with the composition of the England cantos in 1822–3:

> I have no great cause to love that spot of earth,
>   Which holds what *might have been* the noblest nation;
> But though I owe it little but my birth,
>   I feel a mixed regret and veneration
> For its decaying fame and former worth . . ..
>
> Alas! could She but fully, truly, know
>   How her great name is now throughout abhorred;
> How all the nations deem her their worst foe,
>   That worse than *worst of foes*, the once adored
> False friend, who held out freedom to mankind,
> And now would chain them, to the very mind; –
>
> Would she be proud, or boast herself the free,
>   Who is but first of slaves? The nations are
> In prison, – but the jailor, what is he?
>   No less a victim to the bolt and bar.
> Is the poor privilege to turn the key
>   Upon the captive, freedom? He's as far
> From the enjoyment of the earth and air
> Who watches o'er the chain, as they who wear.

> (X, sts 66ff.)

It is from this retrospective point of view and in the disquieting remembrance of 'the impious Alliance which insults the world with the name of "Holy"'[26] that, here and elsewhere, the Byronic *persona* counters Don Juan's praise of Britain as 'the island of the free' and of its capital as 'Freedom's chosen station'. But he does not do so without emphasising that he also believed and believes in the great political principles that once established Britain's former 'fame and former worth' and qualified her for 'What *might have been* the noblest nation'. What he denounces is not her Whig principles but the reactionary policies of her former and present politicians by whom the great ideals were trodden down and the old mind-forged and mind-forging despotism restored. And he does so by using the impressive metaphor of Britain as the turnkey of the imprisoned nations, a metaphor which can be read as an adoption of Swift's and Gay's turnkey-images symbolising urban perversion and corruption under early capitalism or as an inversion of the praise of England and its capital as the 'Scourge of Tyrants and the sole Resource of such as under grim Oppression groan'[27], as we find it, for example, in Thomson's *Seasons*.

After these reflections the narrator turns to the city where he discerns a similar decay:

> The sun went down, the smoke rose up, as from
>   A half-unquenched volcano, o'er a space
> Which well beseemed the 'Devil's drawing-room,'
>   As some have qualified that wondrous place.
> But Juan felt, though not approaching *home*,
>   As one who, though he were not of the race,
> Revered the soil, of those true sons the mother,
> Who butchered half the earth, and bullied t'other.
>
> A mighty mass of brick, and smoke, and shipping,
>   Dirty and dusky, but as wide as eye
> Could reach, with here and there a sail just skipping
>   In sight, then lost amidst the forestry
> Of masts; a wilderness of steeples peeping
>   On tiptoe, through their sea-coal canopy;
> A huge, dun cupola, like a foolscap crown
> On a fool's head – and there is London Town!
>
> But Juan saw not this: each wreath of smoke
>   Appeared to him but as the magic vapour
> Of some alchymic furnace, from whence broke
>   The wealth of worlds (a wealth of tax and paper):
> The gloomy clouds, which o'er it as a yoke
>   Are bowed, and put the sun out like a taper,

Were nothing but the natural atmosphere,
Extremely wholesome, though but rarely clear.

(X, sts 81–3)

Here, in this first description of that 'space/Which well
beseemed the "Devil's drawing room"', the impression of decay,
that undoubtedly triumphs over Don Juan's naive praise, is evoked
by multifarious allusions and correspondences: on the one hand by
its conceptual correspondence to poems equating London with
Hell, like Swift's 'The Place of the Damn'd'[28] or the city passages in
Shelley's *Peter Bell the Third*[29], by its correspondence as regards
point of view and metaphor to Denham's portrait of the city seen
from Cooper's Hill[30] and, most powerfully perhaps, by its allusion
to Genesis (*DJ*, X) which associates London with the Biblical
Sodom, over which 'the smoke . . . went up as the smoke of a
furnace' (Gen. 19:28).

On the other hand, this impression of decay is also conveyed by
the poetic mockery or alienation of popular clichés of London
panegyrics in stanza 82. With its emphasis on London's 'wilderness of steeples', on the 'huge, dun cupola' of St Paul's, on the
'shipping' and 'the forestry of masts', popular verses of famous
panegyrics are recalled and countered at the same time – lines, for
example, like the following in Pope's *Windsor-Forest*:

> The figur'd Streams in Waves of Silver roll'd
> And on their Banks *Augusta* rose in Gold . . .
> Behold! *Augusta's* glitt'ring Spires increase,
> And Temples rise, the beauteous Works of Peace[31]

or, like those of Thomson in *The Seasons*:

> Nurse of art! The City reared
> In beauteous Pride her Tower-encircled Head
>   . . . and on the Thames,
> Like a long wintry forest, groves of masts
> Shot up their spires; the bellying sheet between
> Possess'd the breezy void;[32]

But, here and elsewhere, the Byronic *persona* does not leave it at
that. He does not rest content with allusions to Biblical and

Augustan denunciations and inversions of Augustan praises of the city. His description of 'London Town' is more than a mere paradigm for hard- and soft-core intertextualists. Rather, the 'gloomy clouds which o'er [the city] as a yoke are bowed, and put the sun out like a taper' are rendered emblematic of the unscrupulous policy of her 'sons . . . who butchered half the earth and bullied t'other', the industrial capitalists who transformed the great city into a 'volcano' spouting smoke and dirt. And, at the same time, the destruction of urban life is laid at the door of the church, too, when, for this gloomy yoke of pollution, the metaphor 'sea-coal canopy' is coined, an oxymoron which relates both grammatically and semantically[33] to the 'wilderness of steeples', and reminds us of Shelley's polemics against the churchmen of the hellish city who 'damn themselves to see/God's sweet love in burning coals'.[34]

In his famous debate with Rosencrantz and Guildenstern, the foolish collaborators with the cynical subverter of royal and divine law, Hamlet communicates the decay of his former Renaissance optimism by playing upon and denying the symbolic connotations of the term canopy:

this excellent canopy . . . this majestical roof fretted with golden fire, why, it appeareth nothing to me but a *foul* and *pestilent congregation of vapours* (II, 2, 299ff.)

Coining the term 'sea-coal canopy', the Byronic *persona* plays a similar game. The space over which it is suspended, the metaphor implies, is no longer 'the Pride of aweful State',[35] no longer a city emblematic of divine and royal protection, but one dominated by a well-established trinity of fools: (1) The 'huge, dun cupola' of St Paul's, looking 'like a foolscap crown/On a fool's head', after failing to recognise that while it glorified the promises of industrialisation it was increasingly blackened and blinded by its problems; (2) '"Fum" the Fourth' (XI, st. 78), the very model of that fashionable generation of monarchs who wear their 'crowns . . . instead of a fool's-cap' (XI, st. 84) and who, instead of relying on the 'people's trust' (XII, st. 83) seeks to 'redeem [his] land's distresses' by 'hired huzzas . . . tours . . . and Highland dresses' (X, st. 86); (3) and, last but not least, the Lord Mayor of the City, the bourgeois purse-holder and tourist manager for the 'royal bird' (XI, st. 78), the 'witless Falstaff of a hoary Hal/A fool whose bells have ceased to ring at all' (X, st. 86).

For a city in which Diogenes himself would lose his liking 'to hunt his honest man' (XI, st. 28) the conventional formulae of *laudes urbis* must be laid aside. The alleged beauties and trophies of this 'mighty Babylon' (XI, st. 23) like 'the gentle sound of Thamis' that's 'hardly heard through multifarious "damme's"' (XI, st. 24), like 'the Mansion House . . . [that] stiff yet grand erection' (XI, st. 25), like her 'Parks . . . those vegetable puncheons' (XI, st. 66) or her '"Rows" most modestly called "Paradise"' (XI, st. 21) must either be rectified as blunt misnomers or rendered as valuables 'which Eve might quit without much sacrifice' (XI, st. 21).

Most adequately, the narrator suggests indeed, this 'Babel' (XI, st. 69) ruled by a triumvirate of dunces, is described in terms of the *ubi sunt* motif, in long, winding, 'where are'-formulae that recall her past splendour and lament her present decay:

> 'Where is the world,' cries Young, 'at *eighty*? Where
>   The world in which a man was born?' Alas!
> Where is the world of *eight* years past? 'Twas there –
>   I look for it – 'tis gone, a Globe of Glass!
> Cracked, shivered, vanished, scarcely gazed on, ere
>   A silent change dissolves the glittering mass.
> Statesmen, chiefs, orators, queens, patriots, kings,
> And dandies, all are gone on the wind's wings.

(XI, st. 76)

While 'chaste wives' (X, st. 10) are replaced by 'pedestrian Paphians abound[ing] In decent London' (XI, st. 30), while 'The House of Commons [is] turned into a tax-trap' (XI, st. 84) and 'Both senates see their nightly votes participated/Between the tyrant's and the tribunes' crew' (XI, st. 75), what is maintained are but the institutions that repress the poor multitude and protect the privileged few, and what is supported are but the naïve and committed sectarians who, hoping to discipline the exploited multitude, tolerate 'hardened and imperial sin':

> Oh, Mrs. Fry! Why go to Newgate? Why
>   Preach to poor rogues? And wherefore not begin
> With C[ar]lt[o]n, or with other houses? Try

Your hand at hardened and imperial sin.
To mend the people's an absurdity,
     A jargon, a mere philanthropic din,
Unless you make their betters better: – Fie!
I thought you had more religion, Mrs. Fry.

(X, st. 85)

In portraying the city as the corrupt and corrupting centre of a rotten nation and the urban experience of the 1820s as one of growing perversions and pains, the idea of a political and social revolution suggests itself to the *persona* (cf. XI, 84):

A row of gentlemen along the streets
     Suspended, may illuminate mankind,
As also bonfires made of country seats;
     But the old way is best for the purblind:
The other looks like phosphorus on sheets,
     A sort of Ignis-fatuus to the mind,
Which, though 'tis certain to perplex and frighten,
Must burn more mildly ere it can enlighten.

(XI, st. 27)

Elsewhere in *Don Juan*, we know, the Byronic *persona* repeatedly indulges in playing the part of the aristocratic Whig revolutionary. Here, however, where he deals with the city whose great historical sons, as he admits, supported the Great Rebellion, the Glorious Revolution and the French Revolution, here neither the idea nor even the rhetoric of revolution are allowed to come to the fore. The instant the one or the other is intoned or mentioned we find it being discontinued or unsaid. Or, to be more precise, we find it devalued as 'A sort of Ignis-fatuus to the mind', a delusive and treacherous light more likely to lead astray than to 'illuminate mankind'.

This unusual caution on the part of the *persona* is attributable to the fact that between London's sons of the heroic days and those of his own he finds little or no likeness. 'Our notion is not high', he states, 'Of politicians and their double front' (XI, st. 36). And this notion holds good not only for those in power but also for those he calls 'My friends the Whigs' (XI. st. 9), the descendants of men who once 'bound the bar or senate in their spell' (XI, st. 77) and whom, in the 1820s, he bluntly terms 'the tribunes' crew' (XI, st. 75). And it applies to the multitude, the common people of London whom, in the stanza quoted above, he qualifies as the 'purblind', and, elsewhere, as the 'progenies/Of this enormous city's spreading spawn' (XI, st. 28) or, more alarmingly even, as the 'scum' (XI, st. 8) the city boils over with.

Denouncing all ranks and parties in these terms the Byronic *persona* – who here in the London cantos reflects more about his former fame (XI, st. 55), his fall and his exile (XI, st. 56) than elsewhere in the poem – comes close to another tragic hero of Shakespeare, to Coriolanus, the lion of Rome, who also ends in exile. Coriolanus, it is true, curses the friends of the people as 'dull tribunes' and the lower classes of Romans as 'a multiplying spawn . . . That's thousand to one good one' (II, 2, 78f.) long before his fall. But he, too, like the Byronic *persona*, feels motivated to write off all ranks and parties as 'kites and crows' in exile only. And he, too, uses the term 'canopy' playing upon its senses 'under the sky' and 'royally enthroned' when being asked by Aufidius's serving-man 'Where dwell'st thou?' he answers: 'Under the canopy . . . I' th' city of kites and crows' (IV, 5, 40ff.).

If this does not mean that the Byronic *persona* identifies with the political philosophy of Shakespeare's *Coriolanus*, it does mean, I believe, that, at the end of his portrait of London, he comes closer to that than to the conviction expressed in Brecht's version of the play according to which nothing but class war, the successful revolution of the enslaved people, can resolve the political and social dilemma and advance freedom and welfare.

This is underlined by the imitation of another stock-feature of London panegyrics, the praise of Parliament, at the very end of the London portrait:[36]

> He also had been busy seeing sights –
>   The Parliament and all the other houses;
> Had sate beneath the gallery at nights,
>   To hear debates whose thunder *roused* (not *rouses*)
> The world to gaze upon those northern lights . . .
>
> He saw however at the closing session,
>   That noble sight, when *really* free the nation,
> A king in constitutional possession

Of such a throne as is the proudest station,
Though despots know it not – till the progression
　Of freedom shall complete their education.
'Tis not mere splendour makes the show august
To eye or heart – it is the people's trust.

There too he saw (whate'er he may be now)
　A Prince, the prince of princes, at the time
With fascination in his very bow,
　And full of promise, as the spring of prime.
Though royalty was written on his brow,
　He had *then* the grace too, rare in every clime,
Of being, without alloy of fop or beau,
A finished gentleman from top to toe.

(XII, sts 82ff.)

Here, once more, the urban experience is communicated not
from the narrator's retrospective point of view in the 1820s, but
from the perspective of his hero in the early 1790s which the
persona had almost consigned to oblivion. In two parenthetical
phrases (82, l. 4; 84, l. 1) and with the adverb 'then' printed in
italics (84, l. 6) the *persona* intimates that Don Juan's elevating
experience is without equal in the 1820s. But the quality of the
impression of the past is not ironically undermined or devalued
but reaffirmed by the narrator. 'This patrician panegyric', Malcolm
Kelsall remarks, 'not only reinforces Byron's clear separation from
radicalism, it also indicates how instinctively his criticism of the
social order is grounded in a political outlook which goes back at
least to the 1730s and 1740s – how *conservative* his attitudes are.'[37]
Indeed, Don Juan's reaffirmed praise of 'the *unreformed* parliament,
and . . . the future George IV'[38] bears a striking resemblance to the
politics of the Augustan poets which were shaped mainly by
Bolingbroke. With his most famous work, *The Idea of a Patriot King*
(1738), Bolingbroke fired the imagination of Pope and his fellow
poets with the vision of a great Prince on the throne who would
save a people too corrupted to reform themselves:

Alas! on one alone our all relies,
Let him be honest, and he must be wise;
Let him no trifler from his [father's] school,

Nor like his [father's] [father] still a [fool],
Be but a man! unministered, alone,
And free at once the senate and the throne;
Esteem the *public love* his best supply,
A King's true glory his integrity; . . .
Europe's just balance and our own may stand,
And one man's honesty redeem the land.

Pope's poetic version of the *Patriot King* entitled *One Thousand Seven Hundred and Forty* (1740)[39] is, I believe, the model of Byron's visionary finale of his sardonic, highly sophisticated, and gloomy portrait of the capital. But can it be regarded as its ultimate object or aim after exposing London's 'sea-coal canopy' with her well-established trinity of fools below it, her 'tyrant's' and her 'tribunes' crew', her 'spreading spawn', her 'scum' and so much more? The *'people's trust'* in whom? 'Only at nightfall, aethereal rumors/ Revive for a moment a broken Coriolanus'. It is rather the exile's dream of what Dr Johnson, another Augustan poet, was also craving for in his *Vanity of Human Wishes*: the restoration of 'The golden Canopy, the Pride of aweful State'[40] over the unreal city in the waste land.

Notes

1.   W. Kent, ed., *An Encyclopaedia of London*, (1937), p. 746.
2.   Cf. M. Gassenmeier, 'Faszination und Angst: Anmerkungen zum widersprüchlichen Bild der Großstadt in 7. Buch des *Prelude*', *Studien zur englischen Romantik*, 1 (1985), pp. 71f.
3.   Cf. G. Gernentz, *Laudes Romae*, (Rostock, 1913); cf. C. J. Classen, *Die Stadt im Spiegel der Descriptiones und Laudes urbium in der antiken und mittelalterlichen Literatur bis zum Ende des zwölften Jahrhunderts*, (Hildesheim, New York, 1980), pp. 1–36; cf. M. Gassenmeier, *Londondichtung als Politik: Texte und Kontexte der City-Poetry von der Restauration bis zum Ende der Walpole-Ära*, (Niemeyer, Tübingen, 1989), pp. 2f., 104f., 298f.
4.   Cf. J. D. Bone, 'Historicism and Deconstruction: Two Contemporary Perspectives on Romanticism', *Studien zur englischen Romantik*, 2 (1987), pp. 212ff.
5.   Cf. *London: The Urban Experience in Poetry and Prose*, eds H. Mell und H. Slogsnat, (Paderborn, 1987).
6.   Cf. A. Löffler, *'The Rebel Muse'*: *Studien zu Swifts kritischer Dichtung*, (Tübingen, 1982), pp. 77f. and 84.
7.   Cf. note 3 above.

8. Gassenmeier, op. cit. (see note 3), p. 6.
9. Ibid., p. 6.
10. *Expans'd Hieroglyphicks, A Critical Edition of Sir John Denham's Coopers Hill*, ed. B. OHehir, (Berkeley and Los Angeles, 1969), pp. 110f., i.e. Draft III, ll. 13ff.; italics mine.
11. Gassenmeier, op. cit. (see note 3), p. 20f.
12. Ibid., pp. 45ff.
13. Cf. J. R. Jones, *The First Whigs*, (London, 1961), p. 198.
14. *The Works of Dryden*, eds E. N. Hooker, H. T. Swedenberg Jr. et al., (Berkeley, 1956–83), II, p. 23.
15. *The Works of Dryden*, II, pp. 48ff.
16. *Londinum Heroico Carmine Perlustratum . . . The Renowned City of London, Surveyed, and Illustrated by J. Adamus a Transylvanian*, (London, 167[0?]); cf. Gassenmeier, op. cit. (see note 3), pp. 107f.
16a. Cf. Gernentz, op. cit., pp. 61ff.
17. Cf. Gassenmeier, 'Faszination und Angst', p. 75.
18. *Civitas Militaris, or, A Poem on the City Royal Regiment of Horse*. By John Tutchin, Gent., (London, 1690); quoted in *Londondichtung als Politik*, p. 196.
19. *Augusta Triumphans, or a Hymn to Victory. In a Panegyrical Address to the Honourable City of London, On the Occasion of the Trophies fix'd in Guild-Hall*. By Elkanah Settle, City Poet, (London, 1707); cf. F. C. Brown, *Elkanah Settle: His Life and Works*, (Chicago, 1910), p. 34.
20. Voltaire, *Oeuvres Complètes. Nouvelle Édition*, revue par M. Léon Thiessé, (Paris, 1829), XII, p. 311.
21. Cf. Gassenmeier, *Londondichtung als Politik*, pp. 225; 318; 329.
22. Jonathan Swift, *The Poems*, ed. H. Williams, 2nd edn, (Oxford, 1958), I, p. 125.
22a. Ibid., pp. 138f.
23. *Trivia: or, the Art of Walking the Streets of London*, Bk II, 115ff. and 126ff., in John Gay, *Poetry and Prose*, ed. V. A. Dearing, (Oxford, 1974), I, pp. 146f.; cf. H. Meller, 'Swifts Stadtsatiren und Gays Ursprungsmythos des vierten Standes', *Irland: Gesellschaft und Kultur*, IV, ed. D. Siegmund-Schultze, (Halle, Saale, 1985), p. 165.
24. Alexander Pope, *The Dunciad Variorum with the Prolegomena of Scriblerus* (1729) in: *The Twickenham Edition of the Poems*, Vol. 5, ed. J. R. Sutherland, (London, 1956), pp. 132–41.
25. *The Poems of Samuel Johnson*, ed. D. N. Smith and E. L. McAdam, (Oxford, 1974), p. 73.
26. Lord Byron, *The Complete Poetical Works*, ed. J. J. McGann, V (Oxford, 1986), p. 297.
27. *Thomson's Seasons, Critical Edition*, ed. O. Zippel, (Berlin, 1908), p. 104.
28. Swift, op. cit., II, pp. 575f.
29. Cf. T. Webb, *Shelley: A Voice Not Understood*, (Atlantic Highlands, NJ, 1977), pp. 96f., and Meller and Slogsnat, *London*, pp. 60ff.
30. Cf. above p. 139.
31. Alexander Pope, *The Poems, A one volume edition of the Twickenham text with selected annotations*, ed. J. Butt, (London, 1965), pp. 207f.
32. *Thomson's Seasons*, p. 189.

33. Cf. *Encyclopaedia Britannica* (1978), II, p. 518.
34. *Peter Bell The Third*, Part III – Hell, ll. 230f., i.e. stanza XVII.
35. Cf. *Poems of Samuel Johnson*, p. 120.
36. Cf. Gassenmeier, *Londondichtung als Politik*, pp. 116; 202f.; 313.
37. M. Kelsall, *Byron's Politics*, (Harvester Press, Sussex, 1987), p. 173.
38. Ibid., p. 174.
39. Cf. Pope, *One volume Twickenham*, p. 831.
40. Cf. note 35.

8
Byron, Pope, and the Grand Tour
MICHAEL G. COOKE

Between Pope's birth in 1688, the year of the Glorious (sometimes called the Bloodless) Revolution in England, and Byron's birth in 1788, a year before the French Revolution with its omnipresent guillotine, changes both subtle and wrenching had occurred in the structures of thought and conduct in English life. For one thing, with James Watt's great enhancement of the steam engine (1769) and with continual rapid gains in textile manufacture, the Industrial Revolution had got fully underway, and turbid urban factory centres had begun to replace more stable agricultural communities. More quietly, Sir Robert Walpole, who coined the phrase: 'let sleeping dogs lie', had proved wide-awake to his political opportunities, and slid into the position of first Prime Minister, with effective rule, of England, while the newly-imported House of Hanover commanded neither the native tongue, the native customs, nor the native desire to rule.

In religion and philosophy the empiricist–materialist tradition made steady headway, and in 1785 with *The Principles of Moral and Political Philosophy* William Paley commenced a series of arguments in defence of God as ultimate designer, rather than ultimate Being, of the universe. Dr Johnson's *A Dictionary of the English Language* (1755), rather than 'fixing' and 'preserving' linguistic authority on the grounds of 'use and elegance' (with a caveat against 'useless foreigners' in word-choice), may have helped to stimulate the scrutiny of and initiatives in language that led to so many far-reaching redefinitions in the Romantic era. And didactic poetry, venerable all the way back to Lucretius and Virgil, expired in the hands of Erasmus Darwin (*The Botanic Garden*, 1789). As Shelley forthrightly put it in the Preface to *Prometheus Unbound*, 'Didactic poetry is my abhorrence.'

And yet, in the teeth of the deeply-conditioning *Zeitsachen*, it is common to argue for a genuine likeness between Pope and Byron, when it is nearly impossible to find another pair of writers, let alone poets, linked across a chasm of one hundred years. We do not link Byron and Eliot (b. 1888); in fact Eliot was at pains to distance himself from Byron, in ways that ought to seem suspicious to our psychoanalytic age. Nor do we link Pope and Hobbes (b. 1588). The relationship between Byron and Pope cannot be simple, but it is stubborn, and will repay close analysis.

Not the most obvious but in many ways the most significant feature of likeness between Byron and Pope is that they fall within the small rollcall of uncompromising poets. They do what they do with a resolution and force that cut through aesthetic protections to strike us like veritable natural phenomena: a lightning storm, a flash-flood, a scorpion, a leopard in high grass. The frank and fierce demands they make on our attention and judgement and moral economy can put us off Byron and Pope, as we are put off other uncompromising poets; e.g. Swinburne (in contrast with Arnold), Marlowe (in contrast with Ben Jonson), Pound (in contrast with Eliot), Dickinson (in contrast with Longfellow). We cannot easily like them, or plausibly leave them alone.

In the nature of the case, Byron and Pope are not uncompromising in like ways, or about like things, and the difference goes beyond the surface extreme of social savagery in Pope and clamant subjectivity in Byron. For it could be said that, at bottom, both poets are early orientated toward a conception of a better world, and later press constantly for it. Their poetry presses into the social system and into our lives, with a view to change. But Pope sees the better world as the predictable product of a specific structure marked by right conduct, right order, right reason. He is, by virtue of adherence to a formal conception and structure, a sub-Utopian poet. Byron's better world was to have emerged out of infinite conversions of individuals and out of infinite negotiations among individuals as free people cherishing one another's freedom. He is more properly seen as a sub-idealistic poet, because he imagined the elimination of the very principle of formal system that the Utopian (and therefore system-minded) Pope insisted on.

The obvious shock that Pope and Byron cause, and the obvious association between them, comes with the fact that, despite the changeful century separating their births, they both work in satire (and satire of course has virtually disappeared in establishment

English poetry today). But this association bears closer scrutiny. For in Pope's case satire was a way of life. When he varied from it he did so to cultivate the kindred voice of didactic poetry. Notably, too, more sentimental, semi-narrative pieces like the 'Elegy to the Memory of an Unfortunate Lady' and 'Eloisa to Abelard' can be felt to strain at a leash if they do not quite produce satirical bite.

For Byron, satire was a way of scoring literary points, when he was young, or venting occasional pessimistic or idealistic spleen; and as he turned older it gave another colour or a further reach to his 'versified aurora borealis'. Priding himself on repelling charges of 'monotony and mannerism', he worked gleefully in many ostensibly clashing modes. His versatility not only includes satire, but also unexpected or mutant forms of satire. He blithely plays himself into the satirical structure as victim and butt, as though liability to satire were the human norm, rather than satire being a castigation of departures from a norm into vice and folly: 'Just as I make my mind up, everyday,/To be a *'totus, teres, Stoic, Sage'*,/The wind shifts and I fly into a rage.' In sharp contrast, Pope recognised in satire a point of personal honour and cultural necessity, as the *Epistle to Dr. Arbuthnot* and the 'First Satire of the Second Book of Horace' make plain. If he 'lisped in numbers' as a general thing, he disciplined himself into the Demosthenes of satire.

Ultimately it is no favour to Byron to cry him up as a late avatar of the Popean or neo-classical spirit. His work in that idiom seems rather *fade*, or facetious, or unwieldy by comparison. Besides, he loved Pope on the dubious ground of the 'passion' and 'freedom' in his writing, seeming as eager to make the little Queen Anne's man a proto-Romantic as some later critics have been to make *him* a post-Augustan. Satire links Byron and Pope less through affinity of spirit than through coincidence of gesture. The *frisson* we get from linking these two uncompromising poets need not be denied, but perhaps it would sustain itself better under another aegis.

The phenomenon of the Grand Tour, which Pope barbed in *The Dunciad* for the egregious vulgarity it had descended into, and which Byron in person made even more egregious and vulgar, may help us to consider Byron and Pope afresh. The matter of satire will come into play, in the framework of the physical, social and philosophical concerns both Byron and Pope had to contend with, for better or worse, around the Grand Tour. Studies by writers such as Christopher Hibbert and Jeremy Black have offered rich information concerning the material and social dimensions of the

Grand Tour, but its moral and imaginative valences will require more attention to figures like Byron and Pope than they have so far been accorded.

Pope and Byron both suffered from a physical deformity which served as a focus for self-pity and exasperation with the world, in one respect, but also in another respect as a spur to prowess and heroism. Byron's handicap was a club foot which at one point he sought to have amputated (a pyrrhic remedy, at best). Notwithstanding, he fenced, he boxed, he swam the Hellespont and outswam Angelo Mengaldo from the Lido to the Grand Canal in Venice, and he had his (or possibly *their*) way with hundreds of women – including 23 whose names he retained – in the space of a year in Venice. Pope in turn, because of a tubercle bacillus presumably imbibed with his wet-nurse's milk, had a worsening humpback that required him, at one stage, to be laced into 'linen stays' to keep upright, and later into 'an iron case'.

In contrast to the peripatetic Byron, Pope could expect to travel little. His family demurred even at his going to London to study foreign languages, since he could never go abroad to put those languages to profit. Instead he travelled as a 'gadder' in the summertime, visiting friends' estates and involving himself in plans for improvements which, often, were inspired by knowledge gained on the Grand Tour. Yet Pope, as Maynard Mack observes, in *Alexander Pope: A Life*, achieved great 'eminence . . . in the face of dismaying odds'.

The odds against Pope were not only, perhaps not chiefly physical. He bore the hereditary social handicap of a family in innkeeping and the linen trade, and what was worse his family adhered to the Catholic persuasion when anti-Catholic sentiment and actual Penal Laws meant, as Mack quotes the words of the first Marquis of Halifax, 'no opportunity of showing [one's] own value to the world'. One had 'to live at best an useless, and by others to be thought a dangerous member of the nation'. Even as he satirically upheld the ideal of national good promoted by an uplifting 'commerce with men and cities' on the Grand Tour, Pope was excluded by class and religion more profoundly than by health from joining in. He set out, however, to make himself a spokesman, a normative Englishman in his time, and his poor health perversely helped him to succeed; it was the foil to his genius, not a foil of his ambition.

Byron, we could think, makes a simple contrast with Pope: socially privileged, spoilt, lionised. Let us recall, though, that he set himself up habitually in 'opposition'. There is something symbolic in the fact that his few speeches in the House of Lords were made in defence of *frame-breakers* and Catholic Emancipation. He defended many unlikely views in this feistily liberal spirit. Let us remember, too, what Leslie Marchand rightly stresses, that Byron fell unexpectedly into his peerage, as into so much else in his life. Before he became heir presumptive to the Byron title and estates he was a boy named George Gordon growing up in Aberdeen, in a 'lower-middle-class Scottish world'. We may doubt whether Byron ever fully accepted himself, or felt fully accepted in his elevated social sphere. In fact he seems as diligent about risking or repudiating it as Pope in courting and cultivating it. If Pope comes across as a deliberate, consummate Englishman, Byron appears rather a happenstance exile, a spontaneous invention aptly termed European. Even as he was lining up for the peerage, he was immersing himself, with intuitive propriety, in 'Knolles [*Turkish History*], . . ., Hawkins's Translation from Mignot's History of the Turks, Arabian Nights, all travels, or histories, or books upon the East I could meet with . . .'

Byron's version of the Grand Tour may seem from Hibbert's traditionalist viewpoint 'wayward', since it gave up customary comforts and predictable trophies or at least diluted them with such fresh woods and pastures new as Malta, Portugal, Spain, Turkey, Albania, and even Greece (Italy had been since the Renaissance the great destination, with France, Switzerland, Germany, Austria and the Low Countries clearly subordinate). The Grand Tour that Pope may have wished to preserve or revive in its original design of advancing aristocratic culture by training diplomats, public servants, and military officers in art, architecture, history, landscape design, international relations, and what have you, this Grand Tour Byron took it upon himself to deformalise, personalise, and open up equally to adventure and meditation. Byron, in fact, would have qualified as one of the youths of whom Pope so wickedly wrote: 'Europe he saw, and Europe saw him too.' Except that Byron's spectacle, which Arnold called 'the pageant of his bleeding heart', extended even farther afield.

But the reaction of his age to Byron's version of the Grand Tour brushed Pope's satirical thrust aside, and embraced Byron as a discovery, a discoverer. For Childe Harold or the travelling figure in 'The Dream' is not just a spectacle; he is a prism, a consciousness struggling with his own years, with the age he lives in, with history, and with the unfamiliar and the unknown that convention ignores even while reality demands their notice. In other words, Byron owns the uncertainty on the Grand Tour, and so institutionalises possibility in it, as against the acquisitive materiality and simple plus-or-minus judgements that had prevailed through Pope's time and beyond. The fifth Earl of Exeter, for example, in the last decades of the seventeenth century spent so much on things like Japanese cabinets inlaid with mother-of-pearl and sets of boxwood statuettes, that his estate needed decades to amortise his debts.

The expectation that the Grand Tour would yield measurable benefits for the aristocratic tourist's culture and country estate, and for the state of his country usually went unmet. Objections in principle long antedate Pope's satire. Gibbon was only the most famous among those who thought the tourist was sent over too young, and that the tour was too long and too incoherent to prove profitable. Malleable youth were being shaped amiss, at great expense. Objections in fact were also frequent. As Milton saw it, the youths returned to England 'transformed' into 'mimics, apes, and kickshows'.

The materialistic or utilitarian focus of the Grand Tour admitted of a further, and more troubling objection. Its very teleology caused it to take on an intense insulation from the realities within which it operated. This is nowhere more evident than in the acts of transfer the Grand Tour created. In one direction it transferred a virtual miniature of the tourist's world to the Continent: the Earl of Burlington is reported to have arrived at Dover in the early eighteenth century with 878 pieces of luggage. In the other direction the English tourist transferred gardening and architectural and decorating styles, to the extent of building replicas of Italian villas. Pope, as 'Epistle IV: To Burlington' demonstrates, serenely accepted this gesture of initial transfer, and only balked at further copying: 'Yet shall (my Lord) your just and noble rules/Fill half the land with Imitating Fools.' He had been somewhat less discriminating in *Windsor Forest*: 'Behold! th' ascending *Villa's* on my Side/ Project long shadows o'er the Chrystal Tide.'

It appears that Byron, for his part, early enough intuited the impossibility of the Grand Tour transfer. He prefers to 'recall such visions and create/From what has been, or might be, things which grow . . .', and is full of scorn for 'The artist and his ape [who] teach and tell/How well his connoisseurship understands/The graceful bend and the voluptuous swell:/Let these describe the undescribable' (*Childe Harold* IV, sts 52, 53). He suggests that failure inheres in the act of transfer, regardless of era, treating Hadrian with wonderfully concise disgust as the 'Colossal copyist of deformity' (*CH* IV, st. 152).

Besides, by Byron's time the act of transfer had become too heavily literal, and problematical. The transportation of the Elgin marbles from Greece set off quite an unfavourable outcry, swelled by Keats and Byron himself. In *Childe Harold* II Lord Elgin is likened to Alaric, the Visigoth king who in 395 AD had carted off treasures from occupied Athens. Clearly such a gesture implies respect shapeshifted into rapacity. Smollett, or as Sterne would have it Smelfungus, may have been furnishing a psychic crutch for such rapacity with his determined proof of the odious unworthiness of the foreign people in possession of the transferables.

The insularity of the Grand Tour, in Pope's day, actually took on wilful cultural overtones. There was a complex anthropological and politico-economic traffic taking place *pari passu* with the Grand Tour, and not being acknowledged in its regimen. Swift's *Gulliver's Travels* satirises both the anthropological and the political carryings-on, the taste for which had reached a pitch where the pseudonymous Psalmanazar could invent a foreign people and pass it off as real. As Shaftesbury notes in *Characteristicks*, 'Monsters and monsterlands were never more in request.'

Even apparently sober idealism was producing perverse effects. The Georgia Scheme was intended as an alternative to prison and its 'horrors and brutalities', especially for gentleman debtors who would be sent off to Georgia and a superior life, with whites and blacks and Indians, as the vision went, living in a harmony beyond oppression and racism. But in fact one of the main sponsors of the Georgia Scheme, General James Edward Oglethorpe, was moving rapidly into prominence in the Royal African Company and had the honour of seeing a slave-ship named after him. Another influential sponsor, Bishop Edmund Gibson, who entered Oxford as 'poor serving child', was a noted apologist for black subjugation: his *Two Letters* became the last word on keeping slaves as slaves even if they were baptised, as Christianity in his view furnished every necessary sanction for such rigour. And all this was going on while Pope was otherwise engaged with the great unfolding, incorporating task of *The Dunciad*. The Georgia Scheme enters into the satirical tradition, however, only as an early American satire: *A True and Historical Narrative of the Colony of Georgia* (1741) praises Oglethorpe for keeping the new dwellers free of the 'transitory advantages' of wealth, and ensuring 'the integrity of primitive times' in the form of 'primitive poverty' for them.

Pope himself seems to sense a need for a broader view of the phenomenon of travel in *Windsor Forest*, which by metonymy works as a Grand Tour poem, in which the ships stand not only for nature ('Thy trees, fair Windsor! now shall leave their woods,/And half thy forests rush into thy floods . . .'), but also for the nation the Grand Tour is meant to serve. The nation as metaphor goes on its own Grand Tour, makes its own impact abroad, and brings back its own benefits and trophies (one way to bypass the problems of the individual emissary). *Windsor Forest*, as it winds up, makes a careful sentimental nod to better times for all peoples, as well as singular and dominant glories for England:

> Earth's distant Ends our Glory shall behold,
> And the new World launch forth to seek the Old.
> Then Ships of uncouth Form shall stem the Tyde,
> And Feather'd People crowd my wealthy Side,
> And naked Youths and painted Chiefs admire
> Our Speech, Our Colour, and our strange Attire!
> Oh stretch thy Reign, fair Peace! from Shore to Shore,
> Till Conquest cease, and Slav'ry be no more.

Here is an anthropological Grand Tour, going the other way *into* England, and here is the plastic bubble of the Grand Tour broken to breathe in, however narcotically, the harsh facts of conquest and enslavement. References to Peru and Mexico follow and intensify this theme, but I think we are seeing a gracious afterthought-as-peroration, without concern for the fact, say, that Lord Chandos made £200 000 on the slave trade in 1726 (in the first of the Moral Essays, 'Epistle I: To Cobham', Pope declares that 'gracious Chandos is belov'd at sight').

Unlike Byron, who even in *Don Juan* can be seen developing his own adventitious reverse-Grand-Tour into England, Pope is very subtle about going off the beaten track of nationalism, just as he subtly instructs us in *The Rape of the Lock* (a Grand Tour of the psyche) that the insulated life is not finally available. At bottom his subtlety may be rooted in a certain detachment from problems of basic policy and the temporal process of innovation. That detachment was in fact recommended as a cornerstone of the Grand Tour, as in Ben Jonson's advice in his Epigram 'To William Roe':

> Th'art now, to goe
> Countries, and climes, manners and men to know,
> T'extract, and choose the best of all these knowne,
> And those to turne to bloud, and make thine owne.
> ....
> So, when we, blest with thy returne, shall see
> Thy selfe, with thy first thoughts, brought home by thee,
> We each to other may this voyce enspire:
> This is that good AENEAS past through fire,
> Through seas, stormes, tempests: and imbarqu'd for hell,
> *Came backe vntouch'd*. This man hath trauail'd well.

> (*italics mine*)

And it is that detachment-in-presence that Byron cannot take in. Even when he is away he is not detached, but actively in flight from the endocentric, or actually contending with the real-life difference of the homosexual and the incestuous. Pope can metamorphose Belinda's lost curls magically *upward*, as well as psychosexually downward; trauma is for a moment, consequences vanish away (after all, the curl would have restored itself with a mere few months' seclusion).

In Byron's world, going far afield has strong political and indeed metaphysical implications. He is directly involved, challenging, at risk; he embodies the anthropometric value of travel as a primordial contribution to human development. And so when, in December 1819, Byron cuts or as he says 'curtails' his long hair and sends it in a package to his half-sister Augusta, the act has Samsonian overtones with no prospect of a magical restoration. He indicates that he is older, fainter, lower than when he declared: 'It is not over with me – I don't mean in literature, for that is nothing, and it may seem odd enough to say, I do not think it my vocation. But you will see that I shall do something or other – the times and fortune permitting' (February 1817). That last phrase keeps him from sounding *too* old, like King Lear with 'I shall do such deeds'. Thus, when Byron talks about slavery, he does more than piously wish for change; he recommends it, and with a vengeance. Here is his invocation to Wilberforce in *Don Juan* XIV, sts 82–3:

> You have freed the *blacks* – now pray shut up the whites.
>
> Shut up the bald-coot bully Alexander;
>   Ship off the Holy Three to Senegal;
> Teach them that 'sauce for goose is sauce for gander,'
>   And ask them how *they* feel to be in thrall?

In dealing with the Grand Tour, Pope is dealing with a mastery of foreign space. In going on the Grand Tour, Byron implicates himself in the painful and baffling operations of time. Goethe gives us in the *Italian Journey* a consummate record of the Grand Tour in his time, but it is in *Elective Affinities* that he best expresses what for a Romantic had to be at issue:

> You cannot walk among palm-trees with impunity, and your sentiments must surely alter in a land where elephants and tigers are at home.

A sense of discovery and destabilisation pervades Byron's vision on the Grand Tour. Eventually in 'The Dream' he treats travel as a quintessential metaphor for destabilisation, with all it holds out anthropometrically for stress and development. It makes little difference whether the site he visits is ancient or recent, Rome or Waterloo; both thrust him into quandaries. Metella comes in as the reverse of the Ozymandias scene – nothing is known to begin to match the impressiveness of the monument Byron attached to her name. And Waterloo simply leaves Byron crushed between the appeal of nature and the imperatives of history: 'I turned from all she [nature] brought, to those [the war dead] she could not bring.'

The intensity of Byron's episodic experience in *Childe Harold* can dim the fact that he, or his putative *alter ego*, is not so much visiting sites as going through a learning process. His topical reactions – not in themselves unique – gather into a pattern where he is unwittingly, willy-nilly, learning what time does, and what to do with it. The stanzas on St Peter's, rightly seen as crucial to the design of the whole poem, spell out Byron's epistemology and prove epochal in the story, the now-coming-unto-twilight story of the Grand Tour. Not the national responsibility but the nature of the traveller, and not the site but its mutual engagement with the being of the traveller come to the fore. In effect Byron sums up the mental posture of any but a Procrustean travel, any but a Procrustean experience of life.

We may note that Byron introduces St Peter's as an 'eternal ark'; it also is on a voyage, and one that has no end except to come into the new world that never materialises. As a destination to us, but an 'eternal ark' in itself, the basilica serves to signal the illusoriness of destination. *It* is at risk in time, and the tacit risk it poses for us is compounded by the fact that, entering it, we might be 'climbing some great Alp.' We have the object at hand, but lack the experience of it.

Though Byron lists the attributes of St Peter's, 'Majesty,/Power, Glory, Strength, and Beauty', they remain abstract, and do not register on us: 'its grandeur overwhelms thee not'. The reason is a paradox, in that we exist both intuitively and analytically and cannot readily reconcile the two modes. The very moment of entering St Peter's is sublime, but as Byron brilliantly discerns, the sublime requires an element of conscious detachment, of analysis, whereas his spectator is caught up, intuitively attuned, and so remains in dumb or unconscious mind-expansion.

Analysis, though inferior, remains necessary to appreciation and apprehension. The power or genius of the space that is St Peter's needs time, the field of analysis, to take hold. Byron then can reassure us:

> Thou seest not all; but piecemeal thou must break,
> To separate contemplation, the great whole;
> And as the ocean many bays will make,
> That ask the eye – so here condense thy soul
> To more immediate objects, and control
> Thy thoughts until thy mind hath got by heart
> Its eloquent proportions, and unroll
> In mighty graduations, part by part,
> The glory which at once upon thee did not dart,
>
> Not by its fault – but thine. Our outward sense
> Is but of gradual grasp . . .

(IV, sts 157–8)

The 'gradual grasp' summarises the condition of things for Childe Harold; it also pinpoints the mentality of Byron's work.

For all its fierce commitments and abandon in principle, Byron's is a poetry of incessant corrections and enforced reflection, whether in *The Giaour* and *Mazeppa*, or in *Manfred*, or 'The Dream', or in *Childe Harold* and *Don Juan*. In the St Peter's stanzas Byron is exploring the 'fountains of sublimity', the essential achievements and aspirations of humankind, and so the principle of 'gradual grasp' is more than a simple perceptual construct. It takes the phenomena of the Grand Tour and the very experience of travel into revelatory dimensions. The things of travel, it discloses, are not to be acquired but mysteriously 'entered', and learnt in a way that fuses our innermost capacity with their uttermost powers. Uncertainty and surprise and disarray beset Byron's moments on his way, but his accumulating and emerging sense of time enables him at last to mosaicise, synthesise those moments into a sense of human power, of life itself. By contrast Pope declares that 'In Man, the judgment shoots at flying game,/A bird of passage! gone as soon as found,/Now in the Moon perhaps, now under ground' ('Epistle I: To Cobham').

This is not to suggest that Pope lacks a sense of time, but only that it shows little in his treatment of travel and the Grand Tour, where the stasis of the known good and the normative choice prevails. Pope's sense of time, in fact, tends to be much less educative and evolutionary than Byron's. He offers a negative apocalypse at the end of *The Dunciad*, a positive one at the end of *Windsor-Forest*, and elsewhere scattered apocalyptic phrases: 'Another age shall see . . ./ . . . laughing Ceres re-assume the land' ('Epistle IV: To Burlington'). In a sense, he concerns himself more with the end of time than with time itself.

Not surprisingly, then, when Pope talks about the whole, as Byron comes to do in *Childe Harold*, he operates from a fixed position:

> Vast chain of being, which from God began
> Natures aethereal, human, angel, man,
> Beast, bird, fish, insect! what no eye can see . . .
> . . . .
> From Nature's chain whatever link you strike,
> Tenth or ten thousandth, breaks the chain alike.
> . . . .

All are but parts of one stupendous whole,
Whose body Nature is, and God the soul;
That, chang'd thro' all, and yet in all the same,
Great in the earth, as in th' aethereal frame . . .

(*An Essay on Man*: I, 237–69)

In many respects these lines contain the same theme as Byron's stanzas on St Peter's, but they *contain* it indeed, problematically, as an article of catechism, not as the distillation of what Coleridge calls our lifelong 'struggle to idealize and unify' the welter of experience.

The fact that Pope was rendering a '*short* yet not *imperfect* system of Ethics' may be adduced here, but it chiefly serves to confirm the difference in basic outlook between him and Byron. For Byron bridled at the mere notion of Bentham's *Springs of Action*, pitting his own experience against any system of interpretation. In the 'Dedication' to *Don Juan* he attacked even Wordsworth's 'new system' (perhaps a contradiction in terms), and declared elsewhere that 'when a man talks of system, his case is hopeless'. When encouraged to spend six to eight years working on a subject worthy of his talent (i.e. less mischievous than *Don Juan*), he replied bluntly: 'I hate tasks.' For tasks, presumably, use time by denying its essential feature for Byron, the learning and incorporation of the new.

It is a peculiarity of Romanticism that it neither invented nor perfected any literary form, but proved fluent in virtually every form extant. Romanticism complicated the freight of forms, and in a sense attained formal originality mainly by breaking the prejudice of genre. Ballad and epic and drama, narrative and autobiography and lyric have a watershed at this time. In keeping with such a pattern, Byron recasts the Grand Tour and also, as Jerome McGann has shown, helps to recast its unacknowledged cousin, loco-descriptive poetry, in *Childe Harold*.

But the Grand Tour was, independently, facing critical changes. Travel was no longer 'travail', a change Coleridge captures in the lines: 'A mount not wearisome and bare and steep /But a green mount, variously up-piled.' Here Coleridge represents as well the new popularity of the picturesque, with its softening and deflection of the purposes of the Grand Tour. In addition, the aristocratic presuppositions of the Grand Tour were on the wane, along with its secular political posture. The Cook's Tour, religious and democratic in conception, would replace the Grand Tour in the 1840s and exclusivity (to say nothing of 878 pieces of luggage) could not hold its own in the dawning era of the steam engine and the standardised railway hotel.

The Grand Tour that Pope attempted to chastise into efficacy was being outmoded by social change, and Byron, the outsider aristocrat who made exile not a punishment but a creative way of life, may have pushed the form to an introspective and interpretive extreme that neither he nor any of his immediate company could maintain. In *The Island* (1823) he went back in for escapist romance, although in quasi-Popean couplets. And it is startling to see Wordsworth, in his *Memorials of a Tour on the Continent, 1820*, turning Byron's metaphor of St Peter's as 'an Alp' upside down to make the Swiss Alps a sort of architecture in ruin (as well as mythical beings):

> What are they but a wreck and residue
> Whose only business is to perish! true
> To which sad course, these wrinkled Sons of Time
> Labour their proper greatness to subdue . . .

> (st. XXXVIII)

Clearly there is an emphasis on the interpretive consciousness rather than the material event, and this emphasis repeats itself throughout the series, so that we see cloud-sculptures, or what Wordsworth calls 'sky prospect', instead of works of art, and fancy and 'Fable's dark abyss' either impose upon or substitute for actual landscapes and monuments. In another vein, monuments yield to cottages in Wordsworth, and the aristocracy to the proletariat, in the meditation on 'The Ruined Cottage'. Voltaire's *Candide* had long since deflated the formal pretensions of the Grand Tour, and Sterne's *A Sentimental Journey through France and Italy* had infused it with feeling over purpose.

Pope clearly saw something going wrong with the Grand Tour, as with the Augustan ideal. But ferociously attentive to detail as he was, he represented less a poet of history than a poet of vision, to use the distinction Jules Michelet makes in *The People*. Or say he saw history, what was untidily on the move, with the eyes of vision, timeless and immutable. He responded to dissatisfaction with satire, not re-vision, because he was a poet of holding together, in relation to a system which was not standing on its own but which must not be let fall apart.

He had no inkling that the Grand Tour might be too costly not just in its failings but also in its succeeding. Byron would bring this out in *Don Juan*, showing England enslaved, 'bowed' under the 'yoke' of its own success, and that through the eyes of the idolatrous Juan:

> each wreath of smoke
> Appeared to him but as the magic vapour
> Of some alchymic furnace, from whence broke
> The wealth of worlds (a wealth of tax and paper):
> The gloomy clouds, which o'er it as a yoke
> Are bowed, and put the sun out like a taper,
> Were nothing but the natural atmosphere . . .

> (*DJ* X, st. 83)

The natural atmosphere, we might add, arising as effluvia of unnatural exercises.

In fairness to Pope, though, he seems to have entertained, at the last, some speculative notion of the ironies that radically threatened the Grand Tour. Mack gives a summary of two poems Pope contemplated without ever putting on to paper: 1) Mischiefs of Arbitrary Power, and 2) The Folly of Ambition. The first of these involves what could well have been a detail of a Grand Tour Panorama: a thriving classico-pastoral community on Aetna or Vesuvius, but a sudden annihilating eruption occurs. Such an ironic destruction has a Romantic smack, and the Romantic association is even stronger in 'The Folly', whose simple scene offers a shepherd in a desert landscape marked only by a heap of stones – the remnant of Blenheim and all that commemorates Marlborough, 'The deliverer of Europe'. This poem would have anticipated 'Ozymandias', and could have chimed with *Childe Harold*.

We cannot know how Pope would have articulated either poem, and should not begin to wonder if the great Augustan was turning into a pre-Romantic in his old age, as Wordsworth turned into a veritable Victorian. Pope may just have been competing with Thomson, in the field of socialised nature writing. If it is tempting to think he is challenging the teleological confidence of his earlier scattered invocations of the Grand Tour, it is realistic to see the poems-in-pectore as fresh instances of teaching how to think right with poetry.

For Pope's was, at least as radically as Keats's, a life dedicated to being a poet, and being – like the later Eliot – worthy poet in terms both of admirable utterance and of admirable effect. That excellence may generate the sharpest contrast between Pope and Byron, for Byron always wanted to be other and more than a poet. Pope's excellence springs from an extraordinary, dynastic mating of philosophy and form in poetry. Byron's technical facility with established forms was scarcely inferior to Pope's but in his case it clashed with his psycho-political disposition to discontent. He declared, 'Whatever is, is,' not as a matter of total acceptance and impregnable peace, but as a defiance of people who tried to shape actualities to suit pet, or pat theories. Tension even persisted in his response to the act of writing itself. As his poetic earnings rolled in, he came to declare, '*I loves lucre*', but he could not see in poetry either a life or a livelihood, as Pope with careful cultivation did.

Both Byron and Pope, mercilessly perceptive and eloquent, exposed their times, but in contrasting ways. Pope sought to restore and compose his time. Byron moved to awaken and oppose his time. And in some way this approach freed and also drove Byron to delve into time, and not just the times. It is his penetration of and meditation on time that separates his treatment of the Grand Tour from Pope's, and that gives his poetry with its admixture of humility, opportunism and transcendence a richer if fuzzier image than Pope's, where Pope's with its superb compression and control is sharper and more serene. Even with something as cumbersome and ambitious as the Grand Tour, Pope remained the poet who 'stoop'd to truth and moralized [his] song'. And even with something as specific and busy as the Grand Tour, Byron could not get away from a poetry that expressed 'The Feeling of a former world – and a Future'.

9

Byron in Italy: the Return of Augustus

DONALD H. REIMAN

I

What qualities would identify a neo-Augustan English poet, were one to arise among us today? Would his or her writings be marked by extreme decorum and moderation? (How, then, can we class Swift or Samuel Butler as Augustan writers?) Would this new Augustan's works centre on timeless and universal problems, too abstracted to number the streaks of the tulip? (How, then, can we say that *The Rape of the Lock*, the Isaac Bickerstaff papers, or John Gay's *Trivia* are products of an Augustan sensibility?) Is Augustan poetry centrally marked by imitation of the forms and themes of an earlier era, as the Roman poets in the time of Caesar Augustus turned to the Greeks and as the English wits of Queen Anne's age turned to the age of Augustus himself? If so, how can *The Way of the World* by Congreve – one of the first English authors ever called an Augustan (by Goldsmith in *The Bee*) – and John Gay's *The Beggar's Opera* qualify as masterpieces of the English Augustan stage?[1]

In defining English Romanticism, we have gone beyond trying to enumerate a list of specific qualities that characterise all the Romantic writers and their works and we undertake, rather, to delineate the historical situation in which they found themselves, as liberals, more or less disillusioned by the excesses of the French Revolution and to analyse their confrontation of the philosophical problems – epistemological and ethical – that all shared as the result of their ambivalent reactions to the Enlightenment and the underlying structures of the scientific and industrial revolutions.[2] Just so, in defining the Augustan Age, we need to seek, not a list of qualities common to the writings of all the authors of a period, but a common set of mind and historical circumstances that fostered the development of this mind-set in certain sensibilities whose genius or talents as writers enabled them to define the spirit of their literary age. The central quality that distinguishes the leading writers of the Augustan Age, who began under the aegis of the Glorious Revolution of 1688 (and flourished as long as writers raised in its spirit maintained the values with which this watershed event imbued the psyches of a core of the most talented writers) is, I submit, a sense in the psyches of these writers that they speak for important communal values – that they are not prophets crying in the wilderness (as all the Romantics, of whatever political stripe, felt themselves to be much of the time), but rather that they and their writings possess a moral authority that ought to be recognised by all right-thinking people. Reassured by this sense of moral authority, they can confidently attack as egregious all actions and ideas that deviate from their standards of common sense and right reason, secure in the feeling that all *worthy* members of their audience will applaud the values that they promote and hold in derision the targets of their ridicule.

In the early days of the Roman imperium, the friendship of Caesar himself assured Virgil and Horace that they spoke for society writ large. In England, the religious and socio-economic conflicts of the seventeenth century had divided British society into so many warring factions that no such consensus or authority could be imagined. But after the Glorious Revolution of 1688, a neo-Augustan consensus began to emerge which, by the time of Queen Anne, had attained the assent of a collocation of major writers and their socially secure friends. These writers, whose middle-class origins and moral values had been welded to traditionalist – even aristocratic – tastes and prejudices, came to dominate the literary and social world of London, even though they were sometimes at odds with the reigning political powers.[3]

The death of Queen Anne (1714) led to the installation of the new Hanoverian regime that, backed by the hyper-Protestant commercial interests, was openly hostile to the Tory circle led by Harley (Earl of Oxford) and Bolingbroke who had given *éclat* to Swift and Pope. About the same time, the quarrel between Addison and Steele undercut the unified perspective of even those who did not fall from political grace. At this point there was a change of tone in the works of many of the British Augustans. Swift, shipped off to exile in Dublin, wrote ever more and more savage satires on a social and political ascendancy that he now viewed with the hostility of a political exile. Needless to say, his genius continued to burn brightly in *A Modest Proposal* and *Gulliver's Travels*. (It even illuminated so dull a subject as 'Wood's half-pence' in *The Drapier's Letters*.) But the easy Augustan assurance of *A Tale of a Tub* and *The Battle of the Books* was, in part, consumed by the anger of the frustrated outsider.

Even Pope, in the final edition of *The Dunciad* (1743), produced a vision of national disaster in the fourth book that takes on almost apocalyptic tones, as he damns most of the reigning forces in British society in a condemnation comparable perhaps, to Michelangelo's fresco of 'The Last Judgement' in the Sistine Chapel. In most of the poetry Pope wrote even after 1717, however, he did not abandon his tone of confident moral authority, for he enjoyed the advantage (so far as a capacity to accept political reversals was concerned) of being a non-juring Roman Catholic – and hence an outsider from the start. His personal hopes could not be dashed, as Swift's had been, by the Whig ascendancy, nor did rejection add personal pique to his nationalist, ethical, social, and doctrinal distaste for the Guelf Protestant Succession. Instead of raging or sniping in opposition, Pope continued to write poetry of assured moral superiority in the *Essay on Man* and his *Moral Epistles*; he also found a new voice of quiet but devastating irony by imitating Horatian satires. In his imitation of the First Epistle of the Second Book of Horace ('To Augustus'), he deftly impaled unheroic George II simply by praising him for the same qualities that Horace had regarded as the virtues in Caesar Augustus.[4] Pope had found a viewpoint with which all literate Britons, from low-church Protestants to non-juring Catholics, could agree, and he thereby recreated the common values of his social world, to the acclaim of almost all – except the immediate targets of his satire.

II

Latter-day poets who hoped to reclaim the authority of Pope and his contemporaries had great difficulty because they represented more limited perspectives in a society that was increasingly fragmented by social and political upheavals. William Gifford won widespread praise for *The Baviad* and *The Mæviad* but only by

attacking the most trivial sort of offenders and offences. To satirise
Robert Merry and the Della Cruscan poets for their sentimentality
and bad taste was akin to accusing some scurrilous tabloid newspaper of scandalmongering. All agreed with the judgement but the
widespread response was, 'So, what's new?' By the time Byron
took on the *Edinburgh Review* and the popular poets of his day in
English Bards and Scotch Reviewers, not only did he face a divided
nation in which his political and literary judgements were not
universally upheld, but even he – a Whig as early as his days at
Cambridge – actually disagreed with some of them. Many of those
people whom he singled out for special satire (including Tom
Moore, Francis Jeffrey, Walter Scott, and Lord Holland) were to
become his close friends and allies during the years of fame, while
many of those he praised – notably William Sotheby – plummeted
in his estimation.[5]

As I have recently argued at length in *Intervals of Inspiration*,
Byron's personal *mobilité* resulted initially from his inability to
accept himself as a valuable person. For reasons clearly adum-
brated by Peter J. Manning in *Byron and His Fictions*, each time that
Byron, in the early part of his career, succeeded in defining
himself, he soon afterward turned around to attack the elements of
that self-definition as they existed in others. In *Hours of Idleness*, for
example, he defined himself in terms of his Norman baronial
ancestors (in such poems as 'On Leaving Newstead Abbey' and
'Elegy on Newstead Abbey'), his Scottish heritage and breeding (in
'Lachin y Gair' and 'When I rov'd a young Highlander o'er the dark
heath'), and his Whig politics ('On the Death of Mr. Fox'). But
immediately after Henry Brougham's attack on the book in the
Edinburgh Review, Byron's sense of vulnerability provoked him not
only to attack the Scots (in both *English Bards and Scotch Reviewers*
and *The Curse of Minerva*) and the Holland House Whigs, but to
adopt as his poetic hero William Gifford, a shoemaker's apprentice
turned pimp and classical moralist who had picked as one of *his*
easy targets the crutches of crippled Mary Robinson ('Perdita').[6] In
this gesture, Byron once again flees from what he senses as a point
of weakness in himself, by praising as England's best moralist a
(crippled) poet who had made fun of the crutches of a crippled
woman.

Byron had several reasons to recoil from his identity. As Bryan
Waller Procter ('Barry Cornwall') remembered Byron at Harrow, he
had been nothing but 'a rough, curly-headed boy', 'with an iron

cramp on one of his feet, with loose corduroy trousers plentifully relieved by ink, and with fingernails bitten to the quick.'[7] Before this time, Byron had lived in obscure exile at Aberdeen – a lame provincial whose irresponsible drunken father had abused and abandoned his mother and himself, whose neurotic mother lavished on him equal portions of extravagant affection and abuse, and whose Calvinist nurse 'played tricks with his person'. After unexpectedly becoming heir to his great-uncle in the Byron barony, he entered unprepared into the patrician precincts of Harrow and Trinity College. Even after he had inherited his title, people continued to 'play tricks' with his body, making him wear a torturous shoe to straighten his foot and introducing him into the ways of the 'Greek love' that would prove an alternative outlet for his craving for affection.[8] But the sense that he was an outsider left him unable to assert his identity. In college and afterward, Byron felt even more distant from his central self whenever he participated in the youthful dissipations of the time, for his character had early been moulded – and this is the real mystery of Byron's life – by someone (perhaps an early nurse who read to him, or by a teacher at Aberdeen) who had taught him to look at life as meaningful and had encouraged him to aspire to honour, courage, and integrity.[9] His love affairs, more often than not, had the character of sentimental attachments rather than cynical exploitations, although – because he was so insecure in his personal identity – he was quick to accede to the *mores* of his peers by *pretending* to a callous worldliness.

From Byron's early maturity and through his 'years of fame' in England after the publication of both *English Bards* and the first cantos of *Childe Harold's Pilgrimage*, Byron continued to be the passive recipient of both insults (as when his kinsman the Earl of Carlisle failed to introduce him into the House of Lords) and adulation (as in Lady Caroline Lamb's mad pursuit of him). A round of experiences with his men-of-the-world acquaintances showed him to be (as his retrospective 'Detached Thoughts' testify) an outsider and passive observer of the Dandies, who included him in their dissipations. His active life centred on his reading and writing, by means of which he began to work through his psychological problems. His Mediterranean romances portray his Oedipal struggles against the ghost of his dead father through representations of conflicts between a younger outlaw-protagonist who challenges the authority of an older rival: the Giaour and Hassan in

The Giaour or Selim and Giaffir in *The Bride of Abydos* (both 1813),
Alp and Minotti in *The Siege of Corinth* or Hugo and Azo in *Parisina*
(both 1816). Each pair fight for the affection and allegiance of a
woman who is the wife or daughter of the older protagonist and
the sister or lover of the younger. In 1813–14, amidst this Oedipal
phase of his writing, Byron carried on a protracted and deeply
meaningful affair with his older half-sister Augusta Leigh. By
winning the total love of his father's daughter over the social
taboos of the patriarchal system and then covertly boasting of the
fact in these poems – as well as later in *Childe Harold*, Canto III, and
Manfred[10] – Byron seems to have exorcised the sense of inadequacy
that derived from his feelings of being unloved by his parents.

   At the same time, Byron's success as an author promised him a
surrogate family among the British readers whom he thus made his
confidants. But throughout his years in England, Byron felt the
split between his aristocratic prejudices, morals and associations,
on the one hand, and his basic disapproval of the corruption and
hypocrisy of the British establishment. His radical political incli-
nations – conceived and nourished, no doubt, during his early
years of isolation and poverty – forced him toward the reform
movements led by members of the middle class for whom he felt
only limited sympathy. (His enemy Henry Brougham was one of
these.) Their moralistic cant was even more objectionable to Byron
than was the patriotic cant of the Tories.[11]

                                   III

In 1816, when Byron's marriage failed and the accompanying
scandal drove him from England, he once more lost the sense of
social acceptance that had begun – because of the working-through
of his Oedipal conflicts, his popular acceptance as a poet, and the
growth and stability of his friendships with such more substantive
companions as Hobhouse, Kinnaird, Moore, and Murray – to
promise him psychic security. In Switzerland the efforts of the
Shelleys and Madame de Staël to restore his confidence bore fruit
in the rich produce of 1816, particularly in the final sections of the
Third Canto of *Childe Harold* and *The Prisoner of Chillon*. In Canto
the Third, Byron first asserts without reservation the power of
imaginative language, governed by moral choice, to create a *beau
idéal* that can represent his best and happiest moments and,

thereby, enable him to find community with those separated from him through space and time – notably, at the beginning and end, his infant daughter Ada.[12] In the later stanzas of the poem, inspired by the tour that he and Shelley took around Lake Geneva, Byron contrasts the creative spirit of Rousseau with the critical spirits of Voltaire and Gibbon. Throughout the canto, Byron names those whose lives he considers worthy of honour and remembrance: Rousseau, along with 'young, gallant Howard', who died at Waterloo; Harmodius, the Athenian tyrannicide; Marceau, military hero-martyr of the French Republic; and Julia Alpinula. Those whom he characterises as basically destructive – Hipparchus, Napoleon, Alexander, and, later, Voltaire and Gibbon – he purposely avoids naming, alluding to them by their activities or qualities.[13] Byron thus evokes a humanistic pantheon of imaginative, patriotic, or moral individuals – the noble living and the noble dead with whom he, like Wordsworth in Canto XI of *The Prelude*, can create 'one great society'.[14]

In Canto IV of *Childe Harold*, Byron continued this practice of naming only those persons whom he thinks worthy of emulation, though in this final canto he centres on poets and visual artists of Italy whom he praises as creators of the highest embodiment of humanistic values in their works that confront, even if they must ultimately yield to, the forces of entropy that Shelley's Demogorgon abstracts as 'Fate, Time, Occasion, Chance, and Change', but which Byron images as personal and addresses in the stanzas beginning:

> Roll on, thou deep and dark blue Ocean – roll!
> Ten thousand fleets sweep over thee in vain;
> Man marks the earth with ruin, his control
> Stops with the shore . . .

(IV, st. 179)

Even here, Byron cannot ignore his need for personal community. When he left England in 1816, he had felt 'himself the most unfit / Of men to herd with Man'. But by the end of *Childe Harold*, Canto IV, after viewing the artistic creations of the great imaginative spirits of the past and studying the history of heroic communities – the Swiss who defeated the Burgundians under Charles the Bold and the Roman Republicans who shook off the disaster of Cannæ to vanquish Carthage, he finds hope for the renewal of the human ties he had forsworn. The address to Ocean at the end of *Childe Harold* does not totally swallow up Byron's preceding expressions of admiration for St Peter's and the Vatican, or for the Promethean spirit. Indeed, by the end of those stanzas, he has, in the humanistic tradition, sufficiently tamed Nature to write:

> And I have loved thee, Ocean! and my joy
> Of youthful sports was on thy breast to be
> Borne, like thy bubbles onward . . .
> ....
> For I was as it were a child of thee,
> And trusted to thy billows far and near,
> And laid my hand upon thy mane – as I do here.[15]

As Doucet Devin Fischer and Jerome J. McGann show from two perspectives in their essays and commentaries in Volumes VII and VIII of *Shelley and his Circle*,[16] Byron's earlier picture of Venetian life in *Beppo*, drawn from his personal relationships with Venetian men and women, reflected his commitment to the promiscuous medley of natural Italian social norms, in preference to the calculating formality – and the hypocrisy – of English society. As early as the spring of 1817, in the Fourth Canto of *Childe Harold* and, especially, in *The Lament of Tasso* (his first long poem in which the protagonist is a poet, rather than an aristocrat or man of action), Byron *began* to adopt the Italian aesthetic perspective in which the fine arts and *la bella figura* take precedence over both feudal military prowess and the financial power that had begun to replace it as a social ideal in England and France as they emerged from the Industrial Revolution.[17] After December 1819, when Byron gave up the 'miscellaneous harlotry' of his life at Venice for 'strictest adultery' in his last attachment to Countess Teresa Guiccioli, he found his living society. From his arrival at Ravenna on Christmas Eve of 1819 to take up his role as Teresa Guiccioli's *cavalier servente*, he was totally accepted and soon came to think of himself as a part of the Gamba family, with all its local attachments, customs, and traditional friendships and enmities.[18]

So long as Byron, a baron of militant Norman heritage, remained in England, his social class and friendships had left open to him a choice between only two political courses: (1) he could have joined other landed aristocrats and country squires (by this date, mainly

Whigs of the so-called 'Whig Connexion') in fighting a rearguard action that would preserve their political power and way of life for the present, though with the motto, 'after us, the deluge'; or (2) as one who laid claim to income from coalmines on his Rochdale estates and to friends with entrepreneurial ambitions – both Tories like Scott and Murray and Radicals like Douglas Kinnaird and John Cam Hobhouse – Byron could have allied himself with another group of nobles and with urban industrialists, merchants, bankers, and incipient bureaucrats in reforming Parliament and transferring control of the nation to the emerging capitalist plutocracy.[19] Neither choice was palatable to him. As a poor boy who always had felt like an outsider – and who, at Aberdeen, had doubtless imbibed some egalitarian principles along with the poetry of Robert Burns and the heritage of the Covenanters – he could not remain content as a part of a corrupt and repressive aristocracy. On the other hand, as one whose mother had filled him with stories about the glory of his Gordon forebears and who had inherited an ancient barony at an impressionable age, he found it difficult to surrender his aristocratic prejudices by accepting the value of paper money and credit as being greater than that of name, heritage, and personal honour. Thus, Byron, who talked many friends out of fighting duels, was personally quick to deliver or accept a challenge rather than suffer any imputation upon his courage or his honour.

In Italy, on the other hand, Byron did *not* face the choice between the Scylla of a decadent but obdurate aristocracy and the Charybdis of self-proclaimed reformers with equally self-serving plutocratic – or bureaucratic – values. Particularly in Romagna, where he settled with Teresa Gamba Guiccioli and her family, the landed gentry were actively involved in the revitalisation of a society long held captive by outside powers. All the aristocrats who were not beholden to the papal regime or fearful of the Austrian hegemony had welcomed and participated in the reorganisation of Italy after the French Revolution. Many, in fact, had served in the Italian military units that had fought the Austrians and Russians under the eagles of France.[20] And many – including the Gambas – were prominently involved in the activities of the Carbonari, who now hoped to drive out the Austrians and unseat clerical rule. In this setting, where aristocratic social values combined with liberal political goals, Byron could at last stop being a divided man. Bonded to a strongly unified, aristocratic Italian family, with a surrogate father and a younger brother in Counts Ruggero and Pietro Gamba, Byron finally achieved solidarity with the landed social class whose values had been inculcated by his family heritage and his schooling at Harrow and Cambridge, while at the same time remaining an advocate of progressive political and social change.

The psychic unity provided by this role as aristocratic revolutionary, an ideal embodied for men of Byron's generation by such figures as La Fayette and Kosciusko, was one he was to epitomise in his final journey to Greece. But in Italy, where the accepted form of political expression for generations of foreign domination had been through literature and the fine arts, he could also fulfil his destiny as a poet in perfect harmony with his civic duties. In Canto I of *Childe Harold*, he had mocked not only the British diplomats who had botched the negotiations at Cintra, but the leaders and even those common soldiers, British and French, who had fought and died at Albuera:

> Enough of Battle's minions! let them play
> Their game of lives, and barter breath for fame:
> ....
> Who strike, blest hirelings! for their country's good,
> And die, that living might have proved her shame;
> Perish'd, perchance, in some domestic feud,
> Or in a narrower sphere wild Rapine's path pursu'd.

> (I, st. 44)

Such sentiments betray Byron's sense of guilt at evading his familial heritage by failing to participate in his country's defence. But just as in such later works as *Marino Faliero* he explored the role of an aristocrat and ruler in the forefront of political renovation, so in *The Prophecy of Dante* and in other passages that praise Dante, Milton, and other Italian and British patriotic poets, Byron claims for himself the role of the artist as patriot and political activist, a tradition long sanctified in Italy, heralded in England by Shakespeare and Milton, and at this period being renewed in England under the aegis of Scott and Wordsworth.[21]

IV

Thus at Ravenna, Byron's public roles as lover, aristocrat, political reformer, champion of justice, and poet–prophet were at last united in conjunction with the psychic reintegration that Peter Manning has demonstrated. Byron's psychic growth and confidence evolved partly from his poetic genius and success, which also helped him win a woman as loyal and intelligent as Teresa Guiccioli. And the psychic stability engendered by his Italian sojourn, together with his distance from the divided loyalties of his place in British society, enabled him to achieve the humane and detached tone that helps give *Beppo*, *Don Juan*, and *The Vision of Judgment* their immortality. No longer defensive or petty in his satire, Byron matured in his own life and vision to the point where he could distinguish among the contemporary values that competed for his fealty, and he could recognise as primary, not the passing manners of the age, but the deeper human needs that both generate and give meaning to such arbitrary social patterns. The epic poet of the modern age, Byron could bridge the chasm between the values of feudal aristocracy, Enlightenment rationalism, and the egalitarian existentialism that was to emerge in the twentieth century because he embodied in himself the transmutation of values from one tradition to the others. In seeking personal values that bridged various aspects of his own psyche, he discovered the basis for a new Augustan stance in what he took to be the irrefutable virtue of positive, fundamental human emotions and in the sanctity of the primary ties of love and loyalty to family and friends, rather than in the ideologies that were competing for his allegiance. At the same time, loyalty to such primary relationships also underlay the values of the Gambas and their friends in Romagna, which Byron left only reluctantly months after the Gambas themselves had been exiled to Tuscany.[22]

Protected from both dogmatism and despair by a scepticism that allowed – or forced – him to distrust not only ideologies, but even his own distrust of them, Byron found in Western religious and literary traditions certain fundamental verities that develop from the nature of human beings as social animals: moral people do not betray their families or friends; they affirm positive impulses of love and altruism, whether or not these can be rationally or prudentially explained or justified; they honour courage and integrity, justice and mercy, in the actions of friends and 'enemies' alike (as these categories are defined by social or ideological tests). Above all, moral people resist becoming slaves either to the will of other human beings or to their own selfish desires.

Byron's basic, humane value-system, which he makes the fulcrum for the satire with which he intends to move the world, is embodied in the plot of *Don Juan*, as well as in the poet's commentary on characters and events. Young Juan, fundamentally an honest, idealistic, and loving person, is through a conventionally false education and the manipulations of his mother, led to fall in love with Donna Julia, the young wife of an old husband who is reputed to have been his mother's lover. When Juan and Julia are discovered, the real guilty parties separate them, driving Juan into exile, storm, and shipwreck, and into a struggle for survival that reveals both the heights and depths of human nature, freed from the trammels of social order – what Lear terms 'unaccomodated man'. The lesson taught is that human beings are neither naturally good nor irredeemably bad, but are moral agents who can either discipline themselves for the common good, or, if they fail to do so, can destroy both themselves and others.

On the Greek isle that Juan reaches, he is cared for and loved by Haidée who, in her innocent passion, forgets her love and duty to her father. When Lambro returns home, the island's festivities are seen from *his* point of view, not that of the young lovers, and his reaction of selling Juan into slavery, cruel as it is to Juan and Haidée, appears in the context of paternal love betrayed. Both the seraglio episode, in which Juan is ordered to love the Sultana, and his later stud service at the court of Catherine the Great of Russia are (as recent feminist critics have emphasised) inverted models of the normal situation of male dominance – scenes designed to show how women's feelings are ignored under the social constraints of love.[23] (That both episodes may, as Cecil Y. Lang has argued, reflect Byron's actual homosexual seduction by Ali Pacha simply authenticates Byron's experience and understanding of a woman's dilemma.)[24] But whereas these scenes show the dangers to human integrity of excessive passivity or feminine powerlessness, the intervening sections on the siege and sacking of Ismail by the Russians demonstrate the opposite danger of excessive *machismo*. In responding with natural courage against the armed foe, with respect toward the courageous but vanquished enemy, and with mercy toward the unarmed civilian population, Juan sets a personal standard of values against which to measure the brutalities of war. But Juan's period of powerless *serventismo* at the court of Catherine the Great saps his good nature, and so threatens to corrupt his interior moral code that he grows ill. Having tasted the pleasures and felt the pains of artificial social life from Seville to St Petersburg, he is now seasoned enough to join the Byronic narrator as an observer of the English social scene.

In the English cantos of *Don Juan*, Byron distances himself from the artificial values of the British society as he knew it, but he presents its forms and personalities in detailed particularity. These cantos are impressive in their authorial tone of confident and nondefensive description and analysis that brings each character – all constrained by artificial social values – under the judgement of the *natural* values shown earlier in the poem. In British society, almost everyone is a slave either to artificial conventions, or to 'Cash', or both (XII, st. 14). Even her frolic grace, the Duchess of Fitz-Fulke, merely follows the conventions of the Rakehell Club in her use of monkish garb to seduce Juan at the end of the Canto XVI. The characters in the English cantos both depict individuals whom Byron had known and represent types of the society. Within the poem as it stands, none is finally vindicated or condemned. Byron simply offers his readers a group portrait of his own class, as he had known it a few years earlier during the last period of their ascendancy, with sufficient distance to avoid both idealising and caricaturing. In contrast, Dickens twenty years later was to sketch the faded aristocracy from the outside as evil or self-indulgent, in Sir Mulberry Hawk, Lord Frederick Verisopht (*Nicholas Nickleby*), and Steerforth (*David Copperfield*). In *Don Juan*, on the other hand, the aristocrats are neither the desiccated tyrants of Jacobin reform tracts, nor the frivolous Barbarians of Carlyle's *Past and Present* and Arnold's *Culture and Anarchy*. They are human beings partly chained to traditions and conventions, but on the verge of being seduced into the service of a more insidious and ignoble master – hard cash. That Byron's portraits were fairly drawn from life few denied at the appearance of those late cantos and nobody doubts today.

Italian society's acceptance of Byron as he was, combined with his distance from the turmoil of British society, gave him the security to write truly Augustan satire and social analysis for the first time in his life, not only in *Don Juan*, but also (as Frederick L. Beaty reminds us[25]) in *The Blues, The Irish Avatar, The Age of Bronze*,

and *The Vision of Judgment*. Though the targets of the satire and the
stylistic forms of these works differ, Byron creates in each a tone
appropriate to the situation and wholly without bluster or defens-
iveness. He writes with confidence that his readers will follow his
argument and agree with his judgements. In short, he has become
an Augustan. In *The Vision of Judgment*, for example, Byron –
knowing (and intending) that he will be identified with Satan –
both elevates Satan and concedes his own limitations, just as the
poetic narrator concedes his sins and need for forgiveness. The
poem ends by granting the pathetic George III whatever share of
eternal bliss his blind soul can enjoy. Its conclusion, in which the
King practices the hundredth Psalm (which Byron's readers would
have known from childhood) neatly balances the rewards and
punishments of the monarch; having been used on earth as the
tool of prime ministers (now in Hell), he can only minimally enjoy
the fruits of Paradise. This poetic justice wins assent from readers
across the political spectrum who would have been offended had
Byron either consigned the King to Hell or pictured him as taking
full advantage of the mistake that let him into Heaven. Byron
achieves such masterstrokes of tone simply by treating his audience as a group of friends of different ideals and persuasions
whom he engages in conversation. Understanding the differences
among the values of various members in his audience, he tailors
his argument, not to their particular ideologies but to their common humanity and good sense, thereby achieving a sense of
community with the majority of his thinking readers and recreat-
ing the consensus necessary for Augustan instruction.

The confidence engendered in Byron by the Italians' acceptance
of him, and the aesthetic distance he attained through his removal
from England, enabled him to rise above the level of personal
insults that were being hurled back and forth between bourgeois
reformers and aristocratic reactionaries in the age of Peterloo, the
trial of Queen Caroline, and afterward. Facing British society as he
faced his own friends and correspondents, with whom he was
candid about his own basic values, while remaining tolerant of
their diverse religious and political views, Byron could smile rather
than clench his teeth at his opponents, confident in the ultimate
good-sense and moral truth of his unvarnished humanistic ideals.
That sad smile, replacing the gloomy *Weltschmertz* of his 'years of
fame', marks Byron as the one Romantic who successfully took an
Augustan stance: by adopting the tone of Queen Anne's age,

when the poet's values were those of right-reason and the social norm, he was enabled not only to parallel its artistry, but also to embody in his *ottava rima* poems the humane values that come closest to creating a new social consensus in the twentieth century.[26]

Notes

1. Before writing this paper, I consulted a wide variety of authorities and studies, hoping to extract a meaningful working definition of Augustanism in England. Most agreed in a viewpoint (if not a formal definition) of English Augustanism that attributed to it some of the characteristics I have named. Other speakers at the Trinity College Conference recommended Howard D. Weinbrot's *Augustus Caesar in 'Augustan' England* (Princeton, NJ: Princeton University Press, 1978); when I read it, it told me that many specialised studies I had not consulted also held the same view of Augustanism as my original sources, but that, in fact, the so-called Augustans were *not* great admirers of Augustus, or even of Horace (as compared with Juvenal). Luckily, I need only reply that Byron admired both Horace (see his *Hints from Horace* and the references to Horace in his letters) and the values usually defined as Augustan – especially as exemplified in the poetry of Pope.

2. Both my views on Romanticism and the record of studies that influenced me can be found in my *Romantic Texts and Contexts* (Columbia: University of Missouri Press, 1987) and *Intervals of Inspiration: The Skeptical Tradition and the Psychology of Romanticism* (Greenwood, FL: Penkevill Publishing, 1988).

3. A fine, succinct account of this development appears in the work of one French critic whom few read nowadays: Louis Cazamian's 'Modern Times (1660–1932)' in Emile Legouis's and Cazamian's *A History of English Literature* (rev. ed.; London and Toronto: Dent, 1933).

4. In 1818, Byron identified himself with Augustus (*Byron's Letters and Journals*, ed. Leslie A. Marchand [London: John Murray, 1973–82; henceforth cited as '*Letters*'], VI, 9). In 1821, Byron stated his complex view of Augustus at length in his abortive attempt at an alphabetical listing of his opinions entitled 'My Dictionary', in which he calls Augustus 'a great Man. . . . But not one of *my* great men'; Byron goes on to exonerate him from having destroyed the Roman Republic: 'As to the retention of his power by Augustus – the thing was already settled. – If he had given it up – the Commonwealth was gone – the republic was past all resuscitation' (*Letters*, VIII, 106–7). Byron implies his admiration for Pope's 'Epistle to Augustus' to Lady Melbourne on 11 February 1814 (*Letters*, IV, 53–4).

5. Byron's attempt to find poets to praise in the first edition of *English Bards and Scotch Reviewers* carried him into some strange byways of

literary history. Besides Gifford, Campbell, and Crabbe, Byron lauded Hector MacNeill (a failed West India merchant turned Scottish poet), Martin Archer Shee (a painter), Henry Kirke White (son of a Nottingham butcher, whose reputation was made after his early death by Southey's edition of his *Remains*), Thomas Rodwell Wright, Percy Clinton Smythe (later Viscount Strangford), Byron's friend Francis Hodgson, and his ultimate enemy William Sotheby.

6. The offending lines were these: 'See Robinson forget her state, and move/ On crutches tow'rds the grave, to "Light o' Love"' (*The Baviad*, lines 27–8). Leigh Hunt, in both *The Feast of the Poets* (1814) and in the Preface to *Ultra-Crepidarius: A Satire on William Gifford* (1823) makes much of Gifford's cruelty – and the irony of his attack, considering Gifford's own background and physical condition.

7. Bryan Waller Procter (Barry Cornwall), *An Autobiographical Fragment and Biographical Notes* . . . (London: George Bell and Sons, 1877), p. 135. Procter dates this impression from 'about 1800, when he [Byron] was a scholar in Dr. Drury's house. . . .'

8. On this important subject, see Louis Crompton, *Byron and Greek Love* (Berkeley: University of California Press, 1985).

9. Perhaps also Byron's mother's tales glorifying Byron's Gordon forebears helped create the chivalric *beau idéal* that was probably reinforced by his early reading of such idealised historical biographies as Pierre de Bourdeille de Brantôme's *Vies des hommes illustres et grands capitaines français*. One of the many important desiderata in Byron studies is a book on the subject 'Byron and the Chivalric Ideal'; the research for this study might begin by tracking allusions in his early poetry and letters and then reading the books to which they probably refer; the study might end by comparing Cervantes' and Byron's ultimate reactions to that ideal.

10. Leslie A. Marchand, in *Byron: A Biography* (New York: Alfred A. Knopf, 1957), tells how the allusions to incest in *Manfred* were recognised and pointed out in *The Day and New Times* (II, 699); I reprint the version of that review that appeared in the *Gentleman's Magazine* in *The Romantics Reviewed* (New York: Garland, 1971); Part B, III, 1106–8).

11. In the entry on 'Augustus' in the abortive commonplace book Byron called 'My Dictionary', he concludes his thoughts on the death of the Roman republic and possible forms of government thus: 'As for democracy it is the worst of the whole – for *what is (in fact)* democracy? an Aristocracy of Blackguards' (*Letters*, VIII, 107).

12. 'Albeit my brow thou never should'st behold,/My voice shall with thy future visions blend,/And reach into thy heart, – when mine is cold . . . (III, st. 115). All quotations from Byron's poetry come from *Lord Byron: The Complete Poetical Works*, ed. Jerome J. McGann, (Oxford: Clarendon Press, 1980–), abbreviated *CPW*.

13. There was undoubtedly some classical precedent for this practice; compare Shelley on the reviewer in *Adonais*: 'The nameless worm would now itself disown' and 'Thou noteless blot on a remembered name!' (lines 319, 327).

14. *The Prelude* XI, 393. On the centrality of this concept and the passage embodying it to *The Prelude* – and to the Romantics generally – see *Intervals of Inspiration*, pp. 153–211 (see note 2).
15. On some interactions of philosophical naturalism and the humanistic tradition in British and American poetry of the nineteenth and twentieth centuries, see Reiman, 'A. R. Ammons: Ecological Naturalism and the Romantic Tradition', *Twentieth-Century Literature*, 31 (1985), 22–54.
16. *Shelley and his Circle*, VII–VIII, ed. Donald H. Reiman; Doucet Devin Fischer, Associate Editor; Jerome J. McGann and William St Clair, Contributing Editors (Cambridge, MA: Harvard University Press, 1986).
17. In 1784, William Cowper was shocked to find Handel, a mere artist, honoured in a concert at a church (see Cowper's *Letters*, ed. James King and Charles Ryskamp, II [Oxford: Clarendon Press, 1981], 254, 264–5). But in Italy, artists had been treated as heroes and saints since the Renaissance. As late as May 1819, Byron shows the effects of the British prejudice; though he could accept the Italian habit of honoring dead poets and painters, he commented unfavourably on the enthusiasm of the Venetians when Rossini came to open one of his operas: 'he was Shouted and Sonnetted and feasted – and immortalised much more than either of the Emperors. – . . . Think of a people frantic for a fiddler – or at least an inspirer of fiddles. – I doubt they will do much in the Liberty line' (*Letters*, VI, 132).
18. For the details of Byron's Italian acculturation, see Doucet Devin Fischer's two essays in *Shelley and his Circle*: '"Countesses and Cobblers' Wives": Byron's Venetian Mistresses' (VII, 163–214) and 'Countess Guiccioli's Byron' (VII, 373–487), as well as commentaries to the various letters and documents on which those essays are based.
19. On Hobhouse as a Whig politician, see Robert E. Zegger, *John Cam Hobhouse: A Political Life, 1819–1852* (Columbia: University of Missouri Press, 1973); on the Kinnaird family's transition from Norman–Scottish lairds to London bankers, see *Shelley and his Circle*, VIII, 949–62.
20. Count Alessandro Guiccioli himself had held posts under the French and Antonio Lega Zambelli, first Count Guiccioli's *segretario* and then Byron's steward, had also held various offices under the French. Dr Tommaso Rima, Teresa Guiccioli's physician, and Count Cristoforo Ferri, Teresa's first lover (the summer before she met Byron), had served with the French armies (see their biographies *via* the index to *Shelley and his Circle*, VIII).
21. Of course, Byron played the role, not as Wordsworth and Scott were doing in their support of the *status quo*, but in opposition, as Dante was in exile from Firenze and as Milton, the republican, was during the Restoration. I treat the progression of Byron's feelings toward Great Britain and his *rapprochement* with the Scots and the English in a companion to this paper entitled 'Byron in Italy: The Uses of Refamiliarization', delivered on 8 October 1988 to the bicentennial

198   *Byron: Augustan and Romantic*

conference on Byron held at Hofstra University, Hempstead, New York.

22. Byron's dilatory reluctance to leave the Palazzo Guiccioli in Ravenna after the exile of Teresa Guiccioli and the Gambas has never been satisfactorily explained, but psychologically, I believe, it can be explained by his desire not to be forced into exile again from his recently-adopted home.

23. See Katherine Kernberger, 'Power and Sex: The Implications of Role Reversal in Catherine's Russia', *Byron Journal*, 8 (1980), 42–9; and Susan Wolfson, '"Their She Condition": Cross-Dressing and the Politics of Gender in *Don Juan*', *ELH*, 54 (1987), 585–617.

24. Lang, 'Narcissus Jilted: Byron, *Don Juan*, and the Biographical Imperative', in *Historical Studies and Literary Criticism*, ed. Jerome J. McGann, (Madison: University of Wisconsin Press, 1985), pp. 143–79.

25. Beaty's *Byron the Satirist* (DeKalb: Northern Illinois University Press, 1985) is the concise but comprehensive study of this aspect of Byron's career that was long awaited – perfect for both the teacher and the student preparing to confront any of Byron's satirical poems.

26. On Byron as the central figure of the Romantic movement and as the epic poet who bridged the chasm between the Enlightenment and the twentieth century, see 'Byron and the "Other"', the final chapter in my *Intervals of Inspiration* (note 2).

10

Don Juan Transformed

ANNE BARTON

On 20 January 1822, Byron finished *Werner, or the Inheritance*. It was the fifth in the series of verse dramas to which he had devoted himself since completing Canto V of *Don Juan* in November 1820. He was still bound (or so he pretended) to the promise, extracted from him by Teresa Guiccioli in summer 1821 that *Don Juan* would not be continued beyond Canto V. A few days later, however, probably while Mary Shelley was still labouring over the fair copy of *Werner* that would be despatched to Moore on 29 January, Byron began in secret to write Canto VI, resuming *Don Juan* where he had left off – in the seraglio of the Sultan at Constantinople – more than a year before. The end of Canto V had been a shameless cliff-hanger, with Juan in female dress attracting unwanted attentions from the Sultan, his own ultimate reaction to the Sultaness's passionate advances, his loyalty to Haidée, and indeed his life, all in question. To pick up his poem again at the midpoint of an episode so exciting ought for Byron to have been easy. Yet, as Jerome McGann has discovered (unmasking Byron's own attempts to falsify the chronology), it was to take him an uncharacteristically long time, well over two months, to complete Canto VI.[1]

There were a number of reasons, all of them unpleasant, why Byron might have found it difficult to concentrate on *Don Juan* in the early months of 1822. 'Since the beginning of the year', he wrote to Kinnaird in mid-July, 'one displeasure has followed another in regular succession'.[2] By that time, he had the death of Shelley and his own subsequent illness to add to the list. But the spring had been bad enough, troubled as it was by the continuing uproar over the publication of *Cain*, the death of Lady Byron's mother and ensuing legal complications, the skirmish with the dragoon Masi· at the city gates of Pisa and its unhappy consequences, followed (crushingly) on 20 April by the loss of his daughter Allegra. The need, moreover, to conceal Canto VI even from Shelley, to whom he was now accustomed to show his work as it was written, and who had established himself as the one genuinely appreciative reader of this particular poem, must have been frustrating. But Byron's attention was also distracted during this period by the claims of another and apparently very different literary project: *The Deformed Transformed*, that verse drama begun openly at the same time as his clandestine return to *Don Juan*, which was destined for the remainder of Byron's life to interweave itself sporadically with the greater work, like a kind of dark twin.

The inscription 'Pisa, Jy 1822', in Byron's hand, heads the holograph manuscript of 'The Deformed – a drama' now in the Bodleian.[3] (Byron seems not to have arrived at the present title until much later, when he was ready to publish the play.) This, as far as Shelley and the other members of the Pisan circle were concerned, was the poem occupying Byron in the last days of the month, immediately after the completion of *Werner*. Charles Robinson is correct, I believe, in his supposition that the episode Medwin remembered – Byron seeking Shelley's opinion of the 'Faustish kind of drama' he was writing, Shelley's judgement that it was a bad imitation of Goethe containing, in the bargain, two whole lines stolen from Southey, and Byron's instant consignment of the manuscript to the flames – occurred on or shortly after 6 February.[4] Robinson must also be right (reluctant though one is to associate Trelawny with truth) to accept the latter's indignant amendment, communicated to Murray in 1833, of Medwin's account. It was only half a sheet of *The Deformed Transformed*, Trelawny protested, written the night before, that Byron destroyed in public not, as Medwin had implied, a substantial play.

Trelawny's note to Murray goes on to insist that before this catastrophe Shelley had in fact seen and admired other pages of *The Deformed Transformed*, particularly that lyrical incantation which begins, in the published text, 'Beautiful shadow / Of Thetis' boy! / Who sleeps in the meadow / Whose grass grows o'er Troy', which he singled out as 'incomparable'.[5] It looks very much as though what Shelley reacted against in February was some false turn which he sensed the play to be taking either towards the end of its first scene or in the one that followed, a verdict in which Byron (however annoyed he was at the time) acquiesced. Certainly, the two offending lines from Southey's 'The Curse of Kehama' which Medwin quotes ('And water shall see thee, / And fear thee, and flee thee') are not only nowhere to be found in *The Deformed*

Transformed as printed; it is difficult to see where in that text they could conceivably find a place. As for Shelley's accusation that what Byron showed him on that particular morning was 'a bad imitation of "Faust"', it later provoked a puzzled rebuttal from Goethe himself: the Stranger of *The Deformed Transformed*, he told Eckerman in 1827, 'derives from my Mephistophiles', but the play 'is no imitation. Everything is absolutely original and new'.[6] He might have felt differently had he been able to read the sheet which Byron hurled into the fire.

When finally published, in February 1824, *The Deformed Transformed* was accompanied by an 'Advertisement' in which Byron graciously acknowledged his indebtedness to 'the *Faust* of the great Goethe', as well as to *The Three Brothers*, a minor English novel by Joshua Pickersgill. That was by no means the same as confessing to 'imitation'. Yet it seems quite plausible that in its early stages Byron's play might have begun to gravitate dangerously in the direction of Goethe's. The entire Pisan circle, after all, had been much taken up with *Faust* at the beginning of the year. Byron received his copy of Retsch's *Twenty-Six Outlines, Illustrative of Goethe's Tragedy of Faust, Engraved from the Originals by Henry Moses, and an Analysis of the Tragedy* – the best Murray could do in response to his request for a complete English translation – on 12 January, and immediately shared it with his friends. Shelley was transported by the engravings ('the only sort of translation', he feared, 'of which Faust is susceptible'),[7] yet the inadequacy of Retsch's version, scarcely much better than that other partial translation by Charles Anster which had reached Pisa earlier, soon impelled him to attempt, and read aloud to Byron, his own brilliant rendering of the *Walpurgisnacht* scene.

Shelley's recitation, on 14 January of his translation of certain scenes from Calderón's *El Magico Prodigioso*, together with his account of another play by Calderón, *El Purgatorio de San Patricio*, undoubtedly helped (as Robinson has argued) to shape Byron's handling of the *doppelgänger* theme in *The Deformed Transformed*. The spectre of Goethe's Mephistophilis, however, was the one Byron needed to tame, and not least because, unlike the satanic figures in Calderón, it had been walking about in his imagination for so long. They had their first encounter in 1813, by way of Mme de Stael's 'sorry French translation', as Byron later categorised it to Medwin.[8] Then, more consequentially, in August 1816 at Diodati, 'Monk' Lewis orally translated portions of *Faust* for Byron's benefit, an event which, without exactly explaining *Manfred*, nonetheless seems to have precipitated that work.

Manfred itself, Byron's first adult play, had been written during the interval between Cantos III and IV of *Childe Harold's Pilgrimage*. In this respect, it is like the five plays which extend from *Sardanapalus* (begun in January 1821) through *Werner* in the following year. It is also like *Marino Faliero*, the first of Byron's neo-classical experiments. All seven of these plays, from *Manfred* through *Werner*, came into being during a hiatus in the composition of one or the other of Byron's two major works: *Childe Harold* in the case of *Manfred*, *Don Juan* for the other six, although in the case of *Marino Faliero* the pause in question was the earlier and lesser one, lasting about ten months, which separates Cantos IV and V. *The Deformed Transformed*, however, is unique among Byron's dramas (and indeed in his work generally) by virtue of the fact that Byron began it just when he was turning *back* to *Don Juan* rather than away from it, and also because it remained in suspension throughout the rest of that long poem: shadowing it, in fact, for over two-thirds of its total length. Added to from time to time, proceeding by fits and starts, *The Deformed Transformed* was destined, like *Don Juan* itself, to reach its terminus only with Byron's death. It is (*Heaven and Earth* not excepted) his only unfinished play. Moreover, unlike the other works composed during the various interstices of *Don Juan* – *The Vision of Judgment*, *The Age of Bronze* and *The Island*, as well as the five other plays – it was held back from publication by its author for well over a year. Byron did not send the manuscript of *The Deformed Transformed* to Hunt until 21 May 1823, by which point he knew that he was going to Greece: an expedition from which, as he sensed from the start, he would never return.

After Byron's death, Mary Shelley scribbled a reflective note on the fly-leaf of her copy of *The Deformed Transformed*. 'This', she wrote, 'had long been a favourite subject with Lord Byron. I think that he mentioned it also in Switzerland. I copied it – he sending a portion of it at a time, as it was finished, to me. . . . 'I do not know how he meant to finish it; but he said himself that the whole conduct of the story was already conceived.'[9] Byron apparently sent the first portion to Mary in Albaro shortly before the end of October 1822.

She had only just completed the fair copy of Canto XI of *Don Juan*. Nevertheless, on 30 October she was writing enthusiastically that 'you could not have sent me a more agreeable task than to copy your drama, but I hope you intend to continue it, it is a great favourite of mine'.[10] Byron's own letter accompanying his draft has not survived. Judging, however, from Mary's response, it must have expressed some doubt as to whether he would be troubling her with any more of this play. More important, however, is the fact that Mary's description of the work as 'a great favourite of mine' implies prior acquaintance, lending support to Trelawny's claim that some of *The Deformed Transformed*, at least, had already been read and discussed by Shelley and those close to him early in 1822, before the awkward incident recorded by Medwin.

Byron probably did work on the play between that *débâcle* and his decision in late October to have a fair copy made of what had been achieved so far. The entry in his Journal for 18 May 1822 ('I have written little this year – but a good deal last. . . . I have begun one or two things since – but under some discouragement') must refer to *The Deformed Transformed* as well as to his resumption of *Don Juan*. His confession two days earlier, in a letter to Murray, that Allegra's death had 'driven me into some attempts at Composition – to hold off reality – but with no great success', may also point towards the play. There is one anomalous half-sheet of paper in the Bodleian manuscript which seems tantalising in relation to the Medwin/Trelawny story. It occurs, certainly, at an appropriate place: lines 586 to 602 of the second scene, after the lyric Shelley had thought 'incomparable', and in the middle of an altercation between Arnold and Byron's version of Mephistopheles. More clearly indicative, however, are the three impatient pen-strokes which appear midway through this scene, after 'a goodly rebel!' (line 175). These strongly suggest a break in composition, especially when combined with a change of paper type on the next page, where the play continues.

This, almost certainly, is the point Byron had reached by the end of October, when he had a fair copy made. The decision to do so produced an immediate renewal of interest. On 14 November he was sending Mary Shelley 'the completion of the *first* part – of the drama – as I think it may be as well to divide it – although *intended* to be *irregular* in all its branches'. Between 30 October and 14 November, then, he had picked up his play again, at the first entrance of the Bourbon, and completed its second scene. He had also come to the important conclusion that, like *Heaven and Earth*, it should be structured in parts rather than acts. The concluding section of Part I, scene 2 – Arnold and Caesar talking with the Bourbon and his entourage 'in the cool twilight' outside the walls of Rome the evening before the assault – is comparatively short. On the morning of Saturday, 16 November, Mary was able to tell Byron that she had now copied the whole manuscript, and also how much she preferred what she calls 'your new style' to 'your former *glorious* one'. The terms of praise are interestingly similar to those she was shortly to use of Canto XII of *Don Juan*, a section, she observed, with 'only touches of your *highest* style of poetry' but which she liked 'extremely'.[11] Even more provocative, however, was Mary's observation in her letter of 16 November that 'the "Eternal Scoffer" seems a favourite of yours. The Critics, as they used to make you a Childe Harold, Giaour and Lara all in one, will now make a compound of Satan and Caesar to form your proto-type . . .' She was teasing Byron, but the joke was shrewd.

   In *Manfred*, his first excursion into the territory of the Faust myth, Byron had displayed a singular lack of interest in creating any equivalent to Goethe's Mephistopheles. Arimanes, Prince of Earth and Air, although a dark sovereign, was in no sense a scoffer, a tempter, nor even a companion of the hero. His single appearance, in Act II, is brief. Manfred himself stands alone at the centre of the play, his own dupe and destroyer, a guilt-ridden Byronic hero of the kind familiar from the tales and *Childe Harold* who has somehow managed to find his way into Faust's study. The very word 'devil', together with its cognate forms, is wholly absent from the play, as are the names 'Satan' and 'Lucifer'. Byron was, of course, making a special effort in *Manfred* to devise what the narrator of *Don Juan* would call 'very handsome supernatural scenery' of a determinedly non-Christian kind. It is true, however, of most of Byron's work before *Don Juan* that it avoids mentioning the Great Antagonist, even in jest, by any of his traditional names. 'The Devil's Drive' of 1813, an unfinished satire written in con-scious imitation of Coleridge's 'The Devil's Walk' (which Byron erroneously believed to be the work of Porson) is a striking excep-tion. That poem, however, with its grotesque, essentially comic protagonist – complete not only with hoof but with regulation horns and tail, the connoisseur of 'homicides done in *Ragoût*' – necessarily reproduced the orthodox diabolic vocabulary of its model. In *Childe Harold*, by contrast, in the Tales, and in all the plays up to the point of *Werner*, the more indeterminate word 'demon' is the one for which Byron usually reaches when he means to evoke supernatural powers of a questionable kind.

This is true, perhaps surprisingly, even of *Cain*, set in a world which, although fallen, is still largely unprovided with a vocabulary of evil. Only in stage-directions and speech-prefixes does the dark spirit who lures Cain into a lesser version of his own rebellion have a name. There is nothing comic, either in appearance and behaviour, or in outlook, about Lucifer in this play. Quite a few readers, identifying his voice with Byron's own, resorted to cosmic imprecations based on the idea that his Lordship actually was the Devil incarnate: 'Thou worse than Satan in a serpent's form, / If thou provok'st the thunder – dread the storm. / Oh! that an angel's pow'r, or seraph's might, / Would hurl thee headlong!'.[12] Southey, without going quite as far as the anonymous author of 'A Layman's Epistle to a Certain Nobleman', nevertheless felt impelled to summon up Belial and Moloch in characterising the literary productions of Byron's 'satanic school'. Not, however, until *The Vision of Judgment*, sent to Murray on 4 October 1821 but not published for over a year, did Byron himself give prominence to the words 'Satan', 'Lucifer', 'devil' and 'diabolic'. Like 'The Devil's Drive', the poem in which they found a place was comic, but the suave aristocrat (like 'an old Castilian poor noble'), who parleys so courteously with the archangel Michael over the ultimate destination of George III's soul, bears little resemblance to his Gothic prototype of eight years before.

In joking with Byron about the likelihood that critics would cast him now as a compound of Satan and Caesar just as they had once seen in him a combination of Childe Harold, Lara and the Giaour, Mary Shelley discriminated astutely between the dark spirits of *Cain* and *The Vision of Judgment* on the one hand and, on the other, the Stranger of *The Deformed Transformed*. Caesar, as the Stranger calls himself after the transformation scene,[13] not only claims to possess 'ten thousand names', he equivocates with Arnold – and with the reader – about his diabolic identity. This, although strongly suggested throughout, is never, as it was with the Stranger's predecessors, clear-cut. The word 'devil' appears frequently in *The Deformed Transformed*, running side by side with 'demon', Byron's earlier preference. As one might expect, it clusters about the person of the Stranger, but it does so in ways that are speculative rather than conclusive. The Devil's traditional characteristics, moreover, appear to be indistinguishable from those of large sections of the human race.

That Arnold and Caesar represent warring halves of a single personality has long been recognised. Because the latter perversely insists upon inhabiting the deformed body Arnold has abandoned, Arnold in the godlike shape of Achilles is compelled to see his hideous former self 'for ever by you, as your shadow' (I, 1, 449). According to the bias of the critic, this shadow represents either the Byron for whom fame and adulation could never cancel out the childhood memory of his mother taunting him for his club foot, or Arnold's mortal limitations, his 'potential for self-disintegration and destruction'.[14] Byron's eye must also have been caught by that sentence in the introduction to Retsch's *Twenty-Six Outlines* which claims that 'the easiest clue to the moral part of this didactic fiction is, to consider Faust and Mephistophiles as *one* person, represented symbolically, only in a two-fold shape'.[15] The scene in which Mephistopheles actually disguises himself as Faust and misleads a young scholar was one of those translated in the volume. Shelley, moreover, had already discussed it with Byron back in December 1821. Byron must have had this Mephistophelean impersonation in the back of his mind when he made the devilish Stranger in *The Deformed Transformed* assume Arnold's cast-off shape. From this exchange, central to the play, other pairings were generated: Romulus and Remus, the light and dark pages Huon and Memnon, Eros and Anteros, and 'the mild twins – Gore and Glory' (II, 2, 12). More important, however, was Byron's recognition of another doubling, strange but resonant, linking the Faust story with the other great myth which was absorbing him at the time: that of Don Juan.

The perception of affinity between Faust and Don Juan, those two seekers after the Infinite, whose roads lead them from opposed directions into the same Hell, was a peculiarly nineteenth-century phenomenon. In 1829, five years after the publication of *The Deformed Transformed*, Christian Grabbe wove both stories together in a single play, *Don Juan und Faust*, in which the two men compete for possession of Donna Anna. In Grabbe's tragedy, Faust, with the help of the Devil, spirits Anna away from Rome on the day of her reluctant marriage to Don Octavio, and immures her in a magic castle high up on the slopes of Mt Blanc. She, however, has developed a secret passion for Don Juan, the sexual rather than the intellectual overreacher. She spurns Faust's love and, in his frustration, the magician kills her. Meanwhile, back in Rome, Don Juan has murdered both Don Octavio and Donna Anna's father. Faust, raging against his inability to reanimate Donna Anna, makes a frenzied reappearance at his rival's *palazzo*, where the Devil finds him and bears him off to perdition before making a quick re-entry as the statue in order to account for Don Juan.

Grabbe's drama relates to Byron's in a number of ways, some of them understandable, others almost uncanny. The German dramatist's English was excellent. He had been interested in Byron for some time and, in 1826, he purchased at Brönner's bookshop in Frankfurt a one-volume edition of the *Works*. Grabbe himself had been a premature baby. As an adult, he was given to describing himself bitterly as 'a dwarfish Crab' with 'crooked legs', a 'misbegotten' child.[16] It was predictable that when he opened Brönner's edition, his eye should light upon *The Deformed Transformed*, a late, previously unfamiliar play whose title appears, arrestingly, among the Table of Contents at the top of the righthand column. There can be little doubt of Byron's ultimate responsibility for the existence of *Don Juan und Faust*: for Grabbe's decision to conjoin the two myths, for the Roman setting, and (more surprisingly) for the central idea of a contention between the rake and the magician for possession of the same woman, a rivalry fatal to all three. It is quite extraordinary that Grabbe, who never saw that last, revealing section of *The Deformed Transformed* which was printed for the first time in 1901, let alone Byron's accompanying memorandum about how he meant to continue the story, should nonetheless have felt his way so perceptively in the direction of Byron's unwritten ending. Yet, for all the correspondences between the two plays, Byron's way of relating the Faust and Don Juan myths remains fundamentally different from Grabbe's, and more complex.

During the early stages of composition, before he realised that *Don Juan* was not going to turn out to be another poem of the same range and length as *Beppo*, Byron seems briefly to have entertained the idea of a narrator who also participated as a character in the action: in the form of that rather officious gentleman of Seville who tries unsuccessfully to interfere in the domestic difficulties of Don Jose and Donna Inez in Canto I, and has a pail of housemaid's water overturned on him by the young Juan as a reward for his pains. This pretence was soon abandoned: the narrator distancing himself from his fiction, to become a storyteller who comments, in his own person, upon events he openly fashions and controls. 'For my part', Byron declared in stanzas seven and eight of Canto XIII,

> I am but a mere spectator,
> And gaze where'er the palace or the hovel is,
> Much in the mode of Goethe's Mephistopheles;
>
> But neither love nor hate in much excess;
>   Though 'twas not once so. If I sneer sometimes,
> It is because I cannot well do less,
>   And now and then it also suits my rhymes.
> I should be very willing to redress
>   Men's wrongs, and rather check than punish crimes,
> Had not Cervantes in that too true tale
> Of Quixote, shown how all such efforts fail.

When Byron wrote those lines, on or around 12 February 1823, he had just finished Part II of *The Deformed Transformed*. Mary Shelley received 'a few Scenes more of the drama before begun – for her transcriptive leisure', on 25 January (*L&J*, X, 90). It was the third and possibly the last section Byron asked her to copy, although not the last he was to write. Byron's return to this play, after an interval of two months, was almost certainly what prompted him in stanzas 8 and 9 of Canto XIII to describe himself as Goethe's Mephistopheles overseeing the progress of Don Juan. Yet it only made overt that confluence of the two myths with which Byron had been experimenting now for over a year.

The narrator of *Don Juan* is an unusual Mephistopheles, in that he manipulates his victim from a distance, fashioning but never himself entering Juan's story, never engaging in dialogue with him. In *The Deformed Transformed*, on the other hand, Byron forced that narrator to submerge himself in what gradually reveals itself to be another version of Juan's story, one in which he confronts the protagonist on his own level. Jerome McGann has argued persuasively for Canto VI of *Don Juan* as the turning-point of the entire poem.[17] From this canto onwards, it would be published by John Hunt as opposed to an increasingly apprehensive Murray. This was the moment at which Byron decided that he did, after all, have a plan for the rest of the work, even as (according to Mary Shelley) he did for *The Deformed Transformed*, although in both cases some of the details remained hazy. He also committed himself to a belief in its serious political and moral content.

In general, the action of Byron's play lags behind that of *Don Juan*. By February, Juan had already been launched into London's 'great world'. Arnold, on the other hand, was living through something his twin had already experienced: the taking and sack of a great city. It is part of the odd cross-weaving of poem and play that, back in Canto VIII of *Don Juan*, written some six months earlier, Byron should have allowed Arnold to make a brief, proleptic appearance at the siege of Ismail, in stanza 110. That Tartar Khan who resists so heroically in the last hours of the doomed city sees his five sons cut down, one by one, around him:

> The fifth, who by a Christian mother nourished,
>   Had been neglected, ill-used, and what not,
> Because deformed, yet died all game and bottom,
>   To save a sire who blushed that he begot him.

'Because a hunchback' Byron had written originally. He crossed the word out, but the connection with the hunchback Arnold, whose own mother detests him for his 'hump, and lump, and clod of ugliness' (I, 1, 425), is doubly affirmed.

In *The Deformed Transformed*, Arnold in the superb form of Achilles is the assailant rather than the defender of a city. Consumed, like Juan, with 'the thirst / Of Glory' (VIII, st. 52) he fights with unthinking courage once the battle has begun. Like Juan again, he is among the first to scale the walls, having forgotten his earlier tremor of doubt as to just why he should be hacking and hewing, lopping and maiming, other human beings who are merely trying to defend their homes and families from destruction. Where Juan, however, had been accompanied through the carnage of Ismail by Johnson – a hardened mercenary soldier, even less reflective than Juan and wholly committed to warfare as a profession – Arnold finds himself rampaging through Rome beside a companion whose sardonic, running commentary on human ignorance and folly, on mercenary soldiers, militarism, 'Gore and Glory', and those 'blood-hounds' men call kings, is that of the narrator of *Don Juan*. 'And what dost thou so idly?', Arnold asks this mocking onlooker, irritably, at one point: 'Why dost not strike?' 'Your old philosophers', Caesar replies, 'Beheld mankind, as mere spectators of / The Olympic games' (II, 2, 55–7). This spectator, however, of games far bloodier and more distasteful than those of ancient Greece, observes from within the arena itself. A satirist, anatomising what he cannot check, he sneers at what he sees because (in the words of the narrator of *Don Juan*), he 'cannot well do less'.

   This was the third time Byron had depicted, with indignation, the senseless destruction of a noble city. As with Corinth and Ismail before, he took great pains to establish his historical facts. From the autobiography of Benvenuto Cellini he took the idea that the bullet which struck down Charles of Bourbon, the play's Suwarrow, was fired by the artist/soldier, Cellini himself. He also read widely in other contemporary and subsequent accounts of various kinds, even including popular songs of the period, before beginning to write. The sack of Rome in 1527, however, the work of a rabble of German, Spanish, and Italian mercenary soldiers in the pay of Charles V, was bound to register as a horror and desecration greater than the previous two, and not only because of the atrocities Byron found recorded in his sources. His own visit to Rome, in 1817, had provided him with one of the most intense imaginative experiences of his entire life. 'The Niobe of nations . . . my country, city of the soul', heartrending in her present desolation and decay, but still overwhelming, Rome was for Byron the emotional culmination of Childe Harold's entire pilgrimage, the last object of contemplation before Canto IV and the poem as a whole dissolved themselves in the formless, inhuman swing of the sea. Two visual images in particular burned themselves into his memory: the Colosseum and St Peter's: twin symbols of Rome's greatness as a classical and as a Christian city.

   The impulse which led Byron in *The Deformed Transformed* to reconstruct the violation of this place was related to the one which impelled him in the summer of 1822 to ask Moore for the return of the savage stanzas attacking the Duke of Wellington, written in 1819, which he had previously decided against printing in Canto III of *Don Juan*. These he now placed defiantly at the beginning of Canto IX, explaining to Moore that he wanted them read in juxtaposition with his account of what was done at Ismail by 'those butchers in large business, your mercenary soldiery . . .. With these things and these fellows', he added, 'it is necessary, in the present clash of philosophy and tyranny, to throw away the scabbard' (*DJ*, IX, 191). Although more remote in time, what Charles V did to Rome is, because of the centrality and special character of this city, more painful than the Empress Catherine's wanton destruction of Ismail, or the activities of the Grand Army of the Turks at Corinth. Even Charles of Bourbon, the leader of the Emperor's army, is troubled the night before the assault by a sense that he is about to commit a sacrilege. He commits it all the same. And this time, there are no jokes, of the kind Byron had permitted himself at Ismail and, before that, in 'The Devil's Drive', about women in the fallen city wondering 'wherefore the ravishing did not begin'. Olimpia menaced by the drunken soldiery is in no sense a comic figure. The place, moreover, in which she attempts to find a sanctuary from rape is St Peter's itself: the talismanic building of *Childe Harold* Canto IV, in the contemplation of whose interior space, Byron had declared, the human mind, 'expanded by the genius of the spot', must become 'enlighten'd', by virtue of its effort to comprehend the magnitude of its surroundings. This ennobling effect is lost, however, upon the imperial army which smashes its way into the basilica: men for whom religious bigotry, violence, greed and lust have superseded thought.

Almost all of *Don Juan* was real life, Byron claimed, either his own or that of people he knew. As he went on with the poem, and particularly in what Bernard Beatty has called 'the narrator's cantos' (X through XV, in which digression dwarfs and almost annihilates plot),[18] he seems to have felt increasingly impelled 'to turn back regards, / On what I've seen or ponder'd' (XIV, st. 11). *The Deformed Transformed* parallels this retrospective impulse in its own way: not so much by revisiting Byron's past experience – although the painful, childhood memory of his mother's insults does seem to surface here for the first time in his poetry – as in its assembly of ideas and preoccupations familiar from his own earlier writing. Normally scrupulous to a fault about historical fact, Byron must have decided to endow St Peter's in 1527 with the great Bramante dome it did not acquire until well after the sack, because it was important to him that this should be the same building as the one he had written about in Canto IV of *Childe Harold*. Not only does the play fuse the two distinct types of drama between which Byron had previously alternated – the 'metaphysical' and the historical – it is filled with poetic self-reference, verbal harkings-back to *Childe Harold*, 'The Prisoner of Chillon', *Manfred*, *The Siege of Corinth*, *Marino Faliero*, *Sardanapalus* and *Cain*. Most important of all, Byron's handling of the Stranger as artist, something without parallel in the original Pickersgill tale, seems consciously to reopen an issue crucial in Canto III of *Childe Harold*, where the narrator had also seen his hero as a doppelgänger, but of a very different kind:

> 'Tis to create, and in creating live
> A being more intense, that we endow
> With form our fancy, gaining as we give
> The life we image, even as I do now.
> What am I? Nothing; but not so art thou,
> Soul of my thought! with whom I traverse earth,
> Invisible but gazing . . .

> (st. 6)

In the letters she wrote to Byron after Shelley's death, Mary Shelley alludes on two occasions to one particular lyric in *The Deformed Transformed* as being, in her view, among the most beautiful of all his compositions.[19] Mary never specifies *which* lyric she means, obviously expecting Byron to know without having to be told and, indeed, there is only one plausible candidate: 'Beautiful shadow / Of Thetis' boy! / Who sleeps in the meadow . . .' – the wonderful incantation spoken by the Stranger as he fashions the shape Arnold's spirit is to inhabit. This, according to Trelawny, was the lyric Shelley himself had thought 'incomparable', but even if it had not been associated for Mary with her lost husband, it might have been expected to appeal to the author of *Frankenstein*. In forming a tangible likeness of Achilles, whose phantom form Arnold has chosen, but whose earthly body has dissolved long ago into dust, the Stranger consciously imitates God on the sixth day of Creation:

> From the red earth, like Adam,
> Thy likeness I shape,
> As the Being who made him,
> Whose actions I ape.

> (I, 1, 385–8)

The process, however, seems less like Mephistopheles' dubious rejuvenation of Faust in Goethe's 'Witches' Kitchen', let alone

Frankenstein's creation of a monster, than like the imaginative labours of Cellini, turning and shaping in his hands that wax model by means of which the godlike form of Perseus would be recovered from the past.

In the song Ariel sings to Ferdinand in *The Tempest*, his father's body is transmuted into the precious things of the sea: his bones into coral, his eyes to pearls. The Stranger takes the beautiful things of the earth – violets and hyacinths, birdsong, 'sunshiny water', and the veined marble of the rocks – and turns them into the eyes and hair, the voice, blood, limbs and heart of a resurrected Achilles. At the end, sunbeams 'awaken / This earth's animation! / 'Tis done! He hath taken / His stand in creation!' This is white magic, like that of Shakespeare's Prospero, not black, and indeed Byron had another shadowy but important pairing at the back of his mind when he was writing this opening scene. One of Lady Blessington's most acute observations about Byron concerned the intensely associative nature of his reading. Passing through what she calls 'the glowing alembic of his mind', the ideas and sentences of other authors customarily gave rise to 'chains of thought, the first idea serving as the original link on which the others were formed. – "Awake but one, and lo! what myriads rise!"'[20]

Lady Blessington's description was prompted, significantly, by a conversation she had with Byron about *The Deformed Transformed*, a text of which he apparently allowed her to read in the spring of 1823. It had been at about the time he was beginning that play, that Shelley translated for him the episode in Calderón's *El Magico Prodigioso* in which the Devil creates the illusion of a shipwreck and storm at sea. Calderón's Devil raises this storm as a means of introducing himself, a stranger and apparently sole survivor of the wreck, to the young magician Cyprian, whom he means to ensnare. Byron's Stranger also emerges from the water but the associations with which Byron surrounded him owe less, in fact, to Calderón than to Shakespeare's *Tempest*, the play Calderón's suggestive combination of an illusory storm, a shipwreck, a sorceror and the Devil had awakened in his imagination.

The parallel between Caliban, 'a savage and deformed slave', tormented for bringing his wood in slowly, and Arnold at the beginning of *The Deformed Transformed*, driven out of the house to chop wood for the family by whom he is ostracised, is obvious. Mary Shelley's nameless monster, secretly heaping up firewood for the cottage family from whom he hopes for love, is another link in Byron's associative chain. *Frankenstein*, however, is a less potent influence in this opening scene, less subtly pervasive, than Shakespeare's *Tempest*. I have written elsewhere about the shadowy evocation in Cantos II and III of *Don Juan* of that other island-paradigm of irascible father, shipwrecked lover and disobedient only daughter: a memory Byron uses to intensify the sadness of Haidée's story, which cannot end happily, as Miranda's had.[21] This is not at all the same as the ventriloquism – Byron himself adopting various Shakespearian roles – which so obsessed G. Wilson Knight, leading him to see *The Deformed Transformed* primarily as a working-out of Byron's so-called Richard III complex. Rather, *The Tempest* as a whole colours Part I of Byron's play rather as *Hamlet* colours Canto IX of *Don Juan*. Quotations from Shakespeare, half-remembered or precise, had always been a feature of Byron's poetry and prose. What emerges, however, in *Don Juan* is a tendency to invoke recognisably Shakespearean situations, without necessarily using their words, in order to complicate or add resonance to relationships or attitudes. This is a technique carried over into *The Deformed Transformed*. As they do in Canto IX, fragmentary verbal echoes may nudge at the reader's attention – Ariel's exultant freedom caught up in that of the black horses which bear away Arnold and Caesar ('merrily, merrily, never unsound'), or Caesar's weary reply to Arnold's innocent query, 'What, are there / *New* worlds?' 'To *you*' (I, 2, 10–11). Caesar, however, does not need to repeat any of Prospero's actual words when he accepts as his own Arnold's hideous, cast-off shape. They are there without being spoken: 'This thing of darkness I acknowledge mine'.

It is partly because of this system of unspoken allusion that the ending Byron had in mind for the play can, up to a point, be reconstructed. Although he told John Hunt on 21 May 1823 that he was sending him, through Kinnaird, '*two parts* completed of an odd sort of drama', the edition of *The Deformed Transformed* which Hunt published the following February, just before news reached England of Byron's death at Missolonghi, also included 82 lines of what Byron described in the Advertisement as the 'opening Chorus' of Part III, adding that 'The rest, perhaps, may appear hereafter'. These lines, presumably, together with the Advertisement itself, were written and despatched to England after 21 May. But Byron still retained – or more probably had yet to write – almost 90 lines more of his play, together with a scribbled memorandum indicating the direction in which it would proceed. These lines are, in effect, the equivalent of the fourteen stanzas (also not published until early in this century) of *Don Juan's* last, unfinished Canto XVII.

Lagging, as usual, behind his double in *Don Juan*, Arnold in the final scene of Part II had been left on the brink of that world of complex social and sexual relations in which Juan had been enmeshed ever since he reached London in Canto XI. Juan at the end of Canto VIII carried away with him from the smoking ruins of Ismail the Turkish child he rescued from death: Leila, all of whose friends, 'like the sad family of Hector, / Had perished in the field or by the wall' (VIII, st. 141). Arnold's equivalent action is to preserve the Roman maiden Olimpia from rape, and to take her away from her devastated city to a castle in the Apennines. That castle, surrounded, Byron specifies, 'by a wild but smiling country', may not look exactly like Norman Abbey. It was clearly going to resemble it in being the scene of an unsatisfactory marriage, sexual jealousy, and erotic intrigue. At its centre, moreover, there stands another form of Aurora Raby: an aloof, rather cold and very Catholic heiress.

Arnaud, the hero of Pickersgill's novel, had elected the beautiful form of Demetrius the Macedonian, not that of Achilles. By choosing Homer's hero, Arnold thoughtlessly perpetuated an old vulnerability, his imperfect foot. He also saddled himself with 'rank Thersites', Achilles' mocking follower in Shakespeare's *Troilus and Cressida*, under another name. Ranging by Arnold's side during the battle for Rome in Part II, Caesar came to sound more and more like Shakespeare's Thersites: 'Now, priest! now soldier! the two great professions, / Together by the ears and hearts! I have not / Seen a more comic pantomime since Titus / Took Jewry' (II, 3, 30–33). This particular Thersites, however, unlike his predecessors in Homer and Shakespeare, takes an extraordinary interest in the history of Western civilisation. He has been the fascinated, wry observer of an enormous human past stretching back, beyond the despoliation of Jerusalem by imperial Rome in the first century AD, to the act of fratricide by which Rome herself was founded and, further still, to Troy, the building of the pyramids, Babel, and Adam's Fall. The same mythical and historical territory over which, in *Don Juan*, the mind of the narrator ceaselessly ranges, the Stranger has actually traversed. His omniscience extends, moreover, into the future: not only to America and the scientific inventions of later epochs, but to the way Arnold's particular story is going to end.

Byron, as Mary Shelley reported, clearly did have the catastrophe of his play worked out from its opening scene. There, the Stranger assures an unheeding Arnold that they need no bond between them 'but your own will, no contract save your deeds' (I, 1, 152). This intangible agreement, he intimates, will eventually be signed not in Arnold's blood, but in someone else's, and Arnold's own destruction will follow. In the memorandum published in 1901, Byron made it clear that he meant Olimpia, after her marriage to Arnold, to be attracted to Caesar, despite his distorted appearance, 'owing to the power of intellect', and that Arnold was to become jealous of his own repudiated form. Byron's note to himself goes no further than this, but in the section which follows Arnold, already agonisingly aware that Olimpia, coldly dutiful and patient, 'endures my Love – not meets it' (l. 52) is being taunted in his misery by Caesar. Byron must have intended Arnold, in a jealous fury, to kill Olimpia and then follow this act of violence with another in which, by striking down his mocking doppelgänger, he would in effect commit suicide, and be damned forever. Robinson was obviously right to detect the influence here of Calderón's *El Purgatorio di San Patricio*. Byron was also, however, building upon two other stories, both of them involving (as Calderón's play does not) the death of the woman over whom the hero and his double engage, and both clearly signalled in the text itself.

'Even so Achilles loved / Penthesilea', Caesar observes darkly near the end of Part II (2, 3, 144–5), as Arnold declares his passion for Olimpia. Achilles killed the Amazon Penthesilea, whom he loved. When Thersites mocked him in his grief, Achilles also killed Thersites. Byron must have had this murderous triangle in mind when he departed from Pickersgill by making Arnold choose the shape of Achilles. Early in February 1822, however, just when he was beginning to write *The Deformed Transformed*, Byron had also been involved in rehearsals for what turned out to be an abortive production of *Othello* by the members of the Pisan circle. He played Iago. And that, in what Byron completed of Part III, is the diabolic association Caesar invokes, in a newly social world, to succeed the mask of Thersites. 'You are grave', he tells Arnold, 'what have you on your spirit?' 'Nothing', Arnold snaps. To this disclaimer Caesar, infuriatingly, replies,

> How mortals lie by instinct! If you ask
> A disappointed courtier – What's the matter?
> 'Nothing' – an outshone Beauty what has made
> Her smooth brow crisp – 'Oh, nothing! – a young heir
> When his Sire has recover'd from the Gout,
> What ails him? 'Nothing!' or a Monarch who
> Has heard the truth, and looks imperial on it –
> What clouds his royal aspect? 'Nothing, Nothing!'
> Nothing – eternal nothing – of these nothings
> All are a lie – for all to them are much.

(24–34)

It might, the blank verse set aside, be the voice of the narrator in *Don Juan*, pondering the hypocrisies of London's social scene. In its dramatic context, the speech reads more ominously, reactivating Iago's deceitful 'Nothing, my lord, or if – I know not what' at the beginning of the temptation scene in *Othello*. From it there springs a crucial dialogue between Arnold and his tormentor in which Byron originally, as the manuscript reveals, found himself allowing Arnold to respond to Caesar's accusation of jealousy at line 69 with Othello's disclaimer: 'Not a jot'.[22] He hastily crossed out Shakespeare's words, replacing them with the neutral 'And of whom?'. Yet disjointed fragments from the final scene of Shakespeare's play – 'There is a cause', 'this bright Olimpia – / This marvellous Virgin, is a marble matron – / An Idol, but a cold one to your heat / Promethean, and unkindled by your torch' – continued to crowd in.[23] Not only do they prefigure Olimpia's death but (dizzyingly yet appropriately in a play about doubles) they allow this Iago to corrupt Othello with Othello's own words.

Byron may not, as he insisted, have read Marlowe's *Dr Faustus* at the time he wrote *Manfred*. He certainly read it afterwards. Probably, at that time, he also made his way through the two parts of Marlowe's *Tamburlaine*. Olimpia's name, otherwise unaccounted for, is that of the woman the warrior Theridamas in that play plucks out of the sack of Balsera and, his love for her unrequited, finally kills. Unrequited love was not a problem for Byron himself

during most of his adult life – quite the contrary. His boyhood
rejection by Mary Chaworth, on the other hand, does seem to have
scarred him deeply. It is remembered in a number of poems, and
not least in *The Deformed Transformed*, alongside other painful
childhood memories. The man who wrote that play was, however,
now deeply conscious of his own ageing, and of the death of love.
In the plan for the continuation of *Don Juan* after Canto V that he
outlined to Medwin early in 1822, Byron said that he planned to
send Juan to England with 'a girl whom he shall have rescued
during one of his northern campaigns, who shall be in love with
him, and he not with her'.[24] In *The Deformed Transformed*, propheti-
cally, he reversed their roles.

   Byron once claimed half-jokingly that he did not know whether
to have Juan finish in Hell or in an unhappy marriage, not knowing
which was the worse fate of the two. In the poem as he left it,
Aurora Raby is the only woman among the guests assembled at
Norman Abbey who might conceivably become Juan's wife. She is
also the first in his whole career who seems indifferent to his
charms. For all her sympathetic, Shakespearian qualities, her
integrity and religious calm, it is not impossible that Aurora, once
married to Juan, might have metamorphosed into Annabella
Milbanke, Byron's own disastrously ill-chosen wife. Certainly,
Byron's association of her with the single religious image left
undefaced at Norman Abbey – 'in a higher niche, alone, but
crown'd, / The Virgin Mother of the God-born Child' (XIII, st. 61) –
becomes more disturbing when placed beside Caesar's description
of Olimpia as both 'a marvellous Virgin', 'An Idol', and a 'matron'
disconcertingly marmoreal and cold. Like Olimpia's, however,
Aurora's story remains unfinished. Byron went to Greece and
there (his life, as usual, uncannily entangled with his art) he
became the patron of the Turkish child Hatadje, threatened by the
brutality of the Greeks. He also fell passionately in love with Lukas
Chalandrutsanos and was forced to face the humiliating fact that
this love was not returned. Byron's last important poem – 'On This
Day I Complete My Thirty-Sixth Year', written at Missolonghi –
asks to be read as a dramatic monologue in which Byron wrestles
with the temptations of self-pity, with the pains of loving and not
being beloved, but is finally able to resolve them in a reaffirmation
of his commitment to Greece, and to a war in which, like Cellini
defending Rome from its attackers in *The Deformed Transformed*, he
might justify himself as an artist/soldier in freedom's cause. It was

in Byron's death in the Greek War of Independence that *Don Juan*
was finally transformed.

Notes

1. *Lord Byron. The Complete Poetical Works*, ed. Jerome J. McGann
   (Oxford, 1980–), V, pp. 714–16. All quotations from Byron's poems
   refer to this edition, with the exception of passages from *The Deformed
   Transformed*.
2. *Byron's Letters and Journals*, ed. Leslie A. Marchand (London,
   1973–81), IX, p. 185. All subsequent quotations from Byron's letters
   and journals refer to this edition, and are incorporated in the text.
3. The Lovelace–Byron Papers: 157=aafols. 196–234. I am grateful to
   the Earl of Lytton for permission to consult Byron's manuscript of
   'The Deformed', and to quote from it.
4. Charles E. Robinson, 'The Devil as Doppelgänger in *The Deformed
   Transformed*: The Sources and Meaning of Byron's Unfinished
   Drama', in *The Bulletin of the New York Public Library*, 74 (1970), pp. 182–3.
   For the full text of Trelawny's communication to Murray, see
   Medwin's Conversations of Lord Byron, ed. Ernest J. Lovell (Princeton,
   1966), note on p. 155.
5. In *The Works of Lord Byron: Poetry*, ed. Ernest Hartley Coleridge
   (London, 1901), V, p. 491, ll. 381–4.
6. E. M. Butler, *Byron and Goethe: Analysis of a Passion* (London, 1956),
   p. 189.
7. *The Letters of Percy Bysshe Shelley*, ed. Frederick L. Jones (Oxford,
   1964), II, p. 407 (letter 697).
8. *Medwin's Conversations*, p. 141.
9. Quoted by E. H. Coleridge in *The Works of Lord Byron: Poetry*, V,
   p. 474.
10. *The Letters of Mary Wollstonecraft Shelley*, ed. Betty T. Bennett (Johns
    Hopkins, Baltimore, 1980), I, p. 285.
11. Ibid., pp. 289, 299.
12. 'A Layman's Epistle To A Certain Nobleman', quoted in *The Monthly
    Review* (March 1824), CIII, pp. 103, 321–4.
13. Byron was remembering 'the Stranger' in Pickersgill's novel, a
    mysterious and demonic chevalier revealed at the end to be Arnaud
    transformed. This novel (which Lady Blessington rightly called
    'remarkable') deserves a modern edition. Its influence on Byron went
    deeper than has been recognised, extending to far more than the
    transformation scene usually quoted in relation to *The Deformed
    Transformed*.
14. In addition to Robinson's article and subsequent book, *Byron and
    Shelley: The Eagle and Serpent Wreathed in Fight* (London, 1976), see the
    sections on *The Deformed Transformed* in John W. Ehrstine's *The
    Metaphysics of Byron: A Reading of the Plays* (The Hague–Paris, 1976),
    Bernard Blackstone's *Byron: A Survey* (London, 1974), Peter J.
    Manning's *Byron and His Fictions*, (Detroit, 1978), and the article by

220   *Byron: Augustan and Romantic*

Daniel P. Watkins, 'The Ideological Dimensions of Byron's *The Deformed Transformed*', in *Criticism*, 25 (1983), pp. 27–39.

15. F. A. M. Retsch, *A Series of Twenty-Six Outlines, Illustrative of Goethe's Tragedy of Faust, Engraved From the Originals by Henry Moses, and an Analysis of the Tragedy* (London, 1820).

16. For Grabbe's acquisition of the Brönner edition, see *Werke und Briefe*, ed. Alfred Bergmann, Gottinger Akademie Ausgabe, (Emsdetten, 1970), V, p. 165. Grabbe frequently referred to himself in his letters as 'misbegotten'. See also the bitter self-description in the final scene of his comedy *Scherz, Satire, Ironie und tiefere Bedeutung*. I am deeply grateful to Sheila Stern, who established these references for me.

17. Jerome McGann, 'The Book of Byron and the Book of a World', in *The Beauty of Inflections: Literary Investigations in Historical Method and Theory* (Oxford, 1985), pp. 264–76.

18. Bernard Beatty, *Byron's Don Juan* (London, 1985), *passim*.

19. *Letters*, pp. 299, 311.

20. *Lady Blessington's Conversations of Lord Byron*, ed. Ernest J. Lovell, Jr, (Princeton, 1969), p. 82.

21. See '*Don Juan* Reconsidered: The Haidée Episode', in *The Byron Journal*, No. 15 (1987), pp. 11–20.

22. Byron, as the holograph reveals, originally wrote 'Not a j...', crossing the phrase out before he completed its third word.

23. E. H. Coleridge's transcription of this last section is very inaccurate, in ways that matter. Byron wrote 'matron', not 'maid', in the passage quoted. The opening speech prefix should be 'Caesar', not 'Chorus'; Caesar says 'This' (not 'his') 'shape' at Coleridge's line 22; 'the woman' should be 'this woman' at line 93; and Byron's punctuation and capitalisation have frequently been obscured.

24. *Medwin's Conversations*, p. 165.

11

Byron's 'Wrong Revolutionary Poetical System' and Romanticism

HERMANN FISCHER

To talk of a system in connection with Romanticism is a risky undertaking. Of the many warnings that have been pronounced against any attempt to define Romanticism I am going to quote only the most drastic one: Paul Valéry is reported to have said that 'when a man undertook to define Romanticism he must have completely lost his mind'.

To talk of a system in connection with Byron and his poetry seems equally hazardous. When Leigh Hunt had once tried to defend the strange colloquial style of his *Story of Rimini* against Byron's harsh criticism, by maintaining that this style was 'a system – or upon system', Byron wrote to Moore: 'When a man talks of system, his case is hopeless'.[1]

Now the title of this paper is 'Byron's "Wrong Revolutionary Poetical System" and Romanticism', and I am conscious of the risk I am running in linking both Byron and Romanticism with any system whatsoever: I will either have lost my mind or be a hopeless case.

Most of you will, of course, have realised that the wording 'Byron's wrong revolutionary poetical system' is not a piece of critical arrogance on the part of the present speaker, but a quotation from Lord Byron himself. In a letter to John Murray of 15 September 1817 he wrote: 'With regard to poetry in general I am convinced the more I think of it – that . . . *all* of us – Scott – Southey – Wordsworth – Moore – Campbell – I – are all in the wrong – one as much as another – that we are upon a wrong revolutionary poetical system – or systems – not worth a damn in itself – . . . and that the present & next generations will finally be of this opinion.'

Strong words, indeed; and not to be taken less seriously when we find that Byron tried to mitigate them, after they had been divulged by Murray, in writing to Moore: 'I said, that . . . *all* of "us youth" were on a wrong tack. But I never said that we did not sail well. . . . The next generation (from the quantity and facility of imitation) will tumble and break their necks off our Pegasus, who runs away with us; but we keep the *saddle*, because we broke the rascal and can ride.'[2]

There were even moments when Byron denied that *'all* of "us youth" . . . I mean *all* (Lakers included) except the postscript of the Augustans' (meaning George Crabbe and 'Sam' Rogers) could be lumped together as poets or artists following the same 'system'. When Southey had cried out against Hunt's friends and their 'Epicurean system', Byron protested that the men attacked by Southey – i.e. the Whig section of 'all of "us youth"' – were 'men of the most opposite habits, tastes, and opinions in life and poetry . . . – Moore, Byron, Shelley, Hazlitt, Haydon, Leigh Hunt, Lamb – what resemblance do you find among all or any of these men? and how could any sort of system or plan be carried on, or attempted amongst them?'[3]

However, both the mitigation and the denial of what he had written in the first place were obviously defensive or protective manoeuvres and are therefore not to be taken at their face value. The fact remains that Byron had discerned a system, a common denominator, in the works of all those of his contemporaries who were not part of what he termed 'the postscript of the Augustans' – even in Scott, 'the Monarch of [his] Parnassus';[4] that he included himself in their number; and that – at least in tendency – he disapproved of what they were doing, while he was foreseeing still greater damage from their imitators in his and the next generation.

The purpose of my paper is to find out what system, or systems, Byron meant when he wrote that letter of 15 September 1817: what were its elements; with what kind of romanticism did he identify it (our modern notion of Romanticism or of a 'Romantic School' did not, of course, yet exist in England in Byron's days); and finally, the most important question: was Byron's aversion to that 'wrong system' the reaction of a reconfirmed classicist who, after having for some years 'absorbed and used the fever of Romanticism' – as W. J. Calvert has it[5] – proved that he did not really understand its enormous potential and historic necessity by choosing classical or long-discarded models for his further work: Pulci, Berni and

English Cavalier colloquialism for his poetry, the Greeks and Alfieri for his tragedies? Or were that critical recantation and that poetical conversion of Byron's Italian years rather a proof of Byron's foreknowledge of the consequences that would result from a literary culture based on romantic principles? Was Byron in his aesthetics a reactionary or almost a prophet?

My first step will be an investigation of all those features of the poetry of his contemporaries against which Byron expressed a marked distaste in his letters. Beginning with formal elements such as versification, style and genre, I shall go on to concepts of poetry and of poetic creation. This will lead on to the conclusions to which Byron came when he had taken up residence in Italy, and to the way in which these conclusions are reflected in his poetical and philosophical reorientation. In a final attempt to come to a deeper understanding of Byron's struggle with and affiliation to Romanticism (in the modern sense of the word) I shall try to show in what respects I think Byron can be seen as a prophet of certain after-effects of Romanticism which have been operative right into our century.

What did Byron think was wrong with that 'wrong revolutionary system'?

It certainly had to do with *metre*.

To save time I spare you the many technical details about versification which are to be found in Byron's letters. Here is a brief summary of the results:

1 Writing poetry meant to him 'rhyming'. Apart from his plays written in the Alfieri style almost all his work is written in rhyme. Blank verse was uncongenial to him.[6]

2 He preferred strict and even difficult verse forms and rhyme schemes which help the poet to organise the language rhetorically and intellectually and may even further his conception of thoughts. But he would often sacrifice this predilection to other considerations such as originality or variety,[7] appropriateness for the chosen genre, suitability for the subject-matter, agreement with the dynamic drive of impassioned utterance or the excitement of 'fine wild poems' such as Coleridge's *Christabel*;[8] or simply impatience with 'the minor matters of verse writing', with a striving for constant harmoniousness and 'all that sort of thing'.[9] He did not consider writing poetry a matter of the first importance, and he did not think that polishing his 'rugged'

verse for a public 'who would read such things' as his metrical romances was worth his while.[10]

3   In spite of all these liberties his preference for *Childe Harold* and *English Bards and Scotch Reviewers*[11] rather than the verse romances, some of which he came to despise as 'exaggerated nonsense',[12] shows that he disapproved of the carelessness with which he himself and most of his contemporaries wrote verse. He was fully aware that a certain amount of resistance to the prevailing negligence in matters of versification was indicated, and his battle against William Bowles and others in the Pope controversy of 1820–21 as well as criticism of the Lake Poets,[13] the Cockneys around Leigh Hunt[14] and even Walter Scott[15] were no doubt partly prompted by his worries and personal conflicts pertaining to the metrical riot of the poets of his day.

One might thus almost surmise that the 'wrong revolutionary system' of the letter to Murray written in September 1817 might in fact have been that metrical riot; but although metre – and particularly the irregular narrative tetrameter introduced by Scott in imitation of Coleridge's *Christabel* metre – although metre is certainly one of the symptoms of the 'wrong system' Byron obviously meant something much larger than the irregular measures favoured by his 'romantic' brethren.

Was it *style*?

There again we find that Byron had an aversion to most of the stylistic idiosyncrasies of his time. Here are a few representative examples: Milman's Dramatic Poem *The Fall of Jerusalem* (1820) 'is terribly stilted and affected – with *"very, very"* – so soft and pamby'.[16] On the other hand Scott, Gifford and Moore 'are the only regulars . . . who have . . . no nonsense – no affectation . . . about their manner'[17] – those three indeed admitted more traditional rhetoric in their style than either the Lake Poets or the Cockneys, whose 'vulgarity' was particularly unpleasing to Byron. Leigh Hunt's *Story of Rimini*, for instance, seemed to him a 'trash of vulgar phrases tortured into compound barbarisms which he [Hunt] believes to be *old* English'.[18] One passage in a letter to Moore of 12 September 1821 about the 'vulgarity' of the new school of poetry which Southey had called the 'Epicurean'[19] and *Blackwood's Magazine* the 'Cockney School' of poetry[20] is too well-known to need quoting here in full. Byron is appalled by their 'shabby genteel . . . finery', their 'pettiness' and 'lack of gentlemanliness', and Professor Rutherford says rightly that such passages show Byron feeling his way 'towards a social analysis of tone'.[21]

The clear counterpart to the 'shabby-genteel' tone of the Cockneys, as far as style is concerned, was 'English, sterling genuine English' and Byron prided himself on having 'got so much left' of that.[22] It was obviously part of that 'gentlemanliness' which, he said, was 'only to be defined by examples – of those who have it and those who have it not'.[23]

Besides social there is also historical analysis. Byron tried several times to define the style (or tone or attitude) of the poets of his period by comparing it with particular styles in classical Greek and Latin literature.

When he congratulated Thomas Moore on the style of his *Lalla Rookh*, he classified it as 'poetry of the *Asiatic* kind – I mean Asiatic, as the Romans called "Asiatic oratory", and not because the scenery is Oriental' and said that 'such poetry must be tried by only one test, namely whether the passion was fully effective even if the moral was not quite exact'.[24] In making that comparison he of course identified the emotional and ornate style of Moore's and his own verse narratives with a famous fashion in Roman rhetoric: Asiatic oratory or Asianism was the opposite of the terse and concise Lacedaemonian style. (The difference is best-known to English people from Shakespeare's dramatic use of it in the stylistic opposition of Brutus's and Antony's speeches after Caesar's assassination in *Julius Caesar* III, 2). Byron's veneration for the Augustans and his – often very severe – criticism of contemporary poetry, including his own oriental tales, come very near to suggesting a historical system in which the poets of the Romantic period are the Alexandrians of modern history.[25] He would speak of the 'very uttermost decline and degradation of literature' which he felt he had himself helped to bring about as 'one of the builders of this Babel attended by a confusion of tongues'.[26] That Byron had held such opinions at least since 1817 appears from another comparison in a letter to Murray of 15 September of that year – the very letter in fact in which he condemned the 'wrong revolutionary poetical system'. After praising 'our Classics' and Pope, he there speaks of 'us of the lower Empire' and then writes: 'it is all Horace then, and Claudian now among us – and if I had to begin again – I would model myself accordingly'. Again in a letter to Murray of 25 January 1819 he speaks of the 'Claudians of the day' – Claudian, 375–404 AD, was born in Alexandria, lived in Rome, and throughout the Middle Ages was read as a model of rhetoric; he was often called 'the last poet of Rome'.

Another comparison was with the Italian mannerist Gianbattista Marino (1569–1625), whom Byron accused of having 'corrupted not merely the taste of Italy, but that of all Europe for nearly a century'.[27]

The words that most often turn up in Byron's letters when he gives vent to his indignation about contemporary poetry are *rant*, *unintelligible*, *mad*, and *self-love*. All these have also to do with style, but as they have their roots in other, more general 'Claudian' constituents of contemporary poetry which Byron disliked while he knew that he, too, had allowed them access to his poetry, it is best to proceed to a discussion of another one of these constituents: *genre*.

What Byron became particularly doubtful about when he had settled in Italy were the favourite genres of the period: 'German' drama, melodrama and, above all, the 'tale in verse'.

According to Coleridge's critique of Maturin's *Bertram*[28] German drama was nothing but a conglomeration of English elements: sentimentalism, sensationalism and medievalism of English pre-romantic and Gothic literature boiled up to an *olla podrida* of revolutionary tendency and bad taste. Although Byron – apart from *Werner* – never cultivated that genre and even called Maturin's second tragedy 'mad',[29] his early heroes were no doubt influenced by the storm and stress, guilt and rant, attractiveness and criminal energy of the protagonists of those plays, and he did not even abandon the type entirely when in 1821 he explained to Murray his new 'dramatic system' for the production of tragedy, which was based on the Greek tragedians and Alfieri and expressly not on the old English dramatists.[30]

Melodrama was in Byron's view little better than German drama. He was not a little stung when an anonymous oriental melodrama – *Nourjahad* – was ascribed to him by the *Morning Post*: 'I wonder what they will next inflict upon me. They cannot well sink beyond a Melodrama.'[31]

More than these dramatic genres, however, he mistrusted the 'romantic verse narrative' or 'metrical tale' – a genre in which he had gained, and was still gaining, unprecedented popularity. He had never thought very highly of his oriental romances and, by 1817, had even become allergic to the word 'tale' because of the many imitations of his stories in verse.[32] It is more than likely that

Byron's remarks about the 'wrong revolutionary system' of the poetry of his day were above all directed against the many examples of the 'tale in verse', that fashionable genre which, as Scott wrote in his *Introduction* to the first edition of his *Bridal of Triermain* (1813), in England had become synonymous with the term 'Romantic Poetry'. In 1820 Byron stormed against 'the deluge of flimsy and unintelligible romances imitated from Scott and myself who have both made the best of our bad materials and erroneous system'.[33]

Now it is true that the story in verse, which had become an equivalent to the expression 'Romantic Poetry' was part of what Byron called an 'erroneous poetical system'. But the meaning of that expression goes beyond such technical aspects of poetry as versification, style and genre. There can be no doubt that Byron counted *Manfred* among those of his works that followed that 'wrong revolutionary poetical system'. He called it 'a kind of poem in dialogue (in blank verse) or drama . . . of a very wild – metaphysical – and inexplicable kind . . . I have no great opinion of this piece of phantasy'.[34] Like Maturin's *Manuel* it was 'mad' – 'a drama as mad as Nat Lee's Bedlam tragedy – which was in 25 acts & some odd scenes'.[35] It was 'too much in my old style . . . I certainly am a devil of a mannerist – & must leave off'.[36] His assessment of *Cain* was not much different: 'It is in the Manfred metaphysical style, and full of some Titanic declamation', and Byron calls it 'A Mystery, according to the former Christian custom, and in honour of what it will probably remain to the reader', and he also calls it a 'Rhapsody'.[37]

What follows from all this and, of course, from similar opinions expressed in *English Bards, Hints from Horace, Detached Thoughts* and *Don Juan*, is that Byron for a long time wrote poetry in the style, tone and genres cherished by his 'romantic' contemporaries, but did so somewhat against his critical convictions. In other words: his practice as a poet was often not exactly in accord with his taste.

When we now try to sift his more general theories about poetry and the poet two things will become visible:

(a) the roots of the dilemma he found himself in; and
(b) that his so-called classicism had little of the reactionary or nostalgic, but was rather a clear-sighted analysis of present, and a prophetic (and pessimistic) foreboding of future developments in European literary culture.

Notwithstanding the self-criticism we have been quoting from his letters he did not despise all his 'romantic' works. He used to say that he preferred *Childe Harold* to his other poetry because it was his most original work.[38] He added, however, that *English Bards* (bating the malice) was his *best*.[39]

When in 1819 Murray and Ugo Foscolo had suggested to him that he should undertake 'a great work, an Epic poem', he refused, saying he hated tasks, life was too unsure to plan seven or eight years ahead, he knew better employment for the rest of his lifetime than 'sweating poetry'. Then he added: 'And works too! is Childe Harold nothing? you have so many *"divine"* poems, is it nothing to have written a *Human* one? without any of your worn-out machinery?'[40] Finally in 1821, when Byron had for quite a long time come to the conclusion that he had been 'on a wrong tack' with his 'romantic' work, he cast a melancholy look back on the period he had spent in Switzerland – on a period which, after all, was the time of the composition of *Childe Harold*, Canto III and *Manfred*: 'I was out of the way of hearing . . . either praise or censure, *and how I wrote then!*'[41]

The inference to be drawn from all this is that Byron certainly disowned the 'exaggerated nonsense' of some of his oriental romances and found new lines in his poetry after 1817, but that his repudiation of the 'wrong system' and its effects on metre, style, and genre by no means went so far as to make him despise his and his friends' best work written upon that system. That for quite a long time he was not happy with his new line – or lines, since his classical tragedies and his *ottava rima* poems have very little in common – is a different matter, but throws some additional light on his dilemma. In any case, he knew he had broken the Pegasus of romantic poetry and mostly kept the saddle,[42] and so had Scott and Moore, whatever riding accidents might have happened to their imitators and were going to happen to the 'romantic' poets of the next generation, who, he thought, 'must go back to the riding school and the manège, and learn to ride the "great horse"'.[43] By the 'great horse' he presumably means longer serious poems, higher subjects, a higher moral standard, a less irregular versification – in short a poetry whose style and tone of 'suppressed passion'[44] and whose verse technique does not run away with the feelings of the poet.[45]

The fact that Byron himself did not quite do what he advised the next generation to do is only one of his many inconsistencies – but it is a highly significant one. The essence of that advice is a return to classical standards, and in the dramatic works he wrote in Ravenna in 1820–21 – *Marino Faliero, Sardanapalus* and *The Two Foscari* – as well as in *The Prophecy of Dante*, he did try hard to pursue such a course, whereas he considered *Don Juan* – which was to turn out his way of by-passing the classic–romantic dilemma and conducting poetry into quite a different future – at least initially, as a mere experiment, something 'a little quietly facetious'.[46] He even used for it the same word as for his romantic tales: 'my Babel'[47] and was still doubtful about it in April 1820 when he gave Murray leave to 'put it all into the fire' because of the intense public opposition to it and because 'the new Cantos – (i.e. III and IV) – were *not* good'.[48] The new departure towards classicism in 1820–21, however, was something Byron had to give up after a few attempts, and it is easy to prove that neither were those works really classical nor could he have made them so: the nature and structure of his inspiration did not allow for such a retrograde move. Many passages in the letters permit us to see the reasons. However much he might strain after a poetry of 'suppressed passion'[49] and strict objectivity in drama,[50] however much he might strive to return to 'the riding school and the manège' – he was not made for such a way. His conviction was still that poetry was engendered by strong and violent emotion: 'I can never get people to understand that poetry is the expression of *excited passion* he told Moore;[51] and 'I have written from the fulness of my mind, from passion – from impulse . . .' he told Murray.[52] In other words, he could not but follow the two central premises of Romanticism: on the one hand the 'premises of feeling', as Walter Jackson Bate called them in 1946 in *From Classicism to Romanticism*[53]; M. H. Abrams spoke of the 'expressive theory', in *The Mirror and the Lamp*[54]; and on the other hand, closely, even if, in his case, unphilosophically linked with that, the subjectivism of the sentient individual. The words with which Byron sent Moore his *Journal* on 13 July 1820 might serve as a pregnant formula for his whole attitude as a poet: 'I wrote it with the fullest intention to be "faithful and true" in my narrative, but *not* impartial – no, by the Lord! I can't pretend to be that, while I feel.'

He was far from impartial even in the portrayal of his classical heroes (including Dante), and if he justified their guilty passions by appealing to Aristotle and Rymer, Milton and Shakespeare,[55] he was merely kidding himself: like his romantic heroes they were all expressing not only their but also his own 'excited passions'. His

attempt to return to classical habits of mimesis, decorum, correct-
ness, regularity and impersonality was bound to be an error, nay
almost a stillbirth, precisely because he had to be 'faithful and true'
to his own experience; for 'what is poetry, but the reflection of the
world?'[56] He would have liked, at an age when 'the stimuli of life'
had become indifferent to him (as he told Shelley in 1821), to return
to these classical standards which he had disrespected in his
romantic works, even if he had there endeavoured to hide his
confessional urge behind romantic poses and clichés; but he came
to realise that in doing so he would have had to be unfaithful to the
only two sources of poetry he knew: 'expression of *excited passion*'
and 'reflection of the world'.

Being a convinced agnostic and sceptic he was not in a position
to transfer his emotional egotism on to a higher level of idealism
and sublimity, as did the other major Romantics. Being a fundamentally sincere character he had to bring all the turmoil and
culpability of his troubled soul into his poetry.

It is no wonder that he had no patience with people of less
'tumultous passion' (that is how his tutor at Trinity described his
character).[57] He had no patience with John Keats's *'yielding
sensitiveness'*[58] nor with another young poet's 'sensibility' which
seemed to him 'to be an excuse for all kinds of discontent' as well
as a proof that the young man '[could] know nothing of life'. Such
people were in danger of becoming useless, as poets and as social
beings.[59] Much of Byron's indignation at the authors of 'romantic
poetry' presumably sprang from his realising that the strong
emotions with which they filled their poetical romances were
sham. He had learnt by experience that passion was not a continuous state of mind: 'there is no such thing as a life of passion
any more than a continuous earthquake, or an eternal fever', he
wrote to Moore on 5 July 1821. Passion could not be tapped at one's
convenience like a cask of wine; it resulted from the reactions of the
subjective mind to its encounters with reality; it was the upshot of
experience. Hence Byron's resentment when Campbell,
Wordsworth and Felicia Hemans had written romantic poetry
about countries they had never seen.[60] Hence his affirmation that
he could not continue *Childe Harold* 'unless on the spot'.[61] Hence
his refusal to comply with Tom Moore's request that he, Byron,
should write a dirge for a girl he had never known: 'I could not
write upon anything without some personal experience and foundation. . . . You have both in this case and if you had neither, you
have more imagination . . .'.[62]

Byron was a romantic emotionalist by nature, but he was also a scrupulous realist, and that is why, already in 1808 and again in 1821, he rebuffed anyone who compared him with Rousseau: 'I have no ambition to be like so illustrious a madman'[63] – again he uses the word 'mad' in connection with a romantic author or, rather, with an ancestor of Romanticism.

That he did not approve of a poetry that was produced by merely soliciting one's subjective imagination is testified by his well-known rude and unjust condemnation of Keats:[64] such poetry was a worthless fabrication, a 'Keats and Kangaroo *terra incognita*'[65] and Byron hated 'things *all fiction*'.[66] In his opinion neither the mere titillation of the private imagination nor an unfounded pouring forth of private emotions could serve as a substitute for real experience, and no one could better than Byron confirm Lilian R. Furst's contention that 'In practice the distinction between 'romantic' and 'realistic' is more fluid than critical theory would suggest.'[67]

An unwarranted poetic emotionalism meant to Byron 'self-love' or 'pride' – a self-importance that imposes itself on the readers. This notion pops up in passages about Southey[68] and Wordsworth[69] but also in his criticism of Leigh Hunt.[70] As a consequence he was also extremely antipathetic to contemporaries who advanced exaggerated claims for, or in, their poetry. 'Mr. Coleridge may console himself with the "fervour – the almost religious fervour" of his and Mr. Wordsworth's disciples as he calls it – if he means that as any proof of their merits, I will find him as much "fervour" in behalf of . . . Joanna Southcot [the mad Methodist prophetess] as ever gathered over his pages.'[71]

Byron was convinced that no modern author could possibly be *vates*, a man filled with a divinity, a prophetic poet, ενθουσιαστικός; he accordingly made fun of anyone whom he suspected of laying claim to that title and of such people's *'entusymusy'*.[72] Of his own poetry he would speak as of his 'vaticinations'[73] and he would jokingly assume for himself the title of *vates* when any trivial prediction he had made came true.[74] Again and again he made light of the business of writing poetry, by using a vocabulary belittling it – scribbling, rhyming, composing 'poeshie' or 'pomes'.

He believed in the decline and depravity of the poetry of his time as though it was an incontestable historical fact; and the living representatives of the craft were to him mere 'verse-writers – for we shall sink *poets*'.[75] Writing poetry was 'an *art*, or an *attribute*,

and not' – as Wordsworth proclaimed – *'a profession'*,[76] and for
Byron it was to become a mere 'habit', like riding, reading, bath-
ing, or travelling'.[77]

Being true to experience also meant being alert to the bustle and
variety, the pressures and needs of one's age, and this was something in which the majority of the other poets were most deficient.
Byron was annoyed by the Lakers, those 'mere talkers': 'They are a
set of the most despicable impostors – that is my opinion of them.
They know nothing of the world. . . . What sympathy have
this people with the spirit of this stirring age? . . . Look at their . . .
exquisite stuff, when they clap on sail, and aim at fancy.'[78] A man
could do better: 'No one should be a rhymer who could be any
thing better. And this is what annoys one, to see Scott and Moore,
and Campbell and Rogers, who might all have been agents and
leaders, now mere spectators'.[79] This irritation grew as time went
on. The whole community of the English poets, with the exception
of Gifford, Moore and – sometimes – Scott, became for him 'the
Garrison . . . there [is] always more or less of the author about them
– the pen peeping from behind the ear – & the thumbs a little inky
or so'.[80]

What renders these outbreaks something rather more serious
than the proverbial petulance of the *genus irritabile* is the fact that
Byron was increasingly inclined to see himself as another such
'verse-writer'. As early as 1815 and again in 1818 he showed that he
was worried about the poetical character in general. Poets were 'a
marked race' and 'an addiction to poetry [was] very generally the
result of "an uneasy mind in an uneasy body"'; if poets rarely went
mad that was because 'their insanity effervesc[ed] & evaporate[d]
into verse'.[81] These are quite modern pyschological interpretations
of the 'expressive' practice of the Romantic poets, and the latent
self-analysis of Byron's own poetical character contained in them
reveals him as both a Romantic poet and a prescient critic of the
Romantic poets' manner of producing poetry.

Towards the end of his Italian years he became more and more
dissatisfied with his existence as a poet. Poetry was ineffective –
'who was ever altered by a poem?'[82] The highest reward he had
ever got out of being a poet was the expression of gratitude he had
received from 'a girl . . . given over of a decline', who thanked him
without 'a word of cant or preachment . . . upon *any* opinions', for
his having 'contributed so highly to her existing pleasure'.[83] What
a significant romantic and yet down-to-earth reappearance of the
Horatian formula of the *prodesse aut delectare* of poetry!

'Great' poems were no longer possible, not within the 'wrong revolutionary system' of romantic inspiration, not even to Byron who, when encouraged by Murray, Ugo Foscolo or Shelley to write an epic,[84] would either confess his incapacity – 'I have not the inclination nor the power. As I grow older, the indifference – *not* to life, for we love it by instinct – but to the stimuli of life, increases'[85] – or plead the relative inconsequentiality of poetry in a period in which the political liberty of so many people and nations was at stake; when 'one's years [could] be better employed than in sweating poesy'.[86] Even his hard-earned conviction that with *Don Juan* he was creating a real work of art and – perhaps – earning the acknowledgement of future generations for having found a way out of the romantic dilemma[87] – even that conviction subsided after some time, while he yet wrote on – from 'habit'.[88] If you wanted to 'give the age some lights upon policy, poesy, biography, criticism, morality, theology, and all other *-ism*, *-ality*, and *-ology* whatsoever',[89] you might join forces with others and edit a progressive periodical or newspaper. If, however, you were not made for 'that there sort of thing', if you were fed up with English and disheartened by Italian politics, if you looked for a higher purpose in life, something nearer reality than 'scribbling' or 'sweating poetry' (even if that poetry was *Don Juan*) – then you went to Greece.

We have now studied in some detail the elements of the 'wrong revolutionary poetical system' which Byron criticised from 1817 onward with increasing vexation and self-criticism. That system is, as we found, identical with 'romantic poetry' as it was then understood and practised by Scott and others. It is mainly narrative, often sensational, exotic, or sentimental. It deals with emotions and is created out of the poet's subjective emotional reactions to his subject-matter. It puts wit and formal precision or design in the background in the interest of narrative content and continuity. It leads the reader away from the pressing problems of the day, sometimes into regions that have very little in common with empirical reality. It lacks the gentlemanliness of the much more controlled poetry of the neo-classical age as well as the genuine greatness of the classics or Milton. In seeking to appeal to all classes of readers it dispenses with that degree of literary culture which had made all poetry from Ben Jonson to Samuel Rogers an intellectual pleasure rather than a constant appeal to the feelings. It was thus, we may add, a typical product of that period – of the generation that lived after the French and in the Industrial

Revolution and had witnessed Napoleon's rise and fall and the subsequent restoration.

Byron had, for a number of reasons, contributed to the rise of this new poetry – he was, by his essential nature, his politics and his experience as a creative artist, predestined to be affected by the fashion. But his 'gentlemanliness' (in the most comprehensive sense) erected in him strong barriers against the lower manifestations of it while he failed – as the sceptic and realist he was – to understand the enormous potential contained in its higher achievements; that is, in the idealistic, or rather, transcendental and symbolistic offshoot of the spirit of the age of which we, and of which above all the Yale school of romantic criticism, tend to think when the term 'Romantic Poetry' is pronounced.

Byron's having one foot in classicism and one in romanticism explains many of his difficulties, indecisions and inconsistencies; but that should not cause us to disregard the fact that his eyes were capable of casting some very perceptive looks into the future. If he was not in a position to foresee the philosophical, ethical and aesthetic possibilities contained in the new poetry – he only gave it about twenty years[90] – he at least foresaw the damage that might arise, or was bound to arise, from the basic tenets of romantic poetry as he understood and practised it. In that respect he deserves to be called a prophet.

As regards poetic form he anticipated the consequences of the 'debauch'[91] that came into use in his time, as well as the probability of a later return to the 'riding school and the manège'. The latter prediction did in fact come true with Tennyson in England and with the Parnassiens and Symbolistes in France. As to the former, the disappearance of rhyme, metre and accepted conventions of rhetoric and stylistic decorum in much lyrical poetry of our century surely confirms that Byron's apprehensions relating to a poetry whose only warrant was anybody's subjective sensibility were justified. I leave it to the reader to decide in how far those disappearances are really a debauch, but Byron's complaint about the loss of gentlemanliness has much to do with them and it surely betrays a good insight into the sociology of taste.

(Modern pop poets in Germany have for some time 'sunk' the title of poet. They do not call themselves 'verse-writers', as Byron suggested, for they often do not really write in any distinguishable verse form; but they have assumed the honorific *Liedermacher*, 'song-makers', and gentlemanly they emphatically are not.)

Byron's remark that 'there is no such thing as a life of passion any more than a continuous earthquake or an eternal fever'[92] and that 'no poetry is *generally* good – only by fits & starts – & you are lucky to get a sparkle here & there'[93] was confirmed in his time by the Lake Poets' frequent laments for the loss of their imagination when the fits and starts of their enthusiasm left off. Byron's explicit application of that knowledge to the long poems of Virgil, Milton and Dryden in the same letter may be of doubtful historical value, since those poets did not depend on excited passion for their productions as did the Romantics; but it anticipates E. A. Poe's famous theory advanced in *The Poetic Principle*, by thirty years. In other words, Byron foresaw the death of the long poem.

Byron's conviction that poetry is the reflection of the world and the great importance he attached to factual experience – the importance of having lived in more than one world[94] – led him in the last six cantos of *Don Juan*, to the brink of the realistic social novel, the genre which was to supersede the long narrative in popular favour and which, in many respects, was to supersede literary Romanticism altogether.

If Byron was blind to the potential of idealistic Romantic thought, he nevertheless had a clear foreknowledge of the negative consequences of romantic subjectivity. He foresaw the increasing withdrawal of the poets from political and social reality: some of them, like Wordsworth, withdrew into a sphere of 'mystery & mysticism'[95] which prevented the majority of the public from understanding them, and yet continued to pontificate to a sect of admirers who followed their esoteric thoughts with 'almost religious fervour'. The exaggerated self-love of such overweening 'heads of the profession'[96] induced them to postulate for themselves a privileged position which to Byron seemed totally unwarranted by their social importance or utility. Although most of us will not now support this opinion about Wordsworth, we may yet grant Byron a certain prescience of the later results of that romantic attitude: on the one hand, the ivory tower, the solipsistic and self-contained poetry of Mallarmé or Valéry, their *paradis artificiels* and their refusal of any commitment to material reality: art as a profession becoming *l'art pour l'art*; on the other hand, the 'shabby-genteel' coteries of the literary *bohème*, or, still worse, the 'garrisons' of *literati* who will preach to the masses what is good for them – revolutionary changes of their consciousness and of the social order – while they themselves live apart from the workers in the ghetto of intellectuals and profit from the amenities the welfare-state provides for them. There are lots of them in my country, but an English play, Trevor Griffith's *The Party*, convinced me fourteen years ago that they are to be found in this country, too – those intellectuals who, instead of having 'lived in many worlds' like Byron, live only in one, and whose 'problem is not vision but commitment' as Griffith has his committed communist term it.

It is significant that Griffith uses for the characterisation of his protagonist, the Marxist TV producer whose 'Keats and Kangaroo *terra incognita*' is the revolution, the same unsavoury image as the one Byron had used to express his aversion to Keats's 'visionary Poetry': solitary masturbation.

One further symptom of the 'wrong poetical system' was the cultivation of one's despair or, as Byron said, people who use the word sensibility as 'an excuse for all kinds of discontent'.[97] It is still a very common practice today. Byron did not really indulge in it, though he had more reasons to be discontented than many of our modern sensitive pessimists. Both his psyche and the conditions of his existence, including the political situation, were a heavy burden, heavier than most present-day poets of despair have to bear, and his consciousness of Man's '*Geworfenheit*' (dereliction) was a genuine and an awful discovery and not just the adoption of a fashion. There obviously was a lot of excruciating experience behind the words he wrote to Moore on 28 October 1815: 'What is Hope? nothing but the paint on the face of Existence; the least touch of truth rubs it off, and then we see what a hollow-cheeked harlot we have got hold of.' His putting that experience into poetry in *Manfred* and *Cain* has an imprint of greatness that anticipates Heidegger, Sartre and Samuel Beckett. Even if that existentialist greatness is not quite borne out by Manfred's death and Cain's bewildered despair, it is confirmed by Byron's holding out in the midst of the absurdity of his existence and finding, or rather 'choosing' answers to both his poetical and his existential predicaments, answers which are also anticipatory of twentieth-century positions and great ones for that matter.

In *poetry* his answer was *Don Juan* – not only its social realism but also its 'postmodern' attitude, which a colleague of mine, Jürgen Schlaeger, has expressed in these words: '*Don Juan* is not an epic or anti-epic of the hero, nor is it a literary potpourri by an expatriated playboy; it is, rather, the epically furnished record of an early modern aesthetic consciousness. In the promiscuity of its meanings and modalities this consciousness presents itself as a kind of Don Juan of the established literary conventions. It seizes and uses them, leaving them violated and desecrated, but all the more available for use by others.'[98]

In *life* Byron's answer was Greece, his commitment to the cause of liberty, the risk and sacrifice of his existence for a worthy purpose. In this final act the elements of classical *virtus Romana* and of romantic enthusiasm seem to me to be heroically combined, and the fact that this kind of commitment and this kind of death can be seen as a prefiguration of the answer that many a despondent and bewildered intellectual of the twentieth century chose to give to the absurdity of existence confirms my conviction that Byron was a great anticipator of the best spirit of our time.

Notes

1. To Moore, 1 June 1818.
2. To Moore, 2 February 1818.
3. To Murray, 24 November 1818.
4. 'Postscript' etc.: To Moore, 2 February 1818; 'Monarch' etc.: *Journal*, 24 November 1813; see also 12 January 1821.
5. W. J. Calvert, *Byron: Romantic Paradox*, 2nd edn, (Chapel Hill, 1962), p. 61.
6. To Caroline Lamb, 1 May 1812.
7. See To Murray, 20 February 1816.
8. To Coleridge, 18 October 1815; To Murray, 30 September 1816.
9. To James Hogg, 24 March 1814; see also To Hodgson, 3 October 1810, To Lord Holland, 3 April 1813 and 17 November 1813, as well as the letter to Moore of 2 January 1814 with Dedication of *The Corsair*.
10. To Lord Holland, 3 April 1813 and 17 November 1813.
11. To Murray, 26 April 1814.
12. To Shelley, 20 May 1822; To Holland, 17 November 1813.
13. *English Bards and Scotch Reviewers*, ll. 235ff. and 211ff.; *Hints from Horace*, ll. 471ff.
14. To Moore, 1 June 1818.
15. See *Journal*, 12 January 1821, but see also *Hints from Horace*, ll. 407ff. and 415ff.
16. To Murray, 11 September 1820.
17. To Murray, 25 March 1817.
18. To Moore, 1 June 1818.
19. To Murray, 24 November 1818.
20. The articles 'On the Cockney School of Poetry' in *Blackwood's Magazine* appeared from October 1817 till August 1818.
21. A. Rutherford, *Byron: A Critical Study*, 3rd edn, 1965, p. 110.
22. To Murray, 11 September 1820.

23. Rutherford, loc. cit., see *Letters and Journals* V, pp. 551f.
24. To Moore, 22 June 1821.
25. See To Shelley, 20 May 1822 and To Murray, 11 September 1820 and 4 January 1821.
26. Rutherford, loc. cit.; see *Letters and Journals* V, p. 559.
27. 'Some Observations upon an Article in Blackwood's Magazine', 1819.
28. *Biographia Literaria*, Chapter XXIII.
29. To Murray, 14 June 1817; To Moore 10 July 1817.
30. To Murray, 4 January 1821.
31. *Journal*, 27 November 1813.
32. To Moore, 25 March 1817.
33. 'Some Observations . . .'.
34. To Murray, 15 February 1817.
35. To Murray, 3 March 1817.
36. To Murray, 9 March 1817.
37. To Moore, 19 September 1821.
38. To Murray, 26 April 1814.
39. Ibid.; see also To Kinnaird, 31 March 1817.
40. To Murray, 6 April (b) 1819.
41. To Murray, 24 September 1821.
42. To Moore, 2 February 1818.
43. Ibid.
44. To Murray, 20 September 1821.
45. '. . . like drinking Usquebaugh – & then proving a fountain', To Murray, 4 January 1821.
46. To Moore, 19 September 1818.
47. Ibid.
48. To Murray, 23 April 1820.
49. To Murray, 20 September 1821.
50. 'Cain is nothing more than a drama – not a piece of argument . . . the personages talk . . . according to their characters': To Murray, 8 February 1822.
51. To Moore, 5 July 1821.
52. To Murray, 6 April 1819 (b).
53. Harvard University Press, 1946, 2nd edn, Harper, 1961, Chapter V.
54. Oxford University Press, 1953; Norton Library, 1958, p. 21.
55. To Hodgson, 12 May 1821.
56. To James Hogg, 24 March 1814.
57. To Murray, 19 October 1820.
58. To Moore, 14 May 1821.
59. *Journal*, 23 November 1813.
60. *Ravenna Journal*, 11 January 1821; To Hunt, 30 October 1815; To Murray, 4 September 1817.
61. To Lord Holland, 17 November 1813.
62. To Moore, 5 January 1816.
63. To his mother, 7 October 1808; see also *Detached Thoughts* of 1821.
64. To Murray, 12 October 1820.
65. To Murray, 25 December 1822.
66. To Murray, 2 April 1817.

67. *Romanticism. The Critical Idiom* (London, 1969), p. 6.
68. To James Hogg, 24 March 1814.
69. To Moore, 1 June 1818.
70. Ibid.
71. To Murray, 12 October 1817.
72. To Moore, 5 July 1821 and in several other letters.
73. To Murray, 23 April 1819 and 21 February 1820, etc.
74. To Murray, 23–24 April 1820.
75. To James Hogg, 24 March 1814.
76. To Moore, 1 June 1818.
77. To John Hunt, 17 March 1823.
78. To James Hogg, 24 March 1814.
79. *Journal*, 23 November 1813 (Tuesday morning).
80. To Murray, 25 March 1817.
81. To Leigh Hunt, 4–6 November 1815 (?).
82. To Murray, 3 November 1821.
83. To Moore, 5 July 1821.
84. See To Murray, 6 April 1819 (b) and To Shelley, 26 April 1821.
85. To Shelley, 26 April 1821.
86. To Murray, 6 April 1819 (b) and To Moore, 28 April 1821.
87. To Murray, 31 August 1821, 26 May 1822 and 25 December 1822; To Kinnaird, 26 May 1822.
88. To John Hunt, 17 March 1823.
89. To Moore, 25 December 1820.
90. To Lord Holland, 17 November 1813.
91. Ibid.
92. To Moore, 5 July 1821.
93. To Murray, 23 April 1820.
94. To Murray, 25 December 1822.
95. To Leigh Hunt, September–30 October 1815.
96. To Moore, 1 June 1818.
97. Journal, 23 November 1813.
98. 'Some Remarks on the Aesthetic Structure of Don Juan', in: *Salzburg Studies in English Literature* 80 (1978) = Papers read at the Constance Byron Symposium, 1977.

12

The Quintessential Byron

LESLIE A. MARCHAND

With a personality so mercurial, a mind so volatile, and expression so often governed by flippancy, Byron tends to slip through the fingers of those who attempt to grasp his central character and essential ideas. How do we arrive at the quintessential Byron? The best way, it seems to me, is to examine his fundamental and persistent attitudes, whether expressed with the seriousness of *Childe Harold* and *Manfred*, the facetiousness of his letters, or the banter and irony of *Don Juan*. I would put first his realistic view of Romantic aspirations, which he could still cling to as compensation for life's limitations. He had a liberal mind, and his love of liberty went beyond politics and encompassed the basic human condition. His love of truth was uncompromising. His hatred of cant and hypocrisy was perennial. His spontaneity and honesty continually surprise us because they are so uncommon in common life. His genuine hatred of war did not prevent him from engaging in 'Freedom's Battle'. His tough-mindedness permitted a realistic recognition of his own limitations. His willingness to speculate far and wide opened the way to his independence of judgement. His perception of uncertainty in the large matters of human destiny justified the slight value he placed on consistency. He was suspicious of systems and formalities in literature, philosophy, and religion. His healthy cynicism did not lead to misanthropy but to a balanced view of human nature. His alternate romantic and realistic concept of love often transcends the prejudices of his day. His sense of humour and sense of fun rescued him from an obsessive concern with life's seriousness.

But perhaps we can get to the heart of the matter by concentrating on two attitudes which Byron by his own statement considered paramount. He told Lady Blessington: 'There are but two sentiments to which I am constant, a strong love of liberty, and a detestation of cant, and neither is calculated to gain me friends.'

240

His love of liberty allied him with the oppressed people under despotic governments, and drove him to champion the stocking-weavers of Nottingham, the Neapolitans and the Romagnuolas under the yoke of Austria, and to join the Greeks in their war for independence. But it also caused him to chafe at the restraints placed upon individuals by social custom. It even extended to a protest, recognised as futile, against the limitations ordained by nature on the human condition. 'I can see/ Nothing to loathe in Nature', he wrote, 'save to be/ A link reluctant in a fleshly chain.' This longing for liberty of the spirit, which was part of the Romantic aspiration, carried him further in *Manfred* and *Cain* to a complaint that we, 'Half dust, half deity, alike unfit/ To sink or soar, with our mixed essence make/ A conflict of its elements, and breathe/ The breath of degradation and of pride,/ Contending with low wants and lofty will,/ Till our Mortality predominates/ And men are – what they name not to themselves . . .' This foredoomed longing for freedom from the 'fleshly chain' never left him, even after in *Don Juan* the 'sad truth' of human limitations and imperfections turned 'what was once romantic to burlesque'.

Cain's journey with Lucifer to unknown realms whetted his appetite for 'things beyond *my* power/ Beyond all power of my born faculties,/ Although inferior still to my desires/ And my conceptions.' Cain, 'Intoxicated with eternity', exclaimed:

> Oh God: Oh Gods: or whatsoe'er ye are:
> How beautiful ye are: how beautiful
> Your works, or accidents, or whatsoe'er
> They may be: Let me die, as atoms die
> (If that they die), or know ye in your might
> And knowledge: My thoughts are not in this hour
> Unworthy what I see, though my dust is . . .

Byron's love of liberty in a time of Tory oppression impelled him to the political left. He was a liberal in the dictionary definition of the word: '1. giving freely, generous. 2. tolerant of views differing from one's own; broad-minded. 3. favouring political reforms tending toward democracy and personal freedom for the individual.' Here let us recognise at once that Byron departs in one respect from the liberal creed of our day in that he distrusted democracy as did most of the aristocratic liberals of his time, having been frightened by the unreason of mob rule in the French

Revolution. And yet, unlike many of his contemporaries, he was able to see that the Revolution was in its total effects beneficial to mankind.

> They made themselves a fearful monument:
> The wreck of old opinions – things which grew,
> Breathed from the birth of Time: the veil they rent,
> And what behind it lay, all earth shall view . . .

But while he recognised that 'good with ill they also overthrew,/ Leaving but ruins', and that what resulted was a return to despotism in all of Europe under the shield of the Holy Alliance, he did not stop there. He added:

> But this will not endure, nor be endured:
> Mankind have felt their strength and made it felt.
> By their new vigour, sternly have they dealt
> On one another . . . But they,
> Who in Oppression's darkness caved had dwelt,
> They were not eagles, nourished with the day;
> What marvel then, at times, if they mistook their prey?

He proclaimed his 'plain, sworn, downright detestation/ Of every despotism in every nation'. But he added:

> It is not that I adulate the people:
> Without me there are demogogues enough . . .
> I wish men to be free
> As much from mobs as kings – from you as me.

> The consequence is, being of no party,
> I shall offend all parties: never mind!
> My words, at least, are more sincere and hearty
> Than if I sought to sail before the wind.

In contemplating the European scene in 1814, he wrote in his journal: 'I have simplified my politics into utter detestation of all existing governments . . . The fact is, riches is power, and poverty is slavery all over the earth, and one sort of establishment is no better, nor worse, for a *people* than another.' Here Byron comes close to Pope's lines in the *Essay on Man*:

> For Forms of Government let fools contest;
> Whate'er is best administered is best.

But he may well have had in mind Pope's later apology: 'The author of these lines was far from meaning that no one form of Government is, in itself, better than another . . . but that no form . . . in itself, can be sufficient to make a people happy, unless it be administered with integrity.' For Byron did emphatically denounce monarchy and express his preference for a republic at a time when that idea, even in the Whiggish society he frequented, must have appeared dangerously radical.

As to the second sentiment to which he professed constancy, the hatred of cant, it permeates his poems, both romantic and burlesque. His ridicule of cant, political, religious, sexual, and social, is the most persistent theme in *Don Juan*. To Hoppner he wrote: 'In England the only homage which they pay to Virtue – is hypocrisy.' And in his defence of the frankness of the poem he wrote to his friends in England: 'As to the cant of the day – I despise it – as I have ever done all its other finical fashions . . . If you admit this prudery – you must omit half Ariosto – La Fontaine – Shakespeare – Beaumont – Fletcher – Massinger – Ford – all the Charles the second writers – in short, *Something* of most who have written before Pope – and are worth reading – and much of Pope himself.' And again: '*Don Juan* shall be an entire horse or none . . . I will not give way to all the cant in Christendom.' He succeeded in his attack on the cant of his day by treating it lightly and with irony.

> But now I'm going to be immoral; now
> I mean to show things as they are,
> Not as they ought to be . . .

The best mode of conquering cant, he said, was to expose it to ridicule, 'the only weapon that the English climate cannot rust'.

In that battle he was not intimidated by conventional views. He wrote in his journal in 1813: 'If I valued fame, I should flatter received opinions, which have gathered strength by time, and will yet wear longer than any living works to the contrary. But for the soul of me, I cannot and will not give the lie to my own thoughts and doubts, come what may.'

The cant of patriotism equated with the 'glories of war' stimulated his satiric pen. Byron's hatred of war was founded on his deep-seated and steadfast humanitarian impulses, and his realistic recognition of its horrors as well as the unreason of its origins and motivations. His savage satire is often couched in lighthearted banter. But the description of the battle of Ismail in *Don Juan* is sufficient evidence of the strength of his feeling about the senseless slaughter commanded by ambitious monarchs and generals like Suwarrow, 'who loved blood as an alderman loves marrow'. The heroism of thousands who perished did not alter the fact that 'War's a brain-spattering, windpipe-slitting art', and he was not taken in by the effort to make it appear glittering and noble.

> Medals, rank, ribands, lace, embroidery, scarlet,
>   Are things immortal to immortal man,
> As purple to the Babylonian harlot:
>   An uniform to boys is like a fan
> To women; there is scarce a crimson varlet
>   But deems himself the first in Glory's van.

But deserting satire for the plain statement of his convictions, he concludes:

> The drying up a single tear has more
> Of honest fame, than shedding seas of gore.

Why then did he go to Missolonghi and prepare to capture a Turkish fort with his Suliote soldiers? The reason, he told himself, was that there was a difference between battles for freedom when people were fighting against tyranny and for their rights, and wars of conquest when soldiers and civilians are sacrificed to the ambitions of rulers and military leaders. But in the end his most noble deed was sending Turkish prisoners home and pleading for more humane treatment on both sides.

His tough-mindedness will not allow him to deceive himself and is tied to his hatred of hypocritical pretensions that the real is ideal, or the romantic fiction that the transcendental dream is achievable. This is part of that 'desperate integrity' which Professor Fairchild said should command our respect. Byron's realistic sense always came to the rescue. He followed Lucifer's advice:

> *One good* gift has the fatal apple given –
> Your *reason*:– let it not be oversway'd

By tyrannous threats to force you into faith
'Gainst all external sense and inward feeling.

He was not a profound thinker, but his willingness to speculate knew no bounds. He loved the play of ideas. He confessed: 'I always knock my head against some angle/ About the present, past or future state.' And his championship of freedom of thought was constant. Speaking in his own person in *Don Juan*, he said:

And I will war, at least in words (and should
   My chance so happen – deeds), with all who war
With Thought:– and of Thought's foes by far the most rude
   Tyrants and sycophants have been and are.

Byron was not troubled too much when his speculation led to uncertainties. If that in turn led to scepticism, so be it. He was suspicious of all who were 'hot for certainties'.

He approached all the orthodoxies of his day with an open mind. His journal is filled with his uninhibited free-thinking on religious beliefs. 'Is there anything beyond? – *who* knows? *He* who can't tell. Who tells that there *is*? He who don't know.' He denied being an atheist, but he defended uncertainty and doubt. And he was unsparing in his attack on doctrinal absurdities in the fundamentalism of his day. 'A *material* resurrection seems strange and even absurd except for purposes of punishment – and all punishment which is to *revenge* rather than *correct* – must be *morally* wrong – and when the *world* is at an end – what moral or warning purpose *can* eternal tortures answer?' And he added: 'I cannot help thinking that the menace of Hell makes as many devils as the severe penal codes of inhuman humanity make villains.'

His speculations took curious turns. They were intellectual rather than religious, cosmic rather than theological: '. . . why I came here – I know not – where I shall go it is useless to inquire – in the midst of myriads of the living & the dead worlds – stars – systems – infinity – why should I be anxious about an atom?' In the face of these uncertainties he was willing to question his own doubts, even that concerning immortality which he had so often ridiculed. But it is clear that it was tentative speculation. He wrote in his 'Detached Thoughts' in 1821: 'if we attend for a moment to the action of Mind. It is in perpetual activity . . ... It also acts so very independent of the body – in dreams for instance incoherently and

madly – . . .. Now – that *this* should not act *separately* – as well as
jointly – who can pronounce? – . . . How far our future life will be
individual – or rather – how far it will at all resemble our *present*
existence is another question – but that Mind is *eternal* – seems as
possible as that the body is not so.' After this speculation he
concluded: 'but the whole thing is inscrutable. – It is useless to tell
one not to reason but to believe . . . and then to bully with
torments! . . . But God help us all! – it is at present a sad jar of
atoms.'

We may at this point wish that a record had been kept of those
conversations Byron had with Shelley in their midnight sessions at
Diodati or at Ravenna. And we may wonder how much of
Shelley's depiction of the immortality of Keats in *Adonais* grew out
of that interchange.

Byron's amiable cynicism led him to ridicule the self-deceptions
and hypocrisies he saw in the prevailing conventions of love and
the relations of the sexes. His cynicism was of a mild nature,
usually lightened with humour and based on a recognition of
human frailties, including his own. His irony was leavened with
charity and he usually ended with a forgiving quip. He wrote to
Lady Melbourne: 'we are all selfish & I no more trust myself than
others with a good motive . . .'

But the disillusioned Romantic never died in Byron. Although
under Italian skies and with a new and calmer love he conceded in
the Fourth Canto of *Childe Harold* that 'Existence may be borne . . .',
and an exuberant love of living found expression in *Beppo* and *Don
Juan*, he never abandoned his conviction of the tragedy of human
existence, as he expressed it in 'Prometheus', written at Diodati in
1816:

> Thy Godlike crime was to be kind,
> To render with thy precepts less
> The sum of human wretchedness . . .
> Thou art a symbol and a sign
> To Mortals of their fate and force;
> Like thee, Man is in part divine,
> A troubled stream from a pure source;
> And Man in portions can foresee
> His own funereal destiny;
> His wretchedness, and his resistance,
> And his sad unallied existence.

His longing for the ineffable dream, for the perfection which he did not find in life and love, never left him, and in *Cain* and *Heaven and Earth* he contemplated again the tragedy of human limitations, as poignant as the vision of Egeria in *Childe Harold*. But these moods, sincere as they were, did not govern his life.

Byron's genial tentativeness disturbs some people, particularly those who cling to systems and formalism in life and literature. His contempt for the cant of literary systems is illustrated in his comment on Leigh Hunt's poetry: 'When I saw "Rimini" in MSS. I told him that I deemed it good poetry at bottom, disfigured only by a strange style. His answer was, that his style was a system, or *upon system*, or some such cant; and when a man talks of system, his case is hopeless.' Byron probably would have found Robert Graves's criterion congenial. Graves wrote that 'The only possible test of this or that method of poetry is the practical one, the question, "Did the mountain stir?"'

Throughout his last years Byron's enormous energy, his sharp wit, and zest for living found vent in *Don Juan*, whose broad panoramic view gives us a clear picture of the world we know as well as his own. Even though it was filtered through the vagaries of his own temperament, his view is a sane and healthy one, and that 'versified Aurora Borealis' illuminates our way. The mountain did stir, and will continue to stir for free spirits of the future who read and respond to this freest spirit of their past.

Index